SUNBELT GARDENING

Success in Hot-Weather Climates

TOM PEACE

SUNBELT GARDENING

Success in Hot-Weather Climates

TOM PEACE

FULCRUM PUBLISHING

Golden, Colorado

To my parents, Lucille and Jim Monger,
who always fostered my relationship with the natural world

Library of Congress Cataloging-in-Publication Data

Peace, Tom.
    Sunbelt gardening : success in hot-weather climates / Tom Peace
        p. cm.
    Includes index.
    ISBN 1-55591-356-3 (pbk.)
    1. Gardening—Sunbelt States. I. Title.

    SB453.2.S86 P43 2000
    635.9'52—dc21

                                99-044967

Printed and bound in China
0 9 8 7 6 5 4 3 2 1

Editorial: Daniel Forrest-Bank, Michelle Asakawa
Design: Constance Bollen, cb graphics
Front cover photograph: A striking southwestern garden by Charles Mann.
Back cover garden photographs by Tom Peace:
        top— Hybrid tulips, mere annuals for most in the sunbelt. Nevertheless, they make stunning containers, particularly amidst a winter garden design.
     middle— The white form of tropical sage, 'Snow Nymph', and magenta garden verbena 'Batesville Rose' bloom through the hot southeastern summer months.
    bottom— A rich, dynamic composition of cacti, agaves, and friends in a southwestern garden.
Author photo: Peggy Parks

Fulcrum Publishing
16100 Table Mountain Parkway, Suite 300
Golden, Colorado 80403
(800) 992-2908 • (303) 277-1623
www.fulcrum-books.com

ACKNOWLEDGMENTS

I am grateful for the support and enthusiasm of the following individuals:

Diane Peace, Josh Elrod, Jessica Gilroy, Jim and Lucille Monger, Geraldine and Conrad Ohlendorf, Ken Monger, Rob Proctor, Lauren Springer, Panayoti Kelaidis, Sean Hogan, Parker Sanderson, John Greenlee, Pat McNeal, Gary Hammer, James David, Gary Pease, Greg Starr, Ron Gass, Kim Hawks, Tony Avent, Carl Schoenfeld, David Salman, Edith Eddleman, Doug Ruhren, Kelly Grummins, Charles Mann, Wilma and Tom Finfrock, Donna and Cole Townsend, Sari and Jim Terrusa, Paul and Sarah McCombs, Anne Weckbaugh, Linda Heller, Norma and Wayne Hazen, Chris Woods, Ruth Rogers Clausen, Pat Swansen, Conrad Bering, Peggy Parks, Colleen Belk, Mark Word, Holly Amador, Janet Rademacher, Carrie Nimmer, Nancy Goodwin, and Kitty Lucy.

Special thanks to Scott Ogden and his particularly helpful, informative books, *Gardening Success with Difficult Soils* and *Garden Bulbs for the South*.

C O N T E N T S

PART I
WINTER GARDENING / 30

PART II
SOUTHEASTERN SUMMER GARDENING / 92

PREFACE

Dark, intriguing flowers of Spanish love-in-a-mist comprise part of the many treasures in my garden during the cool season.

GARDENING IS A PASSION for many people, including myself. We choose to enjoy a more intimate relationship with the natural world and endeavor to surround ourselves with it. We know that growth and change are inevitable, and we see it acted out upon the many stages of our gardens. Of course, some changes we may not be very happy about—hail storms, hurricanes, insect pestilence, killing freezes, floods, and droughts to name a few—but gardeners nevertheless keep forging ahead through good times and bad.

Gardeners are enchanted with the mystery of germinating seeds and surprise blossoms from hidden, forgotten bulbs. We celebrate the annual bloom of our favorite flowers and mourn the loss of those that did not make it through the latest brand of adverse weather. We consistently treat each spring with the same innocent wonder and ambition, and pursue the realization of our out-of-doors dreams. We sweat, struggle, toil, and invest our money, time, and very souls in the garden, but it's gardeners out there who are making it all happen.

There is a current upswelling of enthusiasm, however unfounded, for gardens that can be simple, easy, and carefree. Some authors naively promise all the garden beauty with no trouble or work if only we just let go and allow nature to take its course (if you do it this way, there will be no weeding, watering, or work, etc.). The only way to have a great garden without actually doing the work would be to have the resources enabling the hire of inspiration and perspiration necessary to make it happen.

Gardens are defined, instead, as the product of a synergistic interaction between man/woman and nature, together in a co-creative relationship. It certainly sounds tempting to live the dream and have it all without any real effort to create and maintain a garden, but it will not happen easily or instantly, and without human intervention (some weeding and watering are inevitable, and, no, meadows don't come in a can). Work with nature—absolutely; more important, learn from nature—but know that there will be no real garden without an interested, caring person's effort. The only places existing without the ongoing human touch are wilderness (which are vast) and weed lots.

Moreover, those of us who garden do so because we enjoy the process as well as the results. What would we do with all that promised "extra free time" that we will have when we're liberated from the chores of gardening? Watch television or surf the Internet? Good God, I hope not! We garden because we like the experience. It is pleasurable, even therapeutic, for most of us. We like to be outside, touch and smell the soil, and enjoy everything in its season. We may complain about difficult chores during hot, sticky weather, and who wouldn't want someone to give them a hand at sod removal or hauling yards of compost?

No one particular chore does require the greatest amount of a gardener's time. Mostly one spends the time to wander and observe, pull a weed, stake a plant, sow some seeds, water some newly planted flower or shrub, squash a slug, stomp on a snail, tie up a vine, all the while enjoying the butterflies and hummingbirds cavorting about the flowers and watching toads or lizards scurrying through their own private jungle. Usually, in the midst of all that, gardeners are making plans for change; moving this, dividing that, eliminating another, and adding new plants to their domains based upon the inspiration of books, catalogs, or other gardens recently visited.

It all takes time, but it is time well spent. Compared to so many other endeavors in life, gardening is amazingly fulfilling despite the litany of setbacks and frustrations that occur along the way. I think for most of us imbued with inspiration and passion, the process of gardening is as valuable as the resulting garden. The time we spend in the garden may well be the best time we have.

Very few of us readily believe that we will ever be finished with our gardens. Dynamic as they are, gardens constantly grow, evolve, and change. They are not static, like landscapes or lawns, needing simple, casual input to maintain the status quo. We expect change, indeed anticipate it, and are willing to watch as the garden constantly grows. Most of all, it would be impossible to walk away and still have our works survive intact without our ongoing interaction. The garden and the gardener are inseparable.

As much as I love gardening, I garden because I love plants. The variety of species, the diversity of forms and textures, the spectrum of colors; all are a constant source of entertainment. While hardscape, water features, and objets d'art are also essential to a great garden, the plants contained therein are what really intrigue me. I must confess that upon journeying to Versailles, France, and gazing out at the grounds from the Sun King's palace, I asked, "Where are the famed gardens?" I guess I had expected more than just lawns, shrubbery, and fountain pools. That, however, is my particular quirk; I like to see lots of different plants in a garden.

It seems that I am not alone in this compelling interest in the botanical world. Horticulturists travel far and wide to bring back choice new treasures for us to enjoy in our gardens. Some new introductions come from our own greater backyards as adaptable, local native species are discovered out in the wilds or rescued from the onslaught of ever-spreading development. Gardeners are mainly searching for plants, new or tried-and-true, that will prosper in their care and reward their efforts with exciting textures, colors, and forms.

INTRODUCTION

SPRING COMES EARLY to the sunbelt states. While snowstorms and late frosts still plague the northern parts of the country, gardeners in southern realms revel in sun-drenched warmth and the enviable, glorious season. Blossoming fruit trees are joined by azaleas, dogwoods, and honeysuckles in woodland settings throughout the Southeast, while their counterparts in the Southwest consort with desert wildflowers, roses, and irises under spacious skies.

Before long, however, the exciting warmth of springtime bleeds into hot, humid nights and blistering days. The melodious songs of cardinals and mockingbirds surrender to the droning of cicadas as the enchantment of garden and gardener alike fades (and the latter retreats to the refuge of air conditioning). Summer comes early to the sunbelt states. It comes early and stays late, like some unwanted houseguest who does not know when to leave.

There are many not-so-gentle euphemisms and colloquialisms about intense, relentless summer heat. An entire book could be compiled from the long lists of these, which I have gathered in my travels. However, most of the analogies about heat contain rather coarse expletives, and these would give any editor reason to pause. Many references to the underworld (be it Hell, death, or Hades, depending upon with whom I spoke) indicate just how ultimately loathsome extreme heat can be.

Yet the garden is the very metaphor of paradise on earth. Gardeners do chance to glimpse Eden within their private plots of paradise during springtime. No doubt many people suddenly become wary of evil serpents in their gardens as the temperature rises. More than a few cautious Texans have wondered aloud if I was not indeed harboring actual snakes amongst the flowers in my lush garden. While I do confess to liking snakes and other reptiles, I have only found a few, very small ones out back. Nevertheless, even I suspect that there is evil afoot when the spring garden finally wanes, temperatures rise, and it gets hotter than Hades.

THE ENGLISH CANNOT HELP

An unprecedented number of garden books are now available to the aspiring and avid horticulturist. Many of the old and new books on gardening are written from the English perspective on the subject. Although there are many fabulous gardens in Britain, and the combined floral knowledge, experience, and enthusiasm of the English are second to none, they cannot address hot-weather gardening. Their idea of a heat wave is a week of sunshine and temperatures in the eighties, leaving the delicate

Mid-spring in my garden is the apex of the cool growing season. Later, during the long, hot summer, other plants will revel in the same space.

primroses and cherished astilbes besmirched by wilted foliage. In the same vein, anytime one has to drag out a hose and actually water constitutes a drought in England.

Overindulgent viewing of English gardening books leaves us sunbelt horticulturists frustrated and only superfluously inspired. Little tangible information applies to our backyards, and the glorious photos contain a plethora of flowers we can never hope to see growing through a single summer. I am grateful to the English for their historical horticultural pursuits and gardening tradition. They have, no doubt, started many Americans on their own garden paths. However, we can hardly expect British assistance in helping us to navigate among the obstacles, and to understand the many nuances, of gardening in hot climates. Perhaps if the British Raj had stayed in India until the present time, there would be an intrepid English gardener or two who could share with us their secrets of success.

Alas, neither is it possible for us to rely upon the founts of horticultural wisdom springing from the American Northeast. Anyone in warmer parts planting in accordance with a Connecticut calendar, for example, will be completely off schedule in his or her garden timing. March is a bit late to be planting your sweet peas down South. Yet many southern and southwestern gardeners seem to operate by a northeast perspective rather than by one appropriate for their particular region. In Texas, I'm still amazed to see the sudden groundswell of gardening enthusiasm starting in April, when the sensible sunbelt gardener has all but finished planting for the season. Unless one is planting a bog or water garden, it is just plain difficult to give new plantings enough adequate, frequent waterings to get things established once the heat is on. Alas, the majority of horticultural publications (books and periodicals) in this country tend to cater to a homogenized audience, which seldom includes the warmest tier of states.

TWO GROWING SEASONS

Winter plays an important role in the restriction and definition of gardening in cold-weather climates. Very little happens for months on end, except for the wishful perusal of flower catalogs and gardening magazines. This explains the April "spring is planting time" enthusiasm that follows on the heels of winter's chill. Northern gardeners have quite a wait after fall and through winter, until they can plant again in spring. Not so for sunbelt gardeners.

Fall and winter are peak planting opportunities for sunbelt gardeners, and we have a whole second, cool season in which to plant and grow. Cool-season gardening opens the door to a whole new world of flowers and foliage for eager horticulturists. It offers a new palette of colors and textures for our extended gardening pleasure. The good news (for those of us who love to plant and enjoy new flowers) is that we can garden 12 months of the year. The bad news (for those of us who find it all to be a frustrating, arduous task) is that we can garden 12 months of the year. To exclude winter gardening (as any northern informative source would) is to miss out on half of the horticultural picture.

VALUE OF PLANT HARDINESS ZONES

Everyone who has gardened has seen his or her share of plants die. Sunbelt gardeners are particularly experienced at observing death in the garden, as hot temperatures wither many new plantings and high humidity fosters lethal fungus diseases that lay waste to others. Some perennials slowly "melt out" when faced with such relentless forces of horticultural oppression. They looked so good in the pictures of assorted periodicals; so promising in their containerized youth. What is perhaps the most suspicious aspect, however, is the fact that many of the dead and dying in our gardens were listed in various catalogs, magazines, and books as being hardy in our particular zone of the USDA Plant Hardiness Zone Map. The zone information suggests that many plants should be able to grow in this area. Yet when they are attempted, the poor plants don't even get a chance to die during winter's cold. Many of us have bundles of plant labels, like so many tiny tombstones, marking the graves of fallen soldiers from our yearly gardening campaigns. Out of embarrassment, I have gotten to the point where I just destroy all the evidence of failed horticultural experiments.

Does the USDA Plant Hardiness Zone Map lie? Not at all; but the map only displays average minimum temperatures, and it is a way to measure cold hardiness of plants. So we are at fault when we read more into a zone number than is implied. Heat hardiness (and humidity hardiness) is quite another matter. After all, my south-central Texas garden is in the same zone as Seattle, Washington, but I assure everyone that our summers are not at all alike. It is guaranteed that anyone moving from Seattle to my part of Texas would find a brave new world of gardening never before imagined. Neither are the summer growing seasons similar between San Francisco and Fort Lauderdale, although they also share the same "zone."

Another troubling aspect of the USDA zone information is that it reflects minimum temperature averages only, whereas the reality of our gardens is one of extreme temperatures coupled with many other variables of site, soil, and sun. Oddly enough, it also seems that cold hardiness is even variable for particular plants grown in different conditions. Especially in the case of many heat-loving perennials and shrubs, cold hardiness is greater when the plants have enjoyed hot temperatures for a longer period of time. When taken for what it truly offers, the plant hardiness zone concept can be a helpful tool for understanding winter horticultural conditions. However, more information is still necessary for an equal grasp of summer growing conditions.

Finally, as my friend Rob says, "Plants can't read." Do not be surprised if certain flowers grow where the zone information says they should not be able to survive. And to that I add: Just because it is in print does not make it so. There are countless examples in print of misinformation about particular plants' specific cold tolerances. Therefore it is best to use the USDA zone information as a guide, not gospel.

EFFECT OF NIGHTTIME TEMPERATURES

Friends often ask me if their northern or western brand of summer heat is not the same as southern heat: Hot is hot, is it not? So why would southern gardeners be in any different straits than their northern kin? Certainly daytime highs into the nineties and even 100°F occur from Portland, Oregon, to Denver, Colorado, on to Chicago and New York City, but we don't have gardeners from these parts decrying their inability to grow monkshoods, peonies, or Oriental lilies.

I would have to assert that the problem of heat is a bit more complex issue than just that of the daytime high temperature. Indeed, crippling heat is complicated, and relative humidity has an effect on the total picture. Two distinct insights into the debilitating effects of heat on successful horticulture are easily understood. One matter is the prolonged duration of heat (at lower latitudes the heat "wave" lasts for several months), and the other is the less obvious influence of nighttime temperatures.

We know that temperate plants can tolerate some time spent in sweltering heat waves. What makes the high temperature survivable for many plants up north is the ability to cool off at night (also, the naturally shorter duration of hot spells there). During the North's worst 100° heat of summer, temperatures still drop to a mercifully cool respite at night. In the South, however, summertime sees night temperatures slump to only slightly less hot, and the plants get no relief. (The reason is that humid air does not heat up or cool down as rapidly as dry air.) In such conditions, the soil will stay quite warm throughout summer, to the detriment of many nontropical plants.

The early spring performance of many plants, as well as summertime survival of others, is governed primarily by the nighttime temperature. Gardeners eager to set out peppers or okra, caladiums or impatiens in early spring will also see the influence of nighttime temperatures. Not until after the nighttime low temperature rises 60°F or warmer will these and other heat-loving vegetables and flowers begin to grow and thrive. Even though the daytime is plenty hot, if the nighttime lows are sufficiently cool some plants refuse to grow.

Another good example of night temperature influence is how it affects the common garden tomato. Tomato plants will grow and blossom throughout the hottest days of summer, but they will refuse to set fruit when nighttime temperatures remain above the mid-seventies. (This is why sunbelt gardeners need to get tomatoes out early.) Cooler weather brings about a resumption of fruit set on tomatoes. (This is why sunbelt gardeners don't pull up tomatoes when they stop producing mid-season.) Many of the flowers that succeed in our hot southern climate need the warm summer nights in order to thrive. If grown up North, these heat-lovers will only sit and sulk.

HOT SOIL AND ITS IMPACT

As mentioned earlier, when nighttime lows climb, the ambient soil temperature rises. Northern gardeners welcome the warming soil in spring (many seed packets advise, "Do not plant until soil has warmed"), but there is a limit to what is the optimal soil temperature for growth of many temperate plants. If it is 95°F by day and 80°F at night, even shaded soil will begin to get rather steamy. In fact, many seeds refuse to germinate when soil temperatures are too high (for example, spinach, parsley, larkspur, and poppies).

Very warm soils soon become lethal due to their agitated, hyperactive biological components of bacteria and fungus. Populations explode in the soil and become dangerously pathogenic. Indeed, many benevolent, saprophytic microbes (the organisms responsible for breaking down dead organic matter, causing decay) can become parasitic (attacking live tissue) as the temperature of the soil rises and biological activity increases. I am reminded of those television mouthwash advertisements that describe the seething jungle of germs that live inside the human mouth at 98.6°F. Hyperactive microbial dynamics in a hot soil look like that, only you can't cure it with an antiseptic gargle. Although this may not affect plants that thrive in the heat, it definitely influences those that only tolerate hot weather, and many times it pushes them over the edge.

Some gardeners choose to mitigate this condition by keeping available nitrogen levels low enough (by restricting fertilizing) and thereby limiting the dangerous microbial populations through starvation. Others choose to construct lean, well-drained, mineral soil beds (adding no manure) for their at-risk perennials, bulbs, and shrubs. My small garden has various sites containing an assortment of soil blends (clay, sand, and gravel)

Heat-loving plants, such as New Guinea impatiens, perform tirelessly in sultry climates when adequate water is provided.

15

in beds that are raised and also at ground level. This gives me the opportunity to grow the most diverse palette of plants in a small space. I don't choose one particular stratagem exclusively but instead embrace them all in various places in the garden.

There is, ultimately, still the need to experiment a bit in the garden and to try different plants in a variety of sites in order to discover where certain plants prosper. Some of us see the challenge in discovery and are thrilled by it. I am willing to take such chances, even if I add to the mournful stack of plant labels from failed flowers. (I belong to the "Been There, Killed That" club.) We can learn as much from the killing of plants as we do from growing them successfully.

ABOUT DROUGHT

A rising awareness about landscape water needs and drought conditions has been noticed in our communities. This is partially due to some recent dry spells in parts of the country, and partly a result of ever-increasing urban population pressures on a limited resource, especially in the sunbelt. As conservation of water becomes a more reasonable and expedient alternative compared to other costly and environmentally damaging solutions, we hear more about choosing drought-tolerant plants for our home landscape and gardens. Water-wise plantings and xeric (pronounced "zer-ic") gardens are being touted across the United States as worthwhile endeavors in the effort to waste less of our precious water.

It is too bad that there is not even a halfhearted effort by so many urban water boards to promote an alternative to water-guzzling turf lawns. Lawns, the undeniably ultra-American icon of the twentieth century, consume roughly 70 percent of the drinking water in most urban areas in the West and parts of the South. The alternatives to thirsty lawns can and should be explored, promoted, and exemplified. Sadly, it seems that few people will challenge the status quo of "middle-grass" America, lest there be a rush to include an amendment to the Constitution that would prohibit the abolishment of turf lawns.

I am ever mindful of conserving water outdoors (as well as indoors), and I notice that many of my beds require less water than the few remaining vestiges of turf that link the pieces of my garden together. Moreover, I welcome into my garden the trees, shrubs, vines, and perennials that require less water and are adapted to live on our natural rainfall, regardless of whether they are native or exotic. Sometimes my south-central Texas garden receives more rainfall than some plants enjoy, and they perish in conditions that are too wet. Drought adaptation can be a double-edged sword. I must find plants that can tolerate drought (once established) and yet not surrender to drowning during the inevitable wet spells that waterlog my heavy clay soil. Again, if there is an answer, it is not a simple one but rather lies in a diverse horticultural approach. I like to call it a holistic method, embracing variety and complexity in the garden (common and rare plants, natives and exotics). This is the garden that mixes annuals with perennials, includes shrubs and grasses of all sizes, and integrates bulbs, succulents, and ground covers. The year-round resilience of a holistic garden is a result of its greater biological diversity.

IMPORTANCE OF ESTABLISHMENT WATERING

There seems to be a broad area of misunderstanding swirling around the meaning of "drought tolerance" of gardens and landscapes: Many people stand by and watch newly planted xeric trees, shrubs, and perennials perish during their first hot, dry summer. Most folks, it seems, were convinced that the desiccated victim was "drought tolerant" and "needed no other water." It is unfortunately always assumed, and not explained or understood, that certain plants are able to tolerate (perhaps even prosper in) no-water situations once they are established; that is to say, once the roots have left the meager confinement of their pot and have grown far and wide into the soil, whereupon they can supply the plant's water needs.

Container-grown nursery stock is a wonderful luxury for the gardener and home owner, allowing instant additions to our beds and landscapes. Yet, however quickly the new shrubs and perennials may go into the ground, they are not established (rooted in) for quite a period of time. This establishment period can run from a few months for some perennials to several years for trees and shrubs. Especially large trees in rather small containers (demonstrating a large crown-to-root ratio) will require particularly long-term attention—maybe three years—before they are established. These newly planted container specimens will need regular, deep watering, which penetrates the entire root ball, when the weather is hot and dry.

Newly planted trees, shrubs, and perennials are not unlike newborn babies requiring constant vigilance and regular doses of the wet stuff until they are able to fend for themselves. Just imagine what any nursery-grown potted plant would look like if it were not watered on a regular basis. Drought tolerant or not, unless it is a succulent with water stored in the leaves, the abandoned potted plant cannot exist for long. When these same plants are put into holes in the ground, it is no longer obvious to the casual observer that the subject is in need of regular and substantial water while the roots begin to grow into the surrounding soil.

Once roots begin to move out of the root ball and into the soil around it, the plant can be weaned from the hose, slowly and gradually. Just as babies require less frequent nursing as they get older, the establishing shrub or perennial will need fewer waterings (although they should still be deep waterings) until it is finally on its own. Only then can the plant be put to the test as far as drought endurance is concerned.

Drought-loving plants grouped together display the success of healthy specimens inherent to good garden design. Maximillion sunflower prefers dry sites.

HEAT VS. DROUGHT

Many plants that are described as being drought tolerant are automatically assumed to be heat tolerant as well. The converse, too, is often mistakenly the case, as some heat-loving plants are put to death by means of water starvation; people fail to distinguish between the two concepts of heat and drought. It is a common mistake to decide that heat tolerance in plants also translates to drought tolerance. Nothing could be farther from the truth, and it is valuable to understand that the botanical world cannot be pigeonholed quite so easily.

Many alpine flowers must be capable of enduring severe drought, even in sub-zero weather. Perched among rocks and boulders, and exposed to intense, burning sunlight, many alpines must survive with little moisture, as most of the snow is blown away by drying winds. These plants prosper in perennially cool weather: They have adapted to withstand drought, intense sun, and dry winds; but hot temperatures would be their undoing. In contrast, many heat-loving tropicals and subtropicals require constant moisture in order to thrive. Unless the plant has the adaptation of a fleshy rootstock or tuber to retreat to during drought (such as gingers and cannas) or dives deep for moisture (like crinums), it must have additional water when it is dry, or it is toast. Then there are those plants that are able to endure both heat and drought (for example, cacti and yuccas).

This book will explore some of the world's heat-loving and heat-tolerant flowers and foliage that can grace gardens in the southern tier of states as well as be extrapolated further north into other gardens with hot summers). The book is divided into southeastern and southwestern perspectives so that plants with regionally adapted moisture needs and drought tolerances will be viewed in the appropriate context. It is intended to guide, not limit, the reader. Do note that some plants covered in one part of the book (for example, the Southwest) will also grow well in the other region (the Southeast).

RELATIVITY OF DROUGHT

Throughout the Southeast, high humidity accompanies summer heat, and that invariably also includes summer rainfall. Most trees, shrubs, perennials, and annuals considered tolerant of drought within the American Southeast (natives and non-natives alike) are adapted for survival of naturally occurring summer conditions (assuming they are established). These "drought-tolerant" plants would prosper (or at least survive) without any additional watering, even during the worst summer weather. Yet these same trees, shrubs, and flowers would perish if planted west of the Mississippi River without the assistance of additional irrigation. Moving further west, these heretofore "drought-tolerant" plants would be no match for the xeric conditions of the arid Southwest. They would also look strangely conspicuous next to the leaner and meaner native flora of the desert region.

Drought and drought tolerance are both very relative terms in horticulture. It is particularly apparent when moving east to west across a country as large and varied as the United States. Even so, it cannot be assumed that the moisture gradient simply runs from the moist East to the arid West, for other influences occur within these regions on a smaller scale. These are the anomalies of micro-environments in the landscape.

The effect of small-scale environmental nuances or microhabitats (also, microniches) within the realm of larger ecosystems creates additional complexity in nature (and supports additional biological diversity). Ponds, streams, and shady, north-facing slopes occur in otherwise parched desert regions, thus creating varied habitats for moisture-loving plants. Conversely, thin, stony soil, rocky outcrops, and steep southern exposures can make for arid microenvironments even in the wet Southeast. In my garden I re-create many such microniches, thus expanding the variety of horticultural treasures possible for culture.

Oddly enough, the area in which I garden is on the cusp between the arid West and the humid East. This does not necessarily mean that the weather is stable and moderates between the wetter and drier extremes. Rather, it is more like a land contested for and battled over by two opposing armies. Some years the dry side prevails, and my neighbors and I gasp at our proximity to the great Chihuahuan Desert as we feel its hot breath on our backs. Other years we feel more aligned with the Louisiana swamps to the east.

The year 1996 was the driest on record for several decades. Fires swept across the pastures and prairies, and it was 100°F in February. No rain fell that spring or summer, and water was rationed from the rechargeable Edward's Aquifer as lawns, shrubs, and even trees browned in some neighborhoods. Compared to local farmers and ranchers, gardeners at least did not lose everything. Cacti, agaves, aloes, and other desert dwellers did rather well in the garden that year. Strict water restrictions made many of us wonder if it was folly to grow anything else.

However, the following year, 1997, was one of the wettest ever. A stellar spring wildflower season (also one of the coolest in memory) was in turn followed by more rains (most well timed) and even a few floods. Several spring storms left my garden's raised beds a colorful floral archipelago amid temporary lakes. Cannas, gingers, hibiscus, bamboos, and grasses prospered, but as the weather warmed, the excessively wet soils meant quick death to some plants. I was lucky to have grown many of my desert specimens in well-draining pots, which could withstand the deluge of water.

One can only guess what our future weather holds, but I know that my garden will always contain a variety of plants in a variety of sites. There will be low, poorly drained, clay soil pockets for moisture-loving tropicals and subtropicals. Raised beds, constructed of gravel or sand, create well-drained venues for those desert dwellers that like it dry. Again, a holistic approach to gardening, which incorporates diversity, is the best insurance in an unpredictable world.

REGIONAL DIFFERENCES

Anyone who travels across America will tell you that cities, people, weather, and the landscape all differ from one place to another. Indeed, each of our states takes pride in its own particular brand of distinction. Every state has its own emblematic bird, tree, and flower (although sometimes several states share the same icon). Even cities can now revel in the distinction of their particular taste in beer thanks to the microbrewery revolution. Perhaps we will one day see regionalized beer gardens?

One would hardly expect gardens across the sunbelt to be all alike, as if stamped from the same mold. Each state, each region, has its own particular flavor and aesthetics as well as individually variable growing conditions that dictate the bounds of horticulture. Even while the climate is uniformly hot, the soil composition and pH, humidity, and rainfall collectively form the parameters of horticultural potential within which our individual gardens take shape.

Hardy aloe blooms in spring, along with 'Gold Shot' wallflower and pansies. Although native to three different continents, these plants are at home in my garden.

In my part of Texas, three distinct soil zones come together within a small area, resulting in three different growing conditions. The hill country of the Edward's Plateau supports a thin mantle of rich clay soil upon a limestone rock base (very well drained; no chance for deep rooting). The blackland prairie, where I live, sports heavy, black clay soil in a non-hilly setting, so drainage is somewhat lacking (the soil is deep and often very wet). Finally, to the east lays post oak woodland, where the soil is sandy (deep, dry, but not too rich). Although some species of plants tend to occur in all these soil types, the native flora in each area is quite distinct and varied from the others. Creek and river bottomlands in each of the soil zones add yet another aspect to the ecosystems' biodiversities.

Soil conditions dictate obvious differences in the choice of trees, shrubs, vines, and flowers for the gardens in each area. Even though the rocky hill country is less than 20 miles away, and sandy woodlands lie only 5 miles away, there are many plants that our gardens cannot share. Gardens in these three areas will naturally reflect differences between one another due to the cultural boundaries of certain plants. If a small area in Texas can be so diverse, then collectively, the sunbelt states offer quite a panorama of possibilities. It would be a shame to create a homogenized horticulture across the Southeast and Southwest when we can embrace regional differences to attain a greater garden advantage.

A PLACE FOR NATIVES

Making the most of the garden potential in any particular site always includes—but is not limited to—the use of native plants. Unfortunately, the definition of what is, or is not, native seems to be up to personal interpretation. Some people include any plant growing within the state lines as being appropriately "native." (Texans are particularly lucky in this approach since we have such a big state.) This perspective does have limitations since states—especially the big ones—include a vast assortment of sites, soils, climates, and conditions. It is therefore impossible to translate such divergent ecosystem variability into some universal, home-garden archetype that everyone can grow. For example, many plants from all parts of Texas will definitely fail in my south-central, heavy clay garden. Heck, if native plants from 20 or even 5 miles away won't survive in my backyard, then obviously going 200 miles to east Texas hardwood swamps or 500 miles to west Texas deserts may not always yield successful results. Such revelations, unfortunately, only further complicate a rather naive perspective.

Some individuals use a different paradigm for classification of plants as native. These people use the 50-mile radius definition: Plants growing within 50 miles of any garden will be "native" for that person. This view of things used to scare me because of its seemingly overrestrictive nature. There is some obvious merit to this approach, but again, if plant ecosystems can't always translate a distance of 5 or 20 miles, what use is a 50-mile limit? I prefer not to get caught up in unnecessary semantics; I just worry about what works where I live and garden. If that plant is successful, it does not matter if it comes from nearby or far away.

People create artificial systems to classify and specify our natural surroundings for our own understanding and bemusement. Nature simply exists in all its grandeur, diversity, and inexorable complexity. This creates a lot of gray area that falls through the cracks of any "black and white" analysis. It is, therefore, much better to keep the big picture in mind when trying to understand nature. (Remember, there is only one letter's difference between native and naive.) Regardless of whether a plant is native or not, it helps to understand certain things about the wild homes of new arrivals into our gardens.

THE ORIGINS OF THE SPECIES

The flowers gracing our gardens—as well as the trees, shrubs, and grasses—come from all over the world. This is true in northern gardens as well as in gardens with hot weather conditions. From deserts to jungles, and subtropical temperate zones in

Chilean poor man's orchid, Mediterranean gold net toadflax, and Texan red Drummond's phlox surround South African bulb foliage in the winter garden.

between, the world is host to many arid and steamy habitats for heat-loving plants. Mostly, these areas fall along the same latitudinal lines as our sunbelt states, in both the Northern and Southern Hemispheres. Grab a globe and check it out: Find your home state on the spherical map, point, and spin.

I admit to having spent many youthful hours spinning the family globe and pointing to places that I might sometime visit. Now I do it with explorational botanizing in mind. Of course, variables such as the influence of continental landmasses, mountains, and warm or cool ocean currents tend to color the picture differently up or down the latitudinal lines, but this exercise is still very illuminating. It is also good to remember that countless, varied microenvironments can be found within any given hot-weather ecosystem. I may not travel around the world as much as I'd like these days, but in my garden I visit the Orient and Middle East, South America and South Africa, and Australia and New Zealand, not to forget Mexico and the tropical islands.

Understanding plant origins helps the gardener successfully situate newfound treasures. It is helpful to know if the perennial that you just purchased comes from

Mexico or Morocco. And if it hails from Mexico, does it come from the north or the south? If it is from northern Mexico, is it from a low desert or mountain home? Does the native area experience summer rain? Answers to these questions do more than fuel the imagination of my wanderlust soul. Knowledge of a plant's home in the wild makes it easier to successfully cultivate it and find the right place for it in the garden. Moreover, information about any plant communities associated with a particular species also helps us gardeners clue into a greater understanding of the subject.

I recently purchased the wild-type species *Abelia chinensis* for my south-central Texas garden. I wonder what the soil is like in southern China, where this shrub lives in the wild. Does it grow from a well-drained, rocky, limestone outcrop, or along a stream with deep, moist, rich soil? Do weather patterns there include winter freezes, or summer moisture? Is it an understory, shade-loving shrub, or does it revel in sunny meadows? Each species has a particular cultural story behind it. Questions like those above are readily answered once I know a plant's origins. In my garden, the success of many new additions hinges on giving the plants exactly what they need. Our harsh, hot summers with extremes of floods and drought are unforgiving.

Other plants require further inquiries with regard to specific habitat, site, and microenvironment. One recently acquired species of red-hot poker (*Kniphofia*) appears to grow only out from rock faces in its home in the South African mountains (we are talking drainage here). My garden is short on rocky outcrops, and the heavy, waterlogged clay soil would be certain death for such a plant. Therefore, I will make certain that it gets planted in one of my raised gravel beds to ensure good drainage. I am also experimenting with other species of *Kniphofia* from warmer, summer-rain parts of South Africa (the Natal region) with the hope that they will enjoy conditions in my garden.

Microhabitats abound in any particular region on the planet. As pointed out earlier, even the arid West, surprisingly, has moist soil habitats, and the Southeast includes some lean, dry sites. This is a lesson that I appear to be still learning—the hard way. I tortured to death several individuals of a certain South African, Gerber daisy relative (*Haplocarpha scaposa*) by assuming that it liked a dry habitat, only to find out that it comes from moist grasslands (it would tolerate some drought, but not a lot). Now here's a perennial that is more at home in my heavy, clay soil. I just had not associated South Africa (home to gazanias, aloes, and pelargoniums) with moist, grassy microenvironments.

It may not always be possible to come by some of this information. Nevertheless, do search for the perfect spot to plant any newfound, experimental garden treasures. Sometimes intuition is the only help one can get, but it is the savvy gardener's best friend. With new, unknown perennials or shrubs I will sometimes wander the entire circuit of my garden, with plant in hand, looking for what seems like the site that will make it happy. I may go around the garden several times, hoping for a clue or some inspiration (or perhaps just the tiniest whisper from my green friend) to assist me in finding just the right home.

When uncertain about the correct situation for any particular plant, the best course of action will be to watch it carefully after planting. If it needs more sun or water (or less), intervention is still possible, allowing you to move it to a more promising locale. In my garden I seem to always be pushing the limits of a plant's shade tolerance since I don't have enough good sunny sites in which to grow. Also, because my garden is situated on flat terrain with heavy clay soil, I tend to test the moisture limits of a lot of plants.

If I can acquire several individuals to test, I might even plant them along a moisture gradient from lower down in wetter soil, to up in a raised bed with better drainage (or moving from an east-facing position with morning sun to a southern aspect with all-day sun). With this method, it is possible to experiment and find the best site for any particular unknown flower or shrub. "This bed is too dry, this bed is too wet, but this bed is just right!" I call it the Goldilocks approach to gardening, where one tries to find the cultural conditions that are "just right" for any particular plant.

It certainly helps to have different microenvironments from which to choose when searching for a plant's new home. With such flat, undifferentiated topography and restrictive soil conditions as I have, it has been necessary to go beyond the usual horticultural approach in creating varied growing conditions in my garden. Some fortunate people already enjoy gardens with naturally occurring, variable microniches. A little extra moisture here, a little extra drainage there; the gardener's success is based on exploiting each particular site to its best horticultural potential. That is when the plants cultivated there really do thrive. I am glad to have a variety of microhabitats created now in my garden where I can continue to experiment with a variety of plants from different parts of the world.

THE "RANGE" OF GROWING CONDITIONS

Gardening success is measured by the ability to grow plants well. I am not alluding to the fertilizer commercials demonstrating 40-pound cabbages, or the best way to produce tomatoes the size of one's head. Nor is it the greenest, weed-free lawn promised by the application of the super-product-cocktail. Growing something well means giving the specimen ideal, optimal conditions of sun, soil, water, and temperature for it to thrive and give a great performance. That is, after all, what gardening is all about, even if it is a vegetable garden.

Every tree, shrub, vine, grass, succulent, bulb, perennial, and annual can survive and perform within a range, or continuum, of growing conditions. Every living plant will tolerate some of the extremes in the range of growing conditions (barely surviving or performing adequately enough). Yet, every plant has a preference for certain optimal growing conditions in which they are healthy, robust individuals that bloom freely. Such preferences vary from plant to plant. Mind you, there is no universal optimal cultural condition for all plants. The ideal conditions favored by cannas will be radically different from the ideal conditions preferred by cacti.

Moist soil in an open woodland suit these lobelias just fine in North Carolina, but the same plants would need a bog garden setting in the arid Southwest.

There is a difference between preference and tolerance. For example, I prefer world-beat music and eating spicy, exotic cuisine, but I can tolerate Muzak and eating at Denny's (though just barely). The range of growing conditions for plants considers the influence of sun, soil, moisture, and temperature, and the cultural boundaries established by each of them. Too much or too little of each element beyond any specific ideal condition tends to be a limiting factor restricting a plant's potential growth and garden performance.

Plants have a preference for certain conditions, and they perform best when given these. This optimal situation is called the preference zone, where a plant will do its best. On either side of the preference zone is a zone of tolerance. This is where there is too much—or too little—sun, soil, water, or heat, resulting in less-than-ideal growing conditions. Plants will usually survive, but not thrive, when grown in their tolerance zone. When pushed past the limits of tolerance, they die. We all know what that looks like.

For example, butterfly bush (*Buddleia davidii*) prefers sun, but will tolerate some shade; and prefers good soil with adequate moisture, but tolerates poor soil and drought. A butterfly bush, grown well, will have lots of sun and water in good, well-drained soil. It will be full, healthy, and bloom vigorously for a long period of time. If all you have is a dry, shady site with poor soil, you could still plant a butterfly bush, and it will survive (barely) although it will not bloom much, if at all. Better results would come from placing the butterfly bush in a site that has improved soil, only partial shade, and some extra water.

Some species have very wide ranges of tolerance while others do not. Most of the die-hard shrubs and flowers that one sees in the neighborhood are so prevalent because of their resilience. Heavenly bamboo (*Nandina domestica*) is a good example of such a creature. With the ability to thrive in sun or shade, good soil or poor, and wet or dry conditions, this is an adaptable plant. Heavenly bamboo also has its preference for ideal cultural conditions, but it is not stringently bound to them. I like to use it in shady venues in my garden since sunny spots tend to be at a premium. In this case I knowingly give a common plant a less-than-ideal culture, allowing it to still serve a purpose in the garden without using the best sites reserved for rare horticultural dignitaries.

In contrast, some especially rare and choice native species, such as carnivorous pitcher plants of the Southeast (*Sarracenia species*), have narrow, specific cultural requirements. In the wild they survive only in specific microhabitats where sun, soil, moisture, and temperature are just right. Such cultural needs can be replicated in some gardens, and in fact this is the only way one can grow and enjoy these wonderful rarities. With an increased interest in bog gardens and fascination with these unique but threatened species, many gardeners are creating such special niches and making room for them at home.

Usually, a plant's ability to adapt to a site in nature is reflected by its population distribution on the landscape. Wild populations of everything from trees to flowers tend to be the most dense and prolific in the areas where they prefer to grow—that is, where optimal conditions exist. As site limitations move toward those of the tolerance zone, the population thins until that particular species is no longer favored by the prevailing growing conditions. Again, sun, soil, moisture, and temperature are variables affecting plant success either individually or collectively on any given site. Observing natural population distributions in the wild is an illuminating task that helps those of us striving for a better understanding of the plants in our gardens.

In the garden, a plant's ability to adapt by tolerating less-than-ideal growing conditions can result in an acceptable specimen, although flowering is most times reduced. However, when a plant is pushed past the limits of its tolerance, it dies. Some perennials will tolerate the heat of the Upper South (*Geranium sanguinium* and *Veronica incana*, for example) although they may perform even better further north. However, the excessive, torrid heat of Gulf South summers will invariably kill them. (Likewise, although I can tolerate listening to Muzak and eating at Denny's, I fear that prolonged exposure would have a similar effect on me.)

If a flower only tolerates heat, then you may be able to give it just the right home, hopefully with tolerable heat (and perhaps some afternoon shade). But if it is too darned hot, and the heat-tolerant flower falters, perhaps the better bet is a heat-loving flower. Many plants thrive in the heat, rather than just tolerate it, and in areas with long, hot summers these will perform best. Some of these are tropical perennials (Zone 10) that act like annuals for most of us when winter comes around (begonias and impatiens are good examples).

Other plants will thrive in the heat, yet still survive underground during winter. The Mexican firebush (*Hamelia patens*) is actually a small tree in its home in tropical Central America, but where frost occurs this heat-loving plant dies down to the ground, acting more like an herbaceous perennial. I am currently investing more in such tropicals that can tolerate some frost or recover from freezing, since I know that summers will always be painfully hot in my part of Texas and yet a freeze is inevitable, too. Frost tolerance of heat-loving plants is yet another horticultural boundary for sunbelt gardeners to explore.

Another side of this discussion about the range of growing conditions is the issue of drought tolerance. Specifically said, many heat-loving garden subjects are also drought tolerant. They will tolerate drought, but they would prefer some water during tough times, especially in the heat of summer. Many people read between the lines and assume drought tolerance means "this plant needs no water." Still other gardeners feel that they are cheating if they give a drink to a drought-resistant plant during the heat of summer (as if there were some rule of nonwatering for xeric plantings that must be strictly observed, even though the subject is looking bad). It is, however, not a horticultural crime to water wisely, and it may just be that these plants require only one or two well-timed, judicious waterings in order for them to look superb all summer long. Let's not forget that it will still be a low-water garden.

Some desert denizens, such as bear grass (Nolina), desert spoon or sotol (Dasylirion), and century plant (Agave), are assumed by many gardeners to be in little need of summer water. All these heat lovers don't start to grow until the weather warms considerably. At this point, they will tolerate drought and endure blistering heat, but they will not grow without water. Plant growth is governed by cells expanding as they fill with water (cell division, or replication, occurs on a microscopic level and requires little water). Stems and leaves will later become more fibrous, even woody, but it is cellular hydraulics (cell expansion pushed by water) that causes actual growth in all plants. These above-mentioned desert plants prosper in the Sonoran and Chihuahuan Deserts due to summer monsoon rains that create ideal growing conditions; thus, a little summer water in the garden will produce bigger, better specimens.

Other plants actually prefer it dry during the hot season, when they are, for the most part, dormant. Good examples of these are particular bulbs from South African deserts, certain Mediterranean shrubs, and plants of the Mojave Desert; all need perfectly dry conditions during the heat of summer lest they succumb to disease and rot. These species have evolved in environments that experience no summer moisture, and they need similar cultural conditions in the home garden. The rainy, humid summers of south-central Texas will prove fatal for such plants unless grown in containers or specialized beds.

So what does all this mean to the intrepid adventurous gardener? First of all, pay attention. Get the facts about any new horticultural test subjects before placing them in the garden. Find out what the ideal, optimal growing conditions are for any new garden introduction, and find out—if possible—what it will tolerate. Try your best to give your plants what they want by exploring every inch, nuance, and niche of microenvironment in the garden. Don't garden in denial: If you cannot give a subject everything it needs, at least give it some of what it needs, and do so with eyes open (miracles do happen, but don't be shocked if death happens).

A MATTER OF STYLE

Once we know the best sites in the garden for producing well-grown plants, the next consideration is that of aesthetics, design, and style. The best designs and floral combinations fail if the specimens involved are suffering or barely alive; so, growing healthy individuals is always the first concern in garden design. We are therefore encouraged to plan and plant over time, and out in the garden, rather than inside on paper, all at once. After all, everything looks good on paper, where none of the real-world variables of light, moisture, soil quality, and exposure rear their ugly heads.

Gardens are as varied as the gardeners who create and cultivate them. People are imbued with boundless enthusiasm and a full spectrum of taste, which when combined with an interest in plants translates into a myriad of garden styles. Gardens are large or small, and formal, informal, or even wild (some would include crazy and bizarre as likely adjectives). Themes and individual inspirations abound in gardens across the country as Americans embrace the English horticultural tradition and even take it a few steps further. Inasmuch as the garden is the whole, complex botanical world in microcosm, and biological diversity is celebrated by many plant enthusiasts on the home front, an endless, diverse variety of styles should also be encouraged in gardens.

Because I garden 12 months of the year and indulge in both the cool and hot seasons, I am able to have two different garden styles in the same space. I call it the "Gertrude Jekyll and Mr. Hyde" approach. Winter gardening allows me to embrace the sweet, endearing Old World look of the masters. Delicate flowers of bulbs, perennials, and annuals of all the recognizable treasures—irises, daffodils, crocuses, poppies, lupines, phlox, wallflowers, columbines, and daisies—make the garden quaint and charming during the cool season. However, when the heat is on, it transforms into a scary jungle of towering bananas, angel's trumpets, cannas, castor beans, grasses, gingers, and groping vines. I like it that way. I like the change. I also know that with the aid of a hard freeze and a machete, this tropicalismo will be subdued, and the garden will once again be transformed to its genteel state (Gertrude Jekyll returns).

Perhaps not everyone was as influenced by Disneyland's Polynesian Village as I have been, but we do all try to re-create some sort of paradise in our gardens. Because tastes differ, I have tried to include a variety of garden styles in the photographs for this book. Plants can be used in traditional, formal bedding designs or integrated within the informal garden. The main objective is to introduce (or reintroduce) certain plants for use in sunbelt gardens with some personal suggestions for possible combinations. Ultimately the art of gardening, serious or whimsical, is up to each individual.

THE STRUCTURE OF THIS BOOK

This book is divided into three parts. The first portion covers cool-season gardening in all the southern latitudes. From east to west the winter conditions allow for similar cultivation of flowers, and special note is made of those plants capable of enduring light frost or hard freeze. The second part of the book focuses on the hot and humid growing conditions of the Southeast. Many of the plants mentioned in this section will perform exceptionally well in the heat, provided that sufficient moisture is available. This does not preclude these plants from being used in the drier western settings as long as supplemental irrigation is available. The third part of the book is directed toward gardening in the hot but arid conditions of the Southwest. Many of the plants described in this section will perform just as well in more humid regimes farther east. Sometimes site selection will dictate better drainage for these plants in a wetter environment.

Whereas everything in nature tends to exist for its own reason, we humans tend to try to force the natural world into reasonable categories so that we can understand its existence. These tools of botany and taxonomy are useful in our ability to make sense of the wide world of plant life surrounding us. However, these tools are artificial and man-made, and they come with limitations. Understanding the natural world, as realized by the many plants in our gardens, will obviously go deeper than superficial structuring and regimenting. In time all great gardeners gain that insight and understanding that supersede the tools and rules that helped in the beginning. Use this book fully, and do not limit yourself to just those plants that are covered in your region. Let this be a guide to help all hot-weather horticulturists travel farther down the garden path.

PART I
WINTER GARDENING

As the sun traces a lower arc in the southern sky, the seemingly endless heat of summer begins to abate. Shorter days bring cooler temperatures and long, refreshing nights. Because of these shortened days, deciduous trees begin to lose the leaves that have cloaked parts of the garden in shade all summer, allowing even more fall-tempered sun to penetrate the landscape and illuminate new parts of the garden.

With the exception of the real heat lovers, by late autumn most gardens and gardeners in the southern states are burned out. Those plants and people having only tolerated the relentless summer heat are relieved by cooler weather (my bet is that people claiming to be heat lovers possess swimming pools *and* indoor jobs). Short-lived plants, the weak, and the unlucky victims of excessive or forgetful watering are gone altogether, leaving holes in beds and borders. The subtropical plants and "hot-shot" annuals are still looking their best, but even they will yield to shorter days, cooler nights, and eventually, freezing temperatures in most parts of the South. At this time, some parts of the sunbelt are finally granted a reprieve, having received the fall rains that bring life back to the parched earth. It is transition time for southern gardens: from hot season to cool season. This profound shift in the garden calendar is marked by the advent of potted pansies and flowering kale at local garden centers and nurseries. For my garden and myself, it is a time of renewal. It is time for winter gardening; six delightful months full of excitement and rewarded by abundant floral color. And, fortunately, there's a lot more for gardeners to grow and enjoy than simply pansies and kale.

Traditionally, with the end of summer most gardeners are ready to retire for six months and wait until spring's return before they are willing to plant again. Autumn is when I start planting for winter and springtime color. It is the most

OVERLEAF: The demure nature of cool-season flowers comforts those that prefer genteel gardens.

ABOVE: Mild winter weather allows cultivation of a variety of perennials, bulbs, and annuals.

OPPOSITE: Red cabbage becomes the focal point for cool-season annuals and bulbs.

enjoyable time to spend gardening in the sunbelt, and it is also the most horticulturally sensible. Cooler days create an opportunity to relish the hard work of digging, planting, weeding, and soil preparation without the extra sweat. In addition, the end of hot weather is the end of buggy weather. I don't mind gardening alone, without the company of gnats, mosquitoes, biting flies, hornets, and fire ants. Best of all, trees, shrubs, and perennials planted in the cool season have a longer time to become well established and develop deep roots. This enables better growth, thereby improving their ability to survive the next long, hot summer. Also, many winter- and spring-blooming annuals, bulbs, and perennials can only be grown and enjoyed during this cool season. One will not find this type of advice when looking to Connecticut for garden guidance. Their season ends with the coming of winter; ours should not.

Differences between the torrid Southeast and the arid Southwest are moderated during winter. Cold, dry air drifts down from the north and lowers the humidity in states normally dominated by Gulf Coast breezes. Moist Pacific air moves into the dry western states, while rains renew southern California and the inland deserts all the way to west Texas. During wintertime the entire sunbelt enjoys a similar, relatively mild, cool growing season. Therefore, the southern region can be discussed collectively, east and west together. The only variables in this equation are the bold, unpredictable forays of bitter arctic air plunging across the South, and the subsequent hard freezes. These are not necessarily catastrophic events for the savvy winter gardener, since many cold-tolerant flowers are capable of enduring a hard freeze, and these can be planted in gardens at risk. Larkspurs, China pinks, annual lupines, and several different poppies consort in the winter garden without regard to hard freezes. The more common floral workhorses are not the only cold-resistant beauties for winter planting; they are the tip of the iceberg, so to speak.

Some regions of the South are never visited by such frigid blasts (listed as Zones 9 and 10 on the USDA map), and an even greater variety of cool-season garden delights can be enjoyed in these areas during winter. You will know if you live in such a mild zone if there are citrus trees growing in the neighborhood (citrus tolerates only a light frost). Otherwise, growing frost-sensitive flowers in gardens that may be visited by a coldhearted Old Man Winter is playing gardener's Russian roulette. Killing cold snaps are never predictable, and chances are you might have an exceptionally mild winter (one never knows for sure just how severe the cold will be). If you do not invest a large amount of time or money on tender plants, it is perhaps worth the risk; you may get lucky, and the rewards are great.

In spring while the weather is still relatively cool, the garden provides a relaxing atmosphere where we can enjoy its lush exuberance without sweating and swatting bugs.

I love winter gardening. I enjoy the refreshing weather, the garden's crisp new appearance, and the ability to expand the floral palette. Though I, too, am guilty of playing Russian roulette with plants grown past their zone (and I sometimes lose), I make this a small percentage of the overall gardening venture. This is, of course, how I find out what works and what does not. My motto is "Expect the worst, anticipate the best," and I plant accordingly. We gardeners do need to be adventurers at times. We must *learn* from our mistakes and not repeat them, however, so we can move forward in garden knowledge and experience. When certain plants are a success despite adverse weather, I bank on them during following years. Those efforts that fail are chalked up to experience, and the information is exchanged with other gardeners (along with the appropriate condolences).

The winter growing season favors plants from all walks of life that choose an alternate lifestyle. Ephemerals (that is, annual plants) demonstrate one survival strategy allowing a species to escape the heat. California poppies and Texas bluebonnets are famous American wildflower annuals. Similar climates exist in South Africa, the

Mediterranean, and Australia, supplying additional cool-season annuals for our gardens. These plants live when conditions are favorable and moisture is available. After growing, blooming, and forming the next generation's seed, these plants expire. Death is the great escape for these flowers, which leave behind indestructible seeds capable of baking in the sun for years before favorable growing conditions return, enabling the species to live again. Many other plants choose storage organs (bulbs, corms, and tubers) as their vehicle for survival. Narcissus, cyclamen, and Dutch iris demonstrate this modus operandi of cool-season bulbs. They flower and produce seed as well, but they beat the heat annually by retreating below ground, transforming into dormant states with food and water stored for the future. Still other herbaceous perennials retire during the hot weather, having already grown and flowered during the cool season. They use only their crowns or roots to maintain the spark of life while resting. In my garden, jasmine tobacco (*Nicotiana alata*), pink evening primrose (*Oenothera speciosa*), and bear's breech (*Acanthus mollis*) are three such perennials that survive the summer's heat underground.

The garden is a veritable "florgasm" by the end of winter, with container specimens joining the excitement of annuals, bulbs, and perennials.

Texas wildflowers deep in the heart of my "greater backyard" exhibit all these heat survival strategies, and their extravagant springtime display is legendary. March and April bear witness to extensive color carpets composed of a rich, diverse flora. Annuals are plentiful, and many are garden-worthy. Drummond's phlox (*Phlox drummondii*), horsemint (*Monarda citriodora*), bluebonnet (*Lupinus texansis*) plains coreopsis (*C. tinctoria*), black-eyed Susan (*Rudbeckia hirta*), and Indian blanket (*Gaillardia pulchella*) are superb examples of beautiful, resilient, winter-growing ephemerals. The seeds of these flowers germinate with autumn rains, and plants grow throughout the winter months. Spring-blooming bulbs include the onions (*Allium drummondi* and *A. stellatum*) and rain lilies (*Cooperia spp.*). These bulbs break dormancy, initiating root and leaf growth as temperatures moderate in the fall, and grow during the coldest months. Cool-season perennials such as wild blue larkspur (*Delphinium carolinianum*), fragrant phlox (*P. pilosa*), pink evening primrose (*Oenothera speciosa*), and large buttercup (*Ranunculus macranthus*) bloom faithfully every springtime. These Texas natives awaken after a long summer siesta and grow vigorously throughout winter, despite inclement weather.

As in the natural landscape, cooler weather breathes new life into our bedraggled sunbelt gardens. Autumn signals the regrowth of many different seeds, bulbs, and dormant roots that will bloom in winter through spring. Moreover, during the winter season, new and different gardens emerge from the same beds previously graced with a myriad of warm-season plants, and we are thus charmed during the other half of the year.

CHAPTER 1

FLORAL TIME-SHARING

The real beauty of the sunbelt winter garden lies not only in the brilliant array of new flowers that we can enjoy but also in the unique manner in which space can be used. Because so many heat-loving plants tend to go dormant or even freeze down to the ground during cold weather, lots of places in the garden are left vacant for about six months of winter use.

This enables us to indulge in horticultural time-sharing: using the same beds, but for different seasonal plantings. By gardening in this manner we can get twice as much enjoyment from our limited space, and we can delight in a fabulous garden while the people up north are shoveling snow. It does require additional planting, but for those who truly enjoy gardening, it is an added pleasure.

In my USDA Zone 8 Texas garden, a tropical bed filled with bronze-leaf cannas, dwarf banana, Turk's cap (*Malvaviscus drummondii*), white Brazilian plume flower (*Justicia carnea* 'Alba'), red *Lobelia laxiflora*, and yellow Mexican milkweed (*Asclepias curassavica* 'Silky Gold') grows and flowers all through late spring, summer, and fall. However, when cold weather strikes and the frozen plants are cut to the ground, the bed is left desperately barren. That is, of course, until I top-dress the bed with compost and plant it over with orange, yellow, and white Iceland poppies, red Drummond's phlox, red-leaf Swiss chard, and white violas. These charmers fill the bed with the same color scheme through winter and spring, but do so in a comparatively tidy manner (18 inches high instead of 8 feet) not found in their warm-season counterparts.

All the while, the tropicals rest comfortably under a blanket of compost, surviving cold weather, and emerge in midspring to begin another season of growth. By the time the threat of serious competition between the two plantings arises, the weather becomes too hot for the poppies, phlox, and violas, and they exit the stage. The chard becomes dinner. Cleanup is hardly necessary, as the smaller plant remains are quickly covered by foliage and rapidly decompose in a few months of torrid heat. The bed returns to the lush, exuberant look of the tropics, enjoying the heat and flourishing.

In another corner of the garden, cape plumbago (*P. auriculata*) dominates the venue at the sunny, south-facing base of a pecan tree. In summer and fall, the plumbago's slender, arching stems are tipped with clusters of sky-blue flowers, blooming just above the marbled foliage of variegated pittosporum, with purple Mexican heather (*Cuphea hyssopifolia*), Wandering Jew (*Tradescantia zebrina*), and lavender-flowered dwarf, wild petunia (*Ruellia brittoniana* 'Katy') to balance the ensemble. The addition of annuals such as pink or white begonias (*B. semperflorens*) and variegated Cuban oregano (*Plectranthus amboinicus*) completes the scene for the summer months

OVERLEAF: Variegated ginger grows in the shade during summer when the bear's breech is dormant. INSET: In winter the ginger rests while bare tree branches allow sunshine for the bear's breech to prosper.

ABOVE: Red leaves of *Canna indica* reemerge in spring after Iceland poppies have enjoyed the site all winter.

and even into fall, when the sun shines directly on the planting with relentless heat. However, winter's chill ends the performance, and freezing temperatures will kill the plumbago, heather, Wandering Jew, and petunias to the ground, eliminating the begonias and oregano altogether.

The cooler temperatures also resurrect several flowers that have rested throughout summer's heat: Paperwhite narcissus (*N. tazetta*) and pink fragrant phlox (*P. pilosa*) emerge amid their warm-season associates. Later, the grassy foliage of Dutch irises (*Iris x hollandica*) and jonquils (*Narcissus jonquilla*) also rises to join in the cool-season revelry. The plumbago is done for the season, and the rather large void left behind is planted with pink larkspur seedlings. Larkspurs fill the space brightly with green filigree leaves as they grow in winter; they make a smashing display, blooming in spring alongside blue Dutch iris, with the variegated pittosporum and pink phlox in the foreground. The addition of soft yellow and lavender pansies, purple sweet alyssum, and the bold foliage of red cabbage completes this cool-weather color combo. Hot weather's return encourages regrowth of the plumbago, dwarf wild petunia, Wandering Jew, and

Mexican heather as the winter annuals fade and the paperwhites, jonquils, irises, and phlox retire to sleep.

Cool-season bulbs grow hand in hand with warm-season bulbs in the same moist garden spot at different times of the year. Striped-leaf canna 'Pretoria' grows all summer, along with crinums and elephant ears (*Colocasia esculenta*), in a tropical setting where the heavy clay soil is low and boggy. The site need not become vacant, however, when cold weather puts an end to tropical motifs: The ground may be supplanted with Dutch iris, campernelle narcissus (*Narcissus x odorus* 'Campernelli'), Naples onion (*Allium neapolitanum*), and summer snowflakes (*Leucojum aestivum*). These bulbs excel even in the heavy wet soils of the South, prospering for years as they steadily multiply.

Sometimes even before the heat-loving plants are put to rest by a frost, tiny fingers of bulb foliage poke their tips out of the soil in answer to their own autumnal wake-up call. At the same time, almost microscopic seedlings of single, orange opium poppies (*Papaver somniferum*) also arrive at the scene. (These heirloom annuals were found in the garden of my wife's grandparents' homestead not far from our house, where they had been growing for almost a century.) The poppies somehow manage to recover from such a small start and bloom in concert with the blue and white Dutch irises in a lavish, but temporary, color explosion. Fortunately, the linear foliage of the bulbs complements the bold, bluish leaves of the poppies and yields quite a delightful effect when not in flower. The snowflakes, alliums, and campernelles bloom a bit earlier than the irises and poppies, thus lengthening the color parade.

Another flower to make itself at home in this setting is one of the native spiderworts (*Tradescantia gigantea*). Retreating down to the roots during summer, the spiderwort sleeps while cannas and crinums rule. In fall, the starfishlike form of green leaves appears and grows along with the aforementioned flowers, adding yet another foliage texture to the mélange. Blooming in springtime, the spiderwort adds blue and purple flower clusters on top of tall stems before retiring for the summer.

Where the trailing, lavender lantana (*L. montevidensis*) grows, there is a profusion of bloom for months on end during warm weather. The plant grows quickly,

While summer bulbs and subtropical perennials rest, the sweet peas, poppies, larkspurs, daisies, and pansies reign. Blue palm, bamboo muhly, and sweet flag are permanent features.

One bed in two seasons. TOP: winter annuals bloom while heat-loving perennials remain dormant.

BOTTOM: Plumbago, Plectranthus, Cuphea, and Ruellia enjoy months of hot weather.

covering a large area in a single season, but also leaves a big gap in beds after being cut back for winter. I cut mine back by December even if Jack Frost does not, so that the space can be filled with a host of cold-weather treasures. The lantana thrives in hot, sunny sites, so the space it leaves open is ideal for many winter annuals enjoying full sun (as most do). Such an opening is quickly planted with sweet alyssum, stock, bluebonnets, China pinks, South African daisies, and California poppies. New choices for annuals and possible color combinations in the space yield much creative fulfillment from year to year, and every summer the lavender blooms of the lantana faithfully return to cavort with the silver-leafed fluttermill (*Oenothera macrocarpa* var. *Incana*).

Winter cold is certainly never predictable. We don't know when the first frost of the season will occur, and in some years (here, at least) it does not come at all. Of course, gardens in frost-free zones cannot count on Old Man Winter to dispatch some hot-weather plants. In such cases there is no harm done by playing the role with pruning shears in hand, cutting back certain plants to the ground so as to create space in beds and borders (although I know Old Man Winter feels less remorse than I do about the task). The first of December is usually a good time to clean out parts of the garden and replant for winter color, in case a cold north wind hasn't already started the process for you. If certain plants are unfamiliar or new in the garden, do first seek advice on their growth habits. Local nursery people should be able to tell you which plants can be cut back to the ground during winter months and still gracefully recover next summer.

If garden space is particularly limited, yet lots of color is desired, it is best to practice horticultural time-sharing from the start. Designing beds and planting them with the appropriate warm-season flowers will allow those with small yards to garden year-round. It is important to remember that only those plants that will freeze to the ground, or can be cut to the ground in winter, should be placed where open space is desired for cool-season plantings. The persisting shrubs, grasses, and perennials chosen should ideally have as much interest to offer the garden in winter as they do in summer, so that the small space is used to its fullest.

Of course, time-sharing is also possible by planting hot-weather annuals, followed by cold-weather annuals, and back again on a six-month rotation. This approach certainly works wonders in small gardens and containers for those of us who demand variety. Such an approach gives southern gardeners two planting seasons to enjoy, and the ability to change color schemes often. The advantage of planting heat-loving perennials and shrublets, which are then cut back in winter, is that they become well

established and subsequently survive the excessive torture of hot summer with less care. I want to grow everything, so my small garden includes "cut and come again" perennials and annuals for summertime interest. This gives me ample space in which to garden during the cool season.

Many of the really heat-loving, summer-successful flowers are apt to be cut down by cold weather and tend to leave southern gardens bereft after a frost. This seemingly disastrous bane can become a boon to gardeners willing to explore the realm of cool-season flowers. I continue to explore the horticultural world looking for different subtropical and even tropical plants that perform well (even thrive) in summer and yet survive a hard freeze. These plants will give us color galore even in the hottest weather and yet allow us to enjoy flowers in the same spot during the cold weather, after which they faithfully return.

Dutch iris have their day in the sun along with cool-season annuals and perennials, which inevitably yield to hot-weather plants in the same site.

CHAPTER 2

NORTHERN FAVORITES FOR SOUTHERN GARDENS

People who have migrated to the sunbelt from the North are likely to miss some of the flowers near and dear to them. The garden stalwarts of northern climates such as delphiniums, oriental poppies, peonies, lupines, foxglove, and bearded iris fail to survive the infernal heat of summer.

Likewise, the uninitiated human transplant who tries growing sweet peas, stock, snapdragons, candytuft, pot marigolds, Queen Anne's lace, or love-in-a-mist planted at the wrong time of the year will be frustrated by withered failures. Gardeners in the South and Southwest must try different timing in order to enjoy those familiar flowers that evoke nostalgic emotions and conjure such vivid memories of summers gone by.

Many northern garden perennials have annual counterparts that thrive in southern gardens, provided they are winter grown. Fall is the time to sow the seeds of these cool-season annuals, and when they relish their situation in the garden, they will readily self-sow, eliminating the need for further yearly efforts. Some of these flowers are available for sale in small pots and packs at local nurseries, but unfortunately the trend has been toward selling only those annuals that will bloom on compact plants in tiny pots (so as to guarantee sales to an unaware public). This precludes the sale of some flowers requiring substantial time in the garden proper before blooming in all their glory. Persistence in the pursuit of these plants will pay, however, even if one needs to start them from seed.

While delphiniums planted in the South are not long for this world, their close cousins, the larkspurs (*Consolida ajacis*), thrive in southern gardens, reseeding themselves permanently in beds and borders. The more common form, rocket larkspurs, have tall, narrow profiles with some secondary flower branches appearing as the plants start to bloom in spring. Growing through the coldest part of the year, the seedlings survive freezing temperatures even down to zero (I have seen seedlings survive Denver winters unscathed). From March through May, plants ranging from two to four feet tall (half of that being colorful bloom spikes) inject floral spires of white, pink, lavender, rose, and indigo into the garden. It is easy to select and save the seeds of your favorite color(s), replanting them to achieve the desired combinations. I like to use the soft pink along with the silver foliage of Texas sage (*Leucophyllum frutescens*), or blue leaves of Arizona cypress (*Cupressus glabra*). Light pink also complements the pastel, desert greens of *Nolina matapensis, N. nelsoni* (bear grass), or prickly pear cactus (*Opuntia spp.*) and is a knockout with the rich lavender blooms of obscure but delightful *Hesperis steveniana.*

OVERLEAF: Sweet alyssum, violas, lupines, poppy anemones, and phlox are just some of the garden treats during the winter season.

ABOVE: Blue cloud larkspur creates a lovely veil through which to view robust Swiss chard.

RIGHT: Pink rocket larkspur combines well with a variety of foliage colors.

The nomenclature of larkspurs is hazy, with names being changed from the genus *Delphinium* to *Consolida*, and species names vacillating between *ajacis* and *ambigua* and *orientalis*. It is difficult to find the appropriate Latin name for another heavily branched species commonly called cloud larkspur. Distinctively different from the rocket larkspur, this annual does not form a tight, columnar flower spike similar to garden delphiniums. Rather, it branches compoundly with a multitude of tiny bluish-purple or white spurred flowers arranged on each stem's tip. This ethereal effect is as lovely as it is practical, since a single cut stalk will fill a vase (similar to baby's breath). Cloud larkspur is plenty cold hardy, and the two- to three-foot-tall plants knit together the spring garden in the most delightful way. I plant it where the deep purples complement orange flowers of varied Aloe species, California poppies, and *Chasmanthes aethiopica* (a winter-growing South African bulb with no respectable common name).

Wintertime is poppy time in the South, and although oriental poppies won't usually grow for us, we can still enjoy a healthy dose of the enchanting gossamer flowers. Several annual poppies revel in our cool growing season. Iceland poppy (*Papaver naudicale*), although not truly an annual by nature, is a fantastic annual by design for sunbelt gardens. Having grown plenty as perennials up North, I can safely say that there is no better way to enjoy Iceland poppies than to plant them as winter annuals down South. Invincible in cold weather and enthusiastic to flower, this poppy will give you your money's worth after six months of ever-increasing bloom. The basic species has a limited range of colors (orange, yellow, and white), and the plants are undaunted in the face of adversity. Cultivars like 'Champagne Bubbles' deliver an expanded color palette including pink, peach, and soft yellow, but seemingly at the expense of some resilience to wind and cold, which can cripple the blooms.

Although not a true poppy, botanically speaking, California poppy (*Eschscholzia californica*) offers gardeners much the same effect. In spring, plants produce hundreds of silky, golden chalices nestled amid lacy, gray-green foliage (total height 12 to 16 inches). Fall sowing yields beautiful rosettes of frilly leaves on thrifty plants capable of surviving many arctic blasts and adding immeasurable luxuriance to any planting. California poppies prefer well-drained soil and will withstand drought, so they are best used in association with other dryland plants. The soft blues of some yuccas, agaves, desert spoon or sotol (*Dasylirion wheeleri*), and Lindheimer's muhly grass (*Muhlenbergia lindheimeri*) make especially nice foils for the golden flowers. Several poppies juxtaposed with Texas bluebonnets in a naturalized drift create a stunning spring scene. For those wishing for more than orange, the hybrid 'Ballerina' series offers pink, white, yellow, and red shades.

Equally cold hardy (also blooming in spring from a fall sowing) is the Shirley poppy (*Papaver rhoeas*). This classic heirloom annual is often included in wildflower and meadow seed mixes because of its enchanting, ethereal beauty and goof-proof germination. After an inconspicuous, low-profile youth, the plants produce many three-inch-wide blossoms on top of wiry, two- to three-foot-tall stems. The color range includes pinks, lavenders, red, and white, with many bicolors, too, depending on the series planted. The size and ungainly form of Shirley poppies lends them to best use in the middle or back of beds, where the height is compatible with other plantings and one can enjoy gorgeous flowers without gazing at its knobby knees.

Enchanting Iceland poppies hover above the reliable display of resolute China pinks and violas.

Of all the peony hybrids from which to choose, the most successful in the South are the old-fashioned cultivars like 'Festiva Maxima' (double white), 'Big Ben' (red), and 'M. Jules Elie' (medium pink). These hold up well in the heat and require very little winter chilling in order to bloom. Even these selections, however, resent living too close to the Gulf Coast or in the southwestern deserts. For those areas especially, but including the entire South, there is a simple peony substitute: double-flowered opium poppy (*Papaver somniferum*). Individuals with otherwise modest sensibilities can use the euphemism "lettuce poppy," referring to the similarities of foliage between garden lettuce and the poppy. Easy to find and easy to grow, the little seeds seen on bagels and buns are best sown where they are to bloom.

The color range of the peony-flowered poppies includes salmon, white, lavender, red, orange, and pink. This plant has been in human hands for millennia, and a lot of selections have been produced. Single-flowered forms of opium poppy, with only four petals around a button core instead of a plethora of petals, are as variable in color as the doubles. I enjoy opium poppies in the garden, but I refrain from planting too many varieties in one setting for fear of neighborhood suspicion (no doubt they wonder what I am up to out there already). Again, as with *P. rhoeas*, these papavers should be integrated in the middle or rear of borders so the two- to four-foot-tall plants don't awkwardly stand out. (Also, lower leaves wither as the plants begin to bloom; not a pretty sight.) Peeking out from behind small shrubs and midsized ornamental grasses, mixing with larkspurs and Dutch irises, is a fail-safe design use of opium poppies.

The giant, rainbow-colored lupine hybrids love cool climates and fail to thrive south of Zone 7. Personally, I find them just too big to use in most garden settings anyway; I wish modest-sized selections were

Texas bluebonnets and California poppies enjoy celebrity status as state flowers in their respective homes but should be tried by all sunbelt gardeners from coast to coast.

available. The annual lupines, such as bluebonnets and their kin, are the perfect size for most venues, and they offer endless possibilities for the garden. Texas bluebonnets (*Lupinus texensis*) start life in the fall and quickly develop into flattened rosettes of five-fingered, fuzzy foliage, measuring six or eight inches across. At this stage, these plants are invincible, capable of surviving sub-zero temperatures, drought, waterlogged soil, and even truck-tire traffic. (This last observation was made in the pastures by my nursery, not in my garden, thankfully.)

At the end of February, most years, the lovely blue-with-white spikes begin to form, punctuating the garden with short, vertical accents (the inflorescences are about eight inches long). With persistent deadheading, the plants will bloom through the end of May, finally achieving a height of up to two feet. The medium blue color is easy to blend with a variety of flowers; it consorts with cool pastels and hot sunset colors. I am particularly fond of using bluebonnets as a unifying element in the winter garden, and I am comforted with the knowledge that each plant fixes its own nitrogen, enriching the soil. For those wanting more choices, this native lupine is also available in a soft pink form as well as white. Southern California, Arizona, and even west Texas offer their own additional species of annual lupines that would be quite suitable for garden use. Some to look for are *Lupinus hartwegii*, *L. arizonicus*, *L. sparsiflorus*, and *L. subcarrosus*.

Foxgloves, although biennials, are best grown as winter annuals in hot climates. Rather than growing plants the first year and enjoying their blooms the following summer (as it is done up North), foxgloves are started in the fall and grown through winter to bloom in late spring. After this, the plants fade in the heat, as they would if first-stage growth were attempted out of season. Another spring-blooming plant with just as much charm as foxgloves, but better suited for warm-weather gardens, is the Chinese herb hardy gloxinia (*Rehmannia elata*). This spreading perennial forms rosettes of bold-textured leaves that endure the winter weather quite well. For weeks in spring, tall stems bear yellow-throated, bright pink flowers resembling foxgloves. Enjoying the same seasonally shaded venues as yellow columbine (*Aquilegia chrysantha*) and

The gossamer blooms of Shirley poppies are irresistible, but the tall ungainly plants are best matched with other flowers to shield their awkward stems from view.

Louisiana phlox (*P. divaricata*), hardy gloxinia complements the others in color and form and has the same tendency toward summer dormancy. Cool weather initiates the regrowth of new rosettes from the slumbering roots.

Many bearded iris varieties, stalwarts of northern gardens, fail to thrive in hot southern gardens. Luckily, many tough old hybrids and species will be happy in a hot spot and do not become subject to rot. Nurseries are beginning to recognize the value of these enduring treasures, but they remain difficult to find. The best way to acquire such "successful" irises in any particular region is to divide some from a locally growing clump. Other gardeners and friends are usually willing to share some of their stock, or plants may be "rustled" from old, abandoned homesteads, farms, and cemeteries where they have flourished without attention for years. Away from the humid Gulf Coast, try white (and sometimes blue) *Iris albicans*, white *I. florentina*, and purple *I. kochii*, as well as some of the old *I. germanica* crosses, which are mostly found in shades of purple or lilac. Where humidity is a way of life, switch to the Louisiana iris and its kin, coppery

Iris fulva, purple *I. brevicaulis*, and violet *I. virginica*, as well as the somewhat similar white *Iris orientalis*.

Many favorite annuals of northern summers only succeed during the cool season in hot climates. Pot marigolds (*Calendula officinalis*), stock (*Matthiola incana*), and snapdragons (*Antirrhinum majus*) all prosper from a fall sowing and winter growth. Sometimes a sharp, cold blast of arctic air will wither the flowers if the plants are caught in bloom, but they endure and recover from such disasters. As with the pot marigolds, in mild years, stock and snapdragons will bloom midwinter, adding valuable vertical accents to the winter garden. Cold years will delay flowering until it coincides with other plants, like larkspurs and lupines, in spring unison. These winter annuals are easy to find since they flower readily in small packs at nurseries. However nice it is to see exactly what flower color is being purchased, these plants will perform better in the garden if young, preblooming individuals are chosen. They will increase in size in the unrestricted soil of the bed and reward the gardener with substantially larger and longer-lasting displays. Trust the picture tags attached to the flower packs at the nursery, and buy young, not-yet-blooming plants.

Annual candytuft (*Iberis umbellata*), love-in-a-mist (*Nigella damascena*), and annual Queen Anne's lace (*Ammi majus*) grow splendidly during winter. All these are hardy annuals capable of enduring brutal cold, and yet happy to bloom in late spring when the weather gets quite hot. During the cold months, the vibrant green foliage adds a touch of life to an otherwise barren winter landscape, dotting the ground between shrubs, grasses, and hardy perennials and covering the empty spaces where tender crops are frozen down.

I am particularly fond of the feathery texture that *Nigella* lends to the garden, and I add it liberally to most plantings. (This is necessary only once, since it readily self-sows and returns faithfully after that.) The charming, medium-blue flowers of the species mix well with most color combinations in the garden, but there are also white, pink, rose, and light blue selections available for those in search of an expanded palette. After the flowers fade, *Nigella* offers yet another visual treat of decorative, inflated seedpods. Since the hot season of the garden is gearing up by the time they form, it is best to cut the seed heads for indoor enjoyment and let the space be filled by other heat-loving plants.

The Spanish species, *Nigella hispanica*, yields the same foliage effect as its Middle Eastern cousin. With seemingly equal cold hardiness, this plant blooms a month earlier than common love-in-a-mist. The large blue flowers bear intricate black centers, making them eye-catching in the spring garden. The dramatic black and blue flowers coincide with the first bloom of roses, mingling well with hybrid teas and floribundas.

The annual version of Queen Anne's lace is a much better bet for hot climates than its biennial carrot cousin, which needs to endure a full year of growth before blooming

Texas native lupines add a valuable touch of blue to cool-season garden schemes. Young plants bravely face winter temperatures in the single digits.

Easily damaged by frost, the vibrant colorful blooms of Nemesia nevertheless seduce me every winter season. I grow them in pots, which can be readily protected.

the following summer. *Ammi majus* (and related *A. visagna*) forms a rosette of compound leaves during winter, then bolts and blooms in late spring with stems rising up to four feet tall on well-grown plants. Best situated in the middle or back of the border, the flowers can be enjoyed and cut without having to suffer their ungainly appearance. Where happy, *Ammi majus* will self-sow and return every fall.

Annual candytuft *(Iberis umbellata)* is a small-statured plant and almost innocuous in its youth, forming a whorl of tiny leaves along each three-inch stem. In spring, however, the plant branches out and forms an umbrellalike cluster of blooms in pastel pink, purple, and white flowers. This plant is easily lost unless tucked into the front of beds. Larger and perhaps more useful is the hyacinth candytuft *(Iberis amara)*. This annual is much taller (over a foot) and blooms white on an elongated stalk, so that the effect really is quite similar to that of the bulbous hyacinth flower (although the smell of this candytuft comes nowhere close to that of the true hyacinth). It, too, makes a great cut flower.

Sweet pea (*Lathyrus odoratus*) is the only cool-season flowering vine for the winter garden. For those sunbelt gardeners whose olfactory memories are intoxicated by the heady perfume of sweet peas, growing them in the winter is the only cure. Plants are half-hardy, tolerating temperatures to the mid-twenties with little damage and usually rebounding from a hard freeze, which can temporarily burn stems to the ground. It's fun to grow the tendril-clasping vines on fences and trellises otherwise abandoned by the heat-loving, flowering climbers. Often offered as mixed-color cultivars, the white, pink, lavender, red, and maroon flowers blend together very well and also complement other flowers in the cool-season garden. It is nevertheless useful to employ single-color selections, when available, to create vivid effects in the landscape. I continue to plant seed of the heirloom maroon/purple selection, convinced that they smell the best.

FROST-TENDER ANNUALS FOR PROTECTED GARDENS

In special frost-free sites, additional cool-season treasures can be added to the winter garden. Coastal California, the southwestern deserts, south Texas, and south Florida offer safe havens for growing such flowers (most years), but special microclimates in colder areas can work as well. Even in my Zone 8 garden, I can enjoy exotic, cool-season, horticultural treats when these flowers are grown in pots capable of being moved indoors, away from a night or two of freezing temperatures. Like most winter annuals, these plants enjoy bright light and good garden soil.

Two of the most exotic annuals to grace our gardens, the orchidlike *Schizanthus pinnatus* (commonly called butterfly flower or poor man's orchid) and the jewel-toned *Nemesia strumosa* (I call it "jewel flower"), come to us from the cool, coastal climates of the Southern Hemisphere (Chile and South Africa, respectively). They find the California coast to their liking but do well anywhere with cool, not freezing, nights. Clusters of purple, pink, white, and mauve frilly blossoms follow the equally valuable fernlike foliage of *Schizanthus*. Grown with the vibrant colored, linear leaves of New Zealand flax (*Phormium tenax* 'Pink Stripe'), *Schizanthus* creates a stunning display. *Schizanthus* also makes an excellent cut flower with long vase life. *Nemesia* does not stand out with distinctly beautiful leaves, but when the foot-tall plants start to explode in vivid showers of yellow, gold, white, orange, and red, they are riveting. Plants flower with many one-inch blooms grouped together on branched stems, and they need only the texture and color complement of bronze-leaf New Zealand flax (*Phormium tenax* 'Purpureum') or 'Bauer's' *Dracaena* to complete the picture. Other species of *Nemesia* also bring blues and purples to the winter color parade.

If for no other reason, Godetia should be grown for cutting as the splendid silky blossoms last up to two weeks in a vase.

Related to the evening primrose, *Godetia* and *Clarkia* are sometimes placed together in the same genus and other times separated (as I have done for the sake of discussion). Both flowers are native to the Pacific Coast, growing during cool, wet winters, and flowering in spring. Common names such as farewell-to-spring and garland flower are sometimes used for these otherwise little-known treasures. *Godetia grandiflora* (syn. *G. amoena*) sports large, terminally held, four-petal flowers resembling silk (with so many ugly silk flowers around these days, this is perhaps not the highest compliment). Many named hybrids are available; white, pink, carmine, and salmon, usually in bicolored patterns, adorn the simple, foot-tall plants. *Clarkia elegans* is one of several species available to gardeners, and it is the most hybridized. With a color palette like that of *Godetia*, but including magenta, purple, and lavender, *Clarkia* grows twice as tall, with semidouble, frilled flowers appearing with each leaf along the willowy, sinuous stems. In gardens and pots, *Clarkia* adds an informal but enchanting feel to plantings. Both *Godetia* and *Clarkia* make unexcelled cut flowers, lasting two weeks or more in a vase.

Some people cannot get enough of the simplicity and old-fashioned charm that daisies lend to gardens. In mild winter climates, enthusiasts can add white, yellow, orange, blue, and purple daisies to the cool-weather color scheme. *Chrysanthemum multicaule* is a delightfully petite, free-blooming annual with clear yellow flowers held above the low, tight foliage. It is perfect for small beds, and it cavorts well with other demure annuals like sweet alyssum and annual lobelia. Miniature magurite

White hyacinth candytuft makes a wonderful addition to this planting with yellow wallflower and orange *Chasmanthes aethiopica*. Delightful form and long bloom time make up for its ungainly youth.

(*Chrysanthemum paludosum*) attains twice *C. multicaule*'s size (up to a foot), producing masses of snow-white daisies amid filigree leaves on a somewhat less compact plant. When happy, *C. paludosum* self-sows for a repeat performance in future years. Yet another half-hardy annual chrysanthemum is *C. carniatum* (alias *C. tricolor*). This rather rangy, erect grower (two to three feet high) has deeply lobed foliage bedecked by hundreds of two-inch daisies displaying multiple color combinations of white, red, yellow, and black, occurring in concentric bands.

Daisies from the Southern Hemisphere include the Australian Swan River daisy (*Brachycome iberidifolia*) and South African *Dimorphotheca aurantiaca* (syn. *Osteospernum aurantiaca*), commonly called African daisy. Swan River daisies form clean, formal mounds of short stems with threadlike leaves, studded by myriad small, blue, purple, pink, or white flowers. Plants are small enough to warrant placement in the front of beds, or use in containers where they can be highlighted and not lost. Included in many southwestern seed mixes because of their infallible germination and quick, fail-safe bloom, African daisies create an informal color carpet even in lean, desert soils when given enough water to start them. The apricot and butter-yellow flowers commonly seen enhance the soft desert greens and pastel blues found in so many cactus, agaves, and their kin. The addition of a few bluebonnets gives drifts of African daisies a refreshing new look.

Bedding and trailing lobelias (*Lobelia erinus*) used during summer up North can also be grown in the frost-free winter garden. Now hybridized to include white, pink, rose, lilac, and light and dark blues, lobelias are very versatile. The plants and flowers are demure and not at all overbearing; the petite lobelia mixes well with other smaller garden subjects. The addition of a few lobelias into specimen containers and beds to mix with established plantings brings a sparkle to gardens during the cool season. It is especially difficult to find diminutive horticultural subjects for southern gardens during the warm months, when plants grow quickly and big, and everything takes on the threatening air of kudzu. It is thus a treat to indulge in the wintertime niceties of plants like lobelia, sweet alyssum, violas, and the tiny daisies. For a while we can relax into the smaller scale of things beautiful before returning to gardening with giants.

MORE FROST-HARDY ANNUALS FOR EVERY GARDEN

The variety of truly cold-hardy annuals (both native and Mediterranean) for southern gardens is amazing. It is a shame that not more are used by sunbelt gardeners, but it is also rare to find many people indulging in winter gardening at all. Using freeze-tolerant annuals allows for worry-free greenery and texture in winter with a resounding crescendo of color in spring.

Along with pansies and violas (which I hope need no introduction in this book), China pinks (*Dianthus chinensis* hybrids) are one of the most often seen cold-hardy winter annuals. Found in colors that range from white to various shades of pink, red, and violet (with many bicolors, too), China pinks are every nurseryman's dream because of their ability to bloom in small pots in fall—a boon to sales. I prefer not to plant mixed-color flats of these delightful cool-season annuals; the result looks all too much like a cheap, old quilt purchased at a garage sale. The best use of such flowers is to paint sweeping brush strokes of color, adding depth and movement to the garden, and select harmonizing or contrasting combinations with other plants.

Several native American ephemerals can be found in seed catalogs as well as along roadsides and meadows. All prosper from a fall sowing and full sun, rewarding us with sometimes sporadic winter bloom and a knockout in spring. Drummond's phlox (*Phlox drummondii*) has almost been bred past recognition (with the addition of some not-too-desirable traits), but the species is quite flashy all on its own, with white, reds, pinks, and purples found in wild populations. Half-inch-wide flowers clustered on branched stems rise to about a foot in height on plants with simple leaves, blooming from March to June. Oddly enough, Drummond's phlox can be found in more summer borders in the North than as a winter annual in southern gardens, where it grows naturally. One can only wonder why such floral excitement is relegated to fields and pastures, and not brought into more gardens.

Other native prairie "wildflowers" in the family Asteraceae (for those who dare to love daisies) include Indian blanket (*Gaillardia pulchella*), Tahoka daisy (*Macheranthera tanacetifolia*), and calliopsis (*Coreopsis tinctoria*). Like the perennial Indian blanket, the annual *Gaillardia* flowers have wide, yellow- and red-banded petals extending from a rounded central disk; flowers are up to three inches across. Modern hybrids now include double pom-pom flowers that look good enough in the seed catalogs but, with greater surface area to catch water, are destined to be kissing the mud after every spring shower. Loving poor, dry conditions, Indian blankets are a must in every naturalized meadow and petite prairiette. The Tahoka daisy also enjoys dry, lean sites in full sun, but it sports asterlike, lavender flowers on compact plants amid ferny foliage (in fact, some taxonomists now say it is an *Aster*). Great as an addition to containerized cacti, agaves, and succulents during winter, the Tahoka daisy gives a lot and asks for little other than drainage. Calliopsis (annual coreopsis) is a bushy, wiry plant with thin, dissected foliage and two-inch flowers similar in color to *Gaillardia*. Plants are used to cohabitation with grasses and sometimes need staking. Definitely put them where they will have someone to lean on—or select one of the midsized strains, which are more compact. The dwarf, solid maroon selection is quite stunning.

Another plant family, *Hydrophyllaceae*, gives us woodland and desert wildflowers ready to grow in the winter sunshine under leafless branches of trees and scrub. Commonly called blue curls and bluebells, *Phacelia* is a genus of hardy annuals with beautiful foliage and flowers, most often found in deciduous woodlands and along forest margins. *Phacelia congesta* forms a rosette of dark green, fernlike foliage that is an excellent addition to the winter garden. Spring finds two-foot-tall stems of soft blue floral "cups" clustered along tips that unfurl like the fiddleheads of a fern. Related *P. tanacetifolia* has a similar appearance in foliage and flower. The California bluebell (*P. campanularia*) has a lower profile, with slightly bronzed

Satiny red flax is dazzling on its own but also flatters green-foliaged palms, bear grass, or Texas sotol.

leaves bearing less dissection, and with decidedly vibrant, cobalt-blue flowers. Baby-blue-eyes (*Nemophila maculata, N. menziesii,* and *N. phaceliodes*) are collectively similar in stature and form, forming rosettes of flattened, serrated leaves. Flowers are open, five-petaled cups with varied combinations of white and blue (baby blue, of course) along sprawling stems. The charming flowers of all *Nemophila* species are perfect additions to woodland gardens, joining in with the concert of spring-blooming bulbs, wood sorrel, comfrey, and columbine.

Brilliant cobalt blue flowers make up for the diminutive size of California bluebell. It prefers good drainage and full sun, similar to its desert home.

Many cold-hardy annuals from Mediterranean Europe and Asia that are commonly found in northern summer gardens grow well as winter annuals farther south. In the North, *Centurea cyanus* is called bachelor's buttons (a common name used for *Gomphrena globosa* in the South), but we will apply another vernacular: cornflower. Normally seen in the common blue form (that would be cornflower blue), other color selections are also now available, including white, pink, crimson, and nearly black. Cornflowers' semidouble daisy flowers are held aloft on thin, branched stems and are best situated deep in a bed so as to hide their knock-kneed appearance. Annual red flax (*Linum grandiflorum*) has a similarly thin, awkward stature that lends it to use in meadow sites, where grasses can play supporting roles. Plants produce masses of satiny, vermilion blooms and look great interpolated with cornflowers.

Other Old World favorites lending a more vertical floral form to the garden include purple-topped clary (*Salvia viridis*) and toadflax (*Linaria maroccana*). Sown in the fall, the annual clary makes moderate-sized clumps with simple, hairy leaves that are not very interesting at all. However, upon bolting to bloom, the plants branch heavily and produce many erect stems dotted with innocuous flowers and terminated by bold blue, leafy bracts (the effect reminds me of brushes dipped in indigo paint). Both white and pink forms of the *Salvia* are available, but they are not nearly as showy as the original. They all make good cut flowers. From Morocco, as the botanical name implies, toadflax enjoys desert conditions that sometimes include narrow windows of opportunity for growth and lean soils. Toadflax is, therefore, ideally suited for quick growth in less than the best of sites. Flowers look like tiny snapdragons borne on terminal spikes, occurring in a rainbow mix of colors. The plants, however, are wispy and weak, and they must be sown en masse for a good show.

Another species of toadflax, *Linaria reticulata*, has really caught my attention. I find its shorter, densely branching habit easier to use in the garden, but it is the flower color that caught my eye. The tiny, perky blooms are two-toned wine and gold, produced in profusion, and are shockingly brilliant. Plants take some cold, but I have yet to see if

The apricot flowers of African daisy cavort with the symmetrical leaves of a young Mexican grass tree.

they are equally as hardy as their Moroccan cousins. They are an incredible enhancement for the red-spined *Ferocactus pringelii* or red-toothed *Agave bovicornuta* during the cool season. I like to pepper them into the dry gravel bed, where they highlight various aloes and elegant *Yucca rostrata*.

From the cold and hostile climate of the steppes of Eurasia come two unlikely members for southern garden clubs. New on the horticultural scene, *Erysimum perofskianum* (one of the large collection of wallflowers) has been refined to a quick-to-bloom perennial also useful as an annual in the South. This selection, called 'Gold Shot', produces abundant golden-yellow, fragrant flowers from tidy, compact mounds of simple leaves. Long blooming and heat tolerant, this wallflower will brighten up the garden from February to June. *Silene armeria* (one of many catchfly species), embodied by the popular selection 'Electra', is another compact grower. Great in rocky ground, the tight mounds of gray-green, elliptical foliage maintain a low profile until spring, when stems elongate, revealing clusters of hot pink flowers.

The southeast American counterpart of the catchfly, *Silene caroliniana*, is a resilient plant capable of enduring wet or dry conditions with equal aplomb. Low dense mats of foliage imbue the winter garden with subtle shades of purple and red when the weather is cold, and the plants seem unfazed by even harsh freezing temperatures. In late spring, bright pink flowers dot the pest-free leaves and increase in number until forming six-inch mounds of cerise blooms. Although relatively unknown even in its homeland, this native is well worth the effort it takes to find and grow. Carolina catchfly is equally at home in the winter garden as a consort for agaves, sotols, and yuccas as it is with evergreen ferns and columbines.

I find the world of cool-season annuals for the winter garden to be particularly exciting. Taking the lead from ephemeral wildflowers in my own Texas "backyard" and those of the desert Southwest, I have expanded the horizons to include annual flowers from all other continents (except Antarctica). Every year I discover more that I'd love to try.

I start most of the winter annuals for my garden from seed so as to ensure the quantities and varieties of choice. Although the availability of these plants from local nurseries is variable and sometimes limited, the seed can be easily obtained by mail from a number of catalogs.

Sometimes I have crop failures, and sometimes too much success, but mostly the process of starting annuals from seed is rewarding. When I have an abundance of a particular flower, I use it throughout the garden with gusto, creating an overall unifying effect. Every year, however, is different, and that means endless possibilities with selections from ever-expanding choices for annual color and excitement in the winter garden.

A multitude of violet and gold blooms produced by *Linaria reticulata* dance amid violas, sweet alyssum, petunias, and 'Red Bor' kale.

ƀULBS FOR ℳINTER AND ℐPRING Ɛ XCITEMENT

There are, perhaps, no flowering plants that epitomize the excitement and anticipation of the advent of springtime more than bulbs. Although many valuable summer bulbs grace warm-weather gardens later in the season, the cool-weather bulbs personify the very miracle of spring.

The emergence of vibrant, linear foliage, thrusting up from the ground into the sunshine without regard to winter's danger, signals life's pulse. Endurance, fidelity, and charm are the traits that most gardeners come to embrace in hardy bulbs capable of perennializing in our gardens. Tender bulbs, in contrast, are endearing (even though they may not be enduring) and reward our extra efforts to grow them with an effusion of exotic springtime bloom. Certainly, no sunbelt garden should be without the blessing of bulbs during the cool season.

BULBS FOR ALL SUNBELT GARDENS

Starting as early as Christmastime, paperwhite narcissus (*N. tazetta* var. *papyraceus*) punctuates gardens in the South. Reliable bulbs push up fresh, gray-green linear leaves when fall arrives, staking their claim to certain parts of the garden that they will embellish for the next few months with lush foliage and delightful flowers. Individual bulbs bloom for a few weeks, protracted by the cool temperatures of the season, and entire clumps can be in flower for almost two months as they dodge the potentially damaging brutal freeze.

This is the bulb commonly forced indoors all over America. I always purchase some to plant as potted gifts for friends, although they may truly test the friendship of those who find the odor questionable. Each bulb produces several sturdy stems with clusters of small, clear white, fragrant (this is the part in dispute among some people) flowers. In the garden, I find the simple grassy foliage complementary to the lacy leaves of columbines or wood sorrel as well as to the bold texture of white, flowering kale or purple cabbage. Additions of white pansies and alyssum further highlight the paperwhite's glory.

Another early bloomer is the Chinese sacred lily (*N. tazetta* var. *orientalis*). Although it sounds "oriental," it originates in the Mediterranean region. The pale green foliage of the Chinese sacred lily is luxuriantly copious (almost to excess) and takes more space than that of the paperwhite. The sizable flowers are white with a broad, golden-yellow cup, and they exhibit a sweet, fruity fragrance. Also susceptible to damage from a hard freeze, Chinese sacred lilies perform best in the Lower South and West Coast regions.

By the time the last paperwhite flower fades, their close cousins, *Narcissus tazetta* hybrids (actually the

OVERLEAF: Narcissus 'Avalanche' is durable and reliable, reveling in heavy clay soil. The many-flowered stalks inspired the other common name, "Seventeen Sisters."

ABOVE: 'February Gold' is a carefree garden gem that's easy to work into designs anywhere. It prefers raised beds of sandy loam when grown in the South.

results of crossing the two previously discussed narcissi), begin to shower the garden with an effusion of foliage and flower. In comparison to paperwhites, the slightly larger and robust (and more delicately fragrant by most accounts), late-blooming *N. tazetta* strains are more hardy. Strains like 'Grand Primo' and 'Avalanche' give sunbelt gardeners their first undeniable taste of springtime as they brighten up gardens in the cold, dreary days of February. Most flowers have white perianths with ivory to yellow cups, and they blend with most every part of the garden. Try planting them in the foreground of heavenly bamboo (*Nandina domestica*) for a wonderful contrast against winter-bronzed foliage and red berries.

Daffodils show their happy countenances in the garden at about the same time as the *N. tazetta* hybrids. Nothing says "Spring is here!" quite like a healthy clump of glowing, golden daffodils. However, not all daffodils are comfortable calling hot-weather climates home, and the correct choice makes all the difference in the world.

Large trumpet daffodils, such as 'King Alfred', will always bloom the first season from a fall planting, but they are not good at repeat performances in years to come. Far better perennials for sunbelt gardens are those from the Division II class called large-cupped narcissi. These lack the debonair profiles of long trumpets but boast large, flattened cups that make for a handsome face.

Two heirloom varieties are particularly successful in lower latitudes. 'Carbineer' is bright lemon yellow with an orange-red cup, while 'Carlton' is two-toned yellow (it is also the world's most numerous daffodil). The cultivar 'Ceylon', also colored yellow with an orange-red cup, is long-lasting and an extremely strong grower. 'Delibes' sports large, full blooms with lemon-yellow perianths and flat, crimson-banded cups. All these bulbs, fortunately, are quite easy to come by in the nursery trade. Companionship is the key to successfully using these vernal delights in the garden. Plant a drift of bulbs in front of a flowering quince (*Chaenomeles speciosa*), whose synchronous bloom time guarantees a knockout spectacle. Also, combining the yellow blooms of daffodils with an underplanting of blue, purple, or white violas doubles their impact.

For those gardeners who must see spring heralded by the trumpets of yellow daffodils, all is not lost. The Division VI class of narcissi, cyclamineus daffodils, offers the classic shape, with flared-back petals, on vigorous plants. Although these are somewhat smaller than the florist variety, they do not have heavy-handed foliage, which makes the large flowers rather cumbersome in the garden after bloom. In fact, the great advantage of the narrow, green foliage is that it is easy to maintain healthy plantings of perennial-flower cover crops in the same space. The flowers dazzle in early spring but are soon succeeded by *Salvia transylvatica*, *Rudbeckia fulgida* 'Goldsturm', and native

Echinacea species, which maintain an evergreen profile in my Zone 8 garden. Perennials fill in as the withering daffodil foliage recedes.

'February Gold' is a hands-down favorite for me in Texas as well as up North. The sulfur yellow (with orange-yellow cup), undaunted flowers appear in mid- to late February and endure any inclement weather unleashed by the north winds. A drift of bulbs with additional punctuation of Iceland poppies makes quite a show.

Another great all-yellow narcissus for warm-weather gardens is 'Peeping Tom'. This narcissus, and its dwarf form, 'Baby Doll', display long, trumpet-shaped cups with reflexed petals. They appear to be brazenly facing the uncertain spring weather, although this fierce disposition is well deserved, as they are both vigorous and long-lasting. Best luck with perennializing these beauties comes from carefully situating them in raised beds of sandy loam.

The true jonquil (many narcissus varieties are commonly called jonquils), *Narcissus jonquilla*, is a species from southern Europe that loves hot-weather climates where the bulbs can receive a summer baking. Leaves are jade green, thin, and rounded in cross-section rather than flattened like many narcissi. The lax foliage is scant and easily hidden in beds or mixed into naturalized bulb meadows. Flowers are famous for their fragrance (truly honey-sweet), which is perhaps why colonists brought this plant with them to America centuries ago. The small, nodding, golden blooms are clustered on top of erect 12-inch stems and present themselves smartly amid a drought-tolerant ground cover like ice plants (*Delosperma* or *Drosanthemum*).

Another "jonquil" at home in the South is *Narcissus x odorus* (also called campernelle), a naturally occurring cross between *N. jonquilla* and *N. pseudonarcissus*. Bigger and bolder than its humble parent, the campernelle is a best bet for fragrant, golden blooms in warmer climates. The thin, vertical foliage, thrusting out of the soil in winter, is as exciting as the first robin of spring (although it usually precedes the latter) and makes a handsome display in the garden. Yellow flowers bear distinctly loose, spade-shaped petals surrounding small cups; they occur clustered two or three to a stem. Campernelles enjoy moist soil and even thrive in heavy clay.

Large drifts of Narcissus 'Trevithian' (background) prosper in a poorly drained clay soil bed while golden freesias prefer the drier, gravel bed in the foreground.

A more recent jonquil hybrid is 'Trevithian'. Although it has the same narrow, rushlike foliage and delicious fragrance as its parent, 'Trevithian' appears more refined than the campernelle. The clustered blooms exhibit rounded, golden petals surrounding a faintly frilled, flat cup. Clean, quaint, and cute, this heirloom bulb is easy to come by, so plant it by the hundreds. I find 'Trevithian' to be an ideal cohabitant with crinums and cannas, as the vigorous narcissi bloom while the summer-growers sleep (and all prosper in the same conditions).

Related to the narcissus is an altogether unique spring-blooming bulb that is very happy in warm sunbelt gardens. Summer snowflake (*Leucojum aestivum*) seems oddly misnamed, since the hardy, cool-season bulbs emerge in winter and bloom with the jonquils and daffodils of spring. Nevertheless, there could not be found a bulb better suited to our gardens (even heavy, wet clay soil). The foliage is dark, lush, and copious, growing to 10 or 12 inches tall. Upon this grassy stage dance petite, white, pendulous, bell-like flowers in clusters of two to six. Not necessarily effective in small numbers, *Leucojum* should be planted in sizable clumps (ten bulbs per large hole) to get their full impact. The charming blooms and rich foliage illuminate any setting, whether it is bed, border, or lawn.

Spanish bluebells or wood hyacinths (formerly *Scilla campanulata*, then *Endymion*, now *Hyacinthoides hispanica*) are resilient bulbs that endure extreme cold and even shade during their growing season. They produce neat but lavish mounds of dark green foliage, which imparts a verdant spring appeal to the garden while other plants lie dormant in winter. Later, in spring, each whorl of leaves is pierced with a foot-tall spike adorned with pendant lavender-blue, bell-like blooms. Although white and pink cultivars are also available, they do not have the same vigor as the original species, producing slightly smaller flowers. The superb blue flowers mix well with most everything blooming at that time in my garden (and there is usually a lot in bloom then), so it is easy to use them with abandon. Spanish bluebells need only consistent moisture and resent the dry summer baking that some tulips and jonquils enjoy.

Another cold-tolerant bulb to enjoy in the sunbelt is starflower (*Ipheion uniflora*). In autumn, when the weather cools, small, gray-green, flattened leaves sprout from the soil in robust clusters. A quick smell of the foliage will help one to recognize these old friends, which emit the familiar scent of garlic. After growing through the coldest winter chills with aplomb, the bulbs begin to bloom in early spring. Overnight the tidy clumps of grassy leaves are sprinkled with refreshing lilac-hued, six-point stars with golden centers. Though the flowers occur singly on very short stems and last for just a few days, the plants appear to remain showered with pastel blossoms for many weeks. Some expansion of the color has been accomplished, and named cultivars can be purchased in various shades of lavender, mauve, and pale violet, but all look great against silver, blue, and bronze foliage backdrops of the winter garden. The tiny bulbs quickly multiply, so even a few will produce an impressive colony in short order. To maintain good health, starflowers should be allowed a well-drained site for their summer dormancy.

Having the experience of growing Dutch irises (*Iris x hollandica*) up North, I was convinced that they were nothing more than a flash in the pan; the foliage never amounted to much, and the blooms did not last long enough (blooming as they do, there, in midsummer). These are the florist iris commonly seen in the cut-flower trade, usually blue with yellow "tongues" on the falls. In lower latitudes, however, these bulbs are completely different creatures.

Fall sees the tiny fingers of foliage push through the ground as they emerge from their summer's siesta and continue to grow into lovely mounds of hardy, bluish-green, curvilinear foliage. By March (through April, depending on the variety) stems bolt to two feet, produce bullet-shaped buds, and unfurl into magnificent masterpieces of form and color that last for weeks in the cool weather of spring. Dutch irises are hybridized (by the Dutch) from Spanish and Moroccan species, and they bloom in various shades of blue, purple, golden yellow, white, and bronze.

Dutch irises bloom in concert with larkspurs, Byzantine gladiolus, snapdragons, stock, and opium, Shirley, and Iceland poppies. All of these bloom with enough height to give Dutch irises the accompaniment they richly deserve. While young, the grassy foliage also mingles nicely with filigree larkspur greens and luxuriant opium poppy leaves. Planted along with bold-leafed, felty mulleins, clary sage, or jasmine tobacco, Dutch irises add contrast elements to the garden early in fall. Clear blue iris makes a splendid companion plant for the orange, spring-blooming aloes in less frosty regions.

An abandoned, but thriving, old planting of Dutch iris and summer snowflakes demonstrates their ease of cultivation.

63

Dutch irises explode into bloom before a lavender cloud of *Hesperis steveniana*.

Tulips like it colder and drier than most of the sunbelt can provide. Hybrid tulips seen in grand but ephemeral displays are first chilled, then planted out for their season of bloom, after which they are pulled and tossed. I recommend spending your bulb budget on bulbs that will perennialize in the garden, and if you need big tulips, purchase a bunch from the local florist.

A few species of tulips will call warm-weather gardens "home." These are small flowers produced by small bulbs, which will return faithfully for many years. Earliest is *Tulipa sylvestris*, the Florentine tulip, displaying two-inch-wide, fragrant yellow blooms on short plants with thin green leaves. It is happy in raised beds of sandy loam where it can escape excessive summer wetness during dormancy.

The lady tulip, *T. clusiana*, produces candy-striped white and red buds that open wide when bathed in sunshine, forming white stars. Flowers rise on top of foot-long stems with narrow gray foliage. The variety 'Chrysantha' is peach and yellow bicolored on the outside, opening to all-yellow insides on shorter stems. These tulips bloom along with the first bluebonnets, making a lovely spring show between perennials in winter repose. Lady tulips need a well-drained, gritty soil that allows the bulbs to bake during summer dormancy.

Other tulip species that perform adequately in southern gardens (provided they are given good drainage) are *T. saxatilis, T. linifolia,* and *T. eichleri*. The large pink flowers of *T. saxatilis* are particularly stunning, but the bulbs seem reluctant to bloom even the first year (I seem to get only a modest percentage to flower). Both *T. linifolia* and *T. eichleri* produce vivid red blossoms with black centers and are under ten inches tall. They would brightly punctuate a winter planting of white or purple sweet alyssum and yellow Chrysanthemum multicaule.

Though warm-weather gardeners cannot include hybrid tulips as perennial additions to our beds and borders, we can grow many bulbs that fail to survive in northern climates. One such treasure is the Byzantine gladiolus (*Gladiolus byzantinus*). Growing from a corm (rather than a true bulb), this Mediterranean native starts growth in early winter as the first flattened, sword-shaped leaves pierce the cold ground. The hardy foliage slowly compounds itself as second and third leaves join the first in forming the plant that we begin to recognize as a gladiolus.

By midspring, the foot-tall plants achieve the five or six leaves that signal readiness to bloom. Slender spikes emerge from the center of each plant and rise another foot above the rich, dark, emerald foliage as flowers burst onto the scene. The two- to three-inch flowers are a rich wine-magenta with white streaks on the lower petals, tightly stacked on the spikes. The brilliant spires dominate the garden while they reign, accenting almost any vignette composed of annuals, perennials, and bulbs. They are particularly stunning with the silver foliage of Texas sage (*Leucophyllum frutescens*) forming a backdrop, accompanied by tall yellow snapdragons and white Dutch irises.

TENDER BULBS FOR WINTER GARDENS

Many bulblike flowers (those producing tubers and corms) from the mild winter regions of South Africa and the eastern Mediterranean are far more common in florist shops than in gardens. Only moderately freeze hardy (to the low twenties) or frost tender, these plants need protection from brutal cold. They prosper along the West Coast (some are perhaps a bit too prosperous) but are easy to enjoy throughout the South with a bit of planning and protection. Growing these tender beauties in pots for part or all of their cycle is one strategy that helps. All enjoy a good baking during their dry dormancy period in summer (easy enough in the sunbelt) and will be ready again for another season of bloom the next fall. Most are inexpensive enough to warrant purchasing new bulbs each season if necessary.

Almost everyone is familiar with the highly bred florist cyclamen (*Cyclamen persicum*). The large, gaudy flowers crowning richly marbled foliage make for quite an irresistible sales item in the dreary days of winter. As fond as I am of bright red, screaming purple, and lipstick pink, sometimes I just want to cut off the flowers and enjoy the wonderful, intricate patterns of silver and green on the leaves. Fortunately, the newest trend in breeding Persian cyclamens is headed down a somewhat regressive path: creating plants with delicious, silver-mottled leaves and smaller, more delicate blossoms reminiscent of the wild parent. The original Persian cyclamen has the same fabulous foliage with small, blush-pink, nodding flowers with violet mouths,

TOP: Byzantine glads throw their spikes of bloom into the wine-colored fray of old-fashioned petunias, iceplant, winecups, and pansies.

BOTTOM: I much prefer the sweet delicate look of the wild Persian cyclamen to that of its overbred kin. Pity it is not as readily sold.

Every year I grow some of the poppy anemones in the garden—they never fail to please.

each bearing the trademark windswept petals. It is available, but not as readily as the hybridized counterparts.

The best site for growing Persian cyclamen is in containers, which allows the tender plants to be brought in from the cold. In my Zone 8 garden, cyclamen prosper outside in slightly raised beds that allow for drainage (and dry feet) during their summer sleep. Because the foliage is close to the ground during the winter growing season, it is easy to protect from freezes by covering (they tolerate a frost to 30° F). The extra effort is greatly rewarded all season long, as I enjoy the marvelous foliage, and doubles in spring, when the delightful blooms emerge. As wet as it is here in my garden, I consider myself lucky to have plants that have lasted for three years. That is as much as I expect from any of my clothes.

Another cyclamen in my garden is the hardy ivy-leaf cyclamen (*C. hederifolium,* syn. *C. neapolitanum*). It displays similarly rich variegations of silver on dark green leaves, although smaller, and blooms in fall rather than spring (foliage emerges with, and after, flowering). Although I have seen magnificent colonies of this cyclamen under the spreading canopies of trees in the Upper South, the plants in my garden seldom bloom (it is just too hot and moist). Fortunately, the delightful marbled foliage looks splendid mixed with the jade tufts of dwarf mondo grass (*Ophiopogon japonicus* 'Kyoto Dwarf') and richly patterned strawberry begonia (*Saxifraga stolonifera*).

Other denizens of the florist trade well suited for gardens in the sunbelt states are poppy anemones (*Anemone coronaria*) and Persian ranunculus (*Ranunculus asiaticus*). Broad-flowered anemones, with simple or doubled flowers rising above frilly green collars, and turbanlike, many-petaled ranunculus are easy to grow. Both have been in the hands of hybridizers for centuries, producing larger, doubled blooms in rainbow colors (sometimes to ill effect, in my opinion), but the original species still exhibit beautiful simplicity. Even though the wild anemones and ranunculus are difficult to find (I'm still searching for a seed source), it would be well worth the trouble to grow them.

The tubers of hybrid anemones and ranunculus are readily available and are inexpensive enough to justify trying a few every year. Only mildly cold tolerant (to about 20° F), these cool-season growers can be started in small pots in a window, or planted out after Christmas, when the chance of killing frost is diminished, as ways to ensure success. The emerald filigree foliage of both plants imparts a lacy element to plantings. Anemones dotted in among bold-leaf aloes offer dramatic foliage contrast as well as red, blue, or white poppylike flowers to consort with the succulent's orange spring bloom. Yellow, white, or pink ranunculus added to plantings of blue iris (rhizomatus German or bulbous Dutch) give the linear iris leaves a contrasting texture along with floral complement.

South Africa's rich and diverse flora includes a plethora of different members of the iris family. As much as the region is split into summer- and winter-rainfall areas, there are hundreds (indeed, thousands) of species that bloom during the summer- or winter-growing seasons. All of these varied plants come from corms rather than true bulbs. A corm is a modified stem, a storage organ that gives the plant a start in life; it still must grow a while before it has enough energy to flower.

Some of the genera (and each has many individual species and hybridized cultivars) available are *Babiana*, *Chasmanthes*, *Freesia*, *Ixia*, *Homeria*, *Lapeirousia*, *Sparaxis*, and *Tritonia*. All these corms need to be planted in late summer or fall for winter growth and spring bloom. Foliage is linear and flattened (except for the pleated leaves of *Babiana*) and leaves grow opposite each other like bearded iris (except for the unique, monofoliar *Homeria*, which consists of just one very long leaf). Frost hardiness is variable, but it is safe to say none can endure a hard freeze, so they must be grown in protected situations. All of the above corms enjoy a good baking during summer dormancy.

I love the verdant, lime green foliage of *Chasmanthes aethiopica* as it emerges and grows robustly to two feet tall. Admittedly, I do protect it from freezing weather several times during winter with layered sheets and an emergency blanket (these inexpensive mylar, foil-like items are great for keeping in the heat!). February and March yield tall spikes of golden-orange tubular flowers that attract early hummingbirds and flamboyant gardeners like myself. I admit to really liking the color orange, which seems to make some "sensible" gardeners frown. *Chasmanthes* is another one of those plants considered a weed in West Coast gardens due to its vigorous success, but it is tame and even enchanting in mine.

As enchanting as these hybrid freesias may be, I now also grow some of the smaller wild species in the garden, which prove to be quite resilient and fragrant.

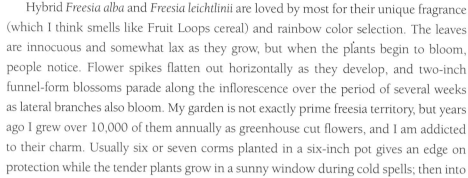

Hybrid *Freesia alba* and *Freesia leichtlinii* are loved by most for their unique fragrance (which I think smells like Fruit Loops cereal) and rainbow color selection. The leaves are innocuous and somewhat lax as they grow, but when the plants begin to bloom, people notice. Flower spikes flatten out horizontally as they develop, and two-inch funnel-form blossoms parade along the inflorescence over the period of several weeks as lateral branches also bloom. My garden is not exactly prime freesia territory, but years ago I grew over 10,000 of them annually as greenhouse cut flowers, and I am addicted to their charm. Usually six or seven corms planted in a six-inch pot gives an edge on protection while the tender plants grow in a sunny window during cold spells; then into

Marriage made in heaven: Mediterranean annual, *Cerinthe major,* nods above blue *Yucca pallida* with hybrid Tritonia flowers glowing below.

the garden they go in spring. Wild species such as *F. alba* and *F. leichtlinii* have proven more frost hardy and content in my garden, though their white flowers are smaller.

Similar to *freesias* on a smaller scale, *Tritonia* leaves form an erect fan of foliage as they go through the first phase of their lives. Thin spikes emerge in spring and flatten out as the white, rose, or pastel orange, funnel-form flowers bloom. Although they lack the fragrance and color range of *Freesia, Tritonia* seem better adapted to garden life in hot climates that still have cold spells in winter. Even more obscure than *Tritonia* is the genus *Lapeirousia*. This iris relative is also small statured, but the half-inch flowers tend to be more open, with a terra-cotta color. It looks best massed where successful colonies can give the appropriate impact.

Ixia has a decidedly upright growth habit, and the thin, grassy leaves look like miniature Siberian iris. The willowy foliage is matched later in spring by an equally graceful bloom. The tall, wiry spikes bear a colonnade of buds and blossoms in shades of rose, pink, cream, and white with dark centers, but the flowers seem shy to open unless coaxed by the sun. When open, Ixia flowers resemble dazzling six-petaled stars swaying on ethereal stems. Any clump of more than a dozen corms planted together should make quite an impact, but they prefer a drier summer dormancy than my garden can provide.

Both *Sparaxis* and *Babiana* sport short leaves in tight fans (the latter having pleated, fuzzy leaves). This certainly makes them more wind-worthy than freesias and easier to cover if protection from the cold is needed. Both plants bloom on loose spikes of only five to ten flattish flowers (again, with six petals, since they are members of the iris family). *Sparaxis* flowers are two inches across, occurring in various shades of red, orange, yellow, and white, with golden centers often accompanied by black bands (hence the common name, harlequin flower). *Babiana* flowers are a bit smaller, in colors ranging from blue and purple to violet and red. Flowers have reddish centers with deep indigo anthers. In the wild, the tasty little corms of *Babiana* are harvested and eaten by baboons (hence the less common name, baboon flower). It also appears that corms of the other plants previously mentioned are palatable to certain birds and rodents—especially in the southwest deserts, where food is more valuable than flowers.

Homeria is called cape iris down in South Africa, where it is so abundant that it covers hundreds of miles with soft yellow and apricot flowers during spring. This plant is an anomaly since the corm (which is poisonous) produces one and only one leaf during its growth. The leaf is folded at the base to give the plant some stability, but it simply grows on out to two or even three feet in length and tends to blow about with the breeze. A rigid, branched stem emerges from the folded leaf base and extends up to 18 inches high. Flowers then play "peek-a-boo" as new blooms emerge from beneath tightly clasped bracts on the stem. After fading, new flowers emerge from other positions on the branched, naked stem.

One South African flower that comes from a tuber, not a corm, is the infamous calla lily (*Zantedeschia aethiopica*). Related to the arums, callas produce bold and beautiful jade-green, arrowhead leaves on fleshy stems. A bog plant, the calla likes rich, wet soils, although it tolerates dry conditions when sleeping in summer. The frost-tender plants need protection from damaging cold, but they reward the gardener who cultures them. Winter and spring blooms of ivory-white funnels, with golden-orange spadix in the center, are favorites everywhere. The calla, too, is so successful in California that it is considered common, but I for one would love to see a huge planting of it growing along with the orange spikes of *Chasmanthes*. Let's put these weeds to good use!

Bulbs are an integral part of my garden in the cool season, and I think they should be included in every sunbelt winter garden. The cold-hardy species and hybrids are almost foolproof and require little care after the initial planting. Yet the extra effort to cultivate some of the more unusual tender, winter-growing bulbs is always time well spent. Their flowers add a touch of class to the spring garden that can be measured by the potful.

The rosy hybrid Ixia bloomed well the first year in my gravel bed, but it tends to be longer lived in pots (stored dry) or in southwest gardens with arid summers.

Cool-Season Perennials for Foliage and Bloom

For many perennials, the renewal of life begins with the cooler days of autumn. The end of blistering heat and the return of rainfall signal the time for revival and growth. These plants grow through winter, enduring errant, frigid blasts with varying fortitude, and contribute foliage color and texture to the garden. Along with spring bulbs and winter ephemerals, these perennials blossom gloriously before beginning their summer slumber in crowns and rootstocks below ground. And, whereas the vagabond seedlings of winter annuals will inevitably sprout in different parts of the garden from one season to the next, the cool-season perennials faithfully return to the same position in beds and borders yearly.

Foliage makes the garden, in any season. The addition of bold foliage, especially, lends the garden a subtle, dramatic beauty that is invaluable. A classic favorite (and I mean it in the Greek sense) is bear's breech (*Acanthus mollis*). Many different species from this mostly tropical plant family (Acanthacea) grace our summer gardens but disappear in winter. However, winter—in the sunbelt, at least—is the season for bear's breech (it also goes by the common name Grecian key plant, but that does not conjure as interesting a mental image).

Being a native of the Mediterranean region, *Acanthus mollis* breaks dormancy in autumn, unfurling large jade-green leaves with deeply cut margins from once-sleeping crowns and thick, fleshy roots. At this point I usually give it a deep drink just to make certain that it has all the water it needs for phenomenal leaf growth. Each successive wave of foliage growth creates an ever-increasing, mounding plant (much like rhubarb) with leaf size also growing steadily larger. Though bear's breech is able to withstand frost, I protect my specimen from the harsh extremes of cold (an old quilt has proven handy). Without the extra help, the plant will recover from the disaster and continue to sprout fresh new leaves from the crown. The incredible bold foliage lends a strong base note to the music of the winter garden, where it contrasts with the melody of holly fern, cast-iron plant, wood sorrel, and cyclamen.

Bear's breech continues growing through winter, and the clump expands in size until it finally sends up spearlike bloom stalks in late spring. The entire inflorescence is bold and structurally beautiful, but the individual flowers are rather anticlimactic (I disappointed one family member who was waiting for the flowers to open, explaining that the plant was indeed almost finished). The plant dominates its position in the shady bed, lording over a host of ground covers. However, the large space left barren upon its retreat into

OVERLEAF: White jasmine tobacco, yellow columbine, and mini-amaryllis 'Scarlet Baby' make an invincible team with complementary foliage and flowers.

ABOVE: Large rounded leaves of clary sage (center) echoes the bold foliage of bronze lettuce and mustard 'Osaka Red'.

slumber can present a problem. Fortunately, quite a few winter-dormant gingers will neatly fill the space at the right time and enjoy the shaded position. My bear's breech time-shares the bed with a variegated pinecone ginger (*Zingiber zermubet* 'Darcey'), which grows through the long, hot summer, then retires for winter. (See photo on page 36.)

Another fine subject for bold foliage interest in the winter garden is the jasmine tobacco (*Nicotiana alata,* syn. *N. affinis*). This is the parent of the often-seen flowering tobacco, but it is taller and with a sweet fragrance capable of casting spells. Without a distinct crown like most other perennials, this tobacco exhibits the remarkable ability to form differentiated growth (that is, sprouting new crowns) along any portion of the root. As a result, in fall, when the resting roots decide to stir, one or several sprouts will appear on the soil where the plant grew in previous years.

The soft, Irish-green, oval leaves start off small but quickly grow to 12 inches long, forming large rosettes on the ground. Although delicate-looking, the plants are very resilient and can endure temperatures in the low twenties without damage. Early spring signals the jasmine tobacco to begin elongation as the somewhat flattened circle of leaves rises into a tentlike form. At this point, multiple branching from the core produces many flowering stems that extend toward the sky, forming branched inflorescences (four feet tall and as wide) bearing hundreds of sweet-scented alabaster flowers. By the time blooming commences in midspring, every evening has an air of enchantment as perfume permeates the entire garden (and any bedroom with a window left open to the magic).

Although jasmine tobacco flowers are white by nature, color has been imparted to its many compact, hybrid forms (most of which do not persist in the garden). Colored forms of the jasmine tobacco sometimes arise from the seed of parent plants grown near the hybrid flowers as the night-flying hawk moths cross-pollinate the blooms. The offspring then has all the qualities of the perennial parent with the added bonus of mauve, pink, or blush flowers on towering stalks. The blossoms will act the same as regular jasmine tobacco, with a tendency to wilt a bit during the day but at dusk exploding with color and scent.

A contrast of color or texture (or both!) against the leaves of jasmine tobacco yields the greatest rewards. Fine linear foliage of evergreen bear grass (*Nolina*), lilyturf (*Liriope*), spring bulbs, or even yuccas enhances the look of jasmine tobacco during winter (by springtime people notice only the myriad flowers). Dark green, bronze, or burgundy-colored foliage enlivens the quiet gaiety of jasmine tobacco's light green leaves. Mustard 'Osaka Red' and red-leaf lettuce make quick annual additions to any site where the vibrant rosettes grow.

Whereas many New World salvias are valuable components of hot gardens, some of the Old World members of the genus offer resilient winter-foliage interest. Clary sage (*Salvia sclera*) is a biennial or perennial (depending upon the variety chosen) that produces large, olive-green, rounded, hairy leaves arranged as a flattened rosette. Enjoying sun and drought, but enduring some shade and heavy soil, clary sage is a versatile plant. Winter rosettes are usually about a foot across and complement smaller ornamental grasses, minor bulbs, red yucca (*Hesperaloe parviflora*), and a host of winter annuals.

In sunbelt winters, the leaves of clary sage remain evergreen and crisp, and warmer days of spring bring on increased growth. New leaves tend to be less horizontally positioned as the plant begins to assume a more jumbled look. Soon after, however, the formation of unique flower spikes gives clary sage a new, interesting look. From the center of each plant arises thick, crook-necked stems covered with white and pastel-colored bracts, resembling shrimp (uncooked, of course). These flower stalks eventually straighten, branch out, and produce myriad pink, white, and lavender bracts surrounding smaller flowers (the color depends upon the variety chosen). After flowering, the perennial forms tend to wither to almost nothing, but they maintain a small rosette that waits for cool fall weather before regrowing.

The silver clary (*Salvia argentia*) and its hybrids offer gardeners the same delightful form as clary sage, but with silvery white foliage. Silver clary is less forgiving of wet soil than its cousin but nevertheless makes a great addition to well-drained beds where the large, felty leaves accent pastel-toned winter annuals and perennials like globe mallow (*Spheralcea ambigua*) and lavenders. The flowers of silver clary are white and without the panache of colorful bracts, but still garden-worthy.

Fuzzy gray rosettes of silver clary create stunning counterpoints even for familiar petunias.

Delicate fernlike leaves add charm and intimacy to the garden plantings, yet such foliage is rarely seen during cold-weather months. Several winter-season perennials with delicate airs and ironclad constitutions grace the beds of sunbelt gardens. One such perennial native to the southern region is the yellow columbine (*Aquilegia chrysantha* and *A. chrysantha* var. *Hinkleyana*). Yellow columbine is tougher and

Early fall sees the emerging foliage of yellow meadow rue, sometimes with subtle rainbow hues. The delicate fernlike leaves belie an ironclad constitution.

longer-lived than any other member of the usually short-lived genus. In autumn, summer-dormant, fleshy roots sprout crowns of dissected foliage resembling maidenhair fern. The plants keep a rather low profile as they endure all the worst of winter, adding touches of lace to the beds where they consort with other woodland denizens. Late winter commences the growth of another whorl of larger leaves, as the columbine doubles and triples its size in preparation for flowering.

In midspring, the yellow columbine throws its hat into the flowering fray with a solitary, long-spurred, nodding bloom. As the flower stalk branches and expands, the columbine adds exponentially more and more clear yellow blossoms to the springtime madness. The two-foot-tall plants are just the right size to grow in front of jasmine tobacco, and their winter foliage mélange is also worthwhile. Yellow columbine also blooms in concert with the hardy garden amaryllis (*Hippeastrum x johnsonii*) and modern miniature amaryllis hybrids such as 'Scarlet Baby'. These flowers benefit greatly from the companionship of the columbines, which envelop the bold, red blooms in clouds like yellow hovering angels.

Other columbine species perform admirably in warm southern climates. A non-native species from Europe, the granny bonnet (*Aquilegia vulgaris*), enjoys the climate as long as the soil is well drained. This columbine has gray-green, felted leaves and short-spurred, funnel-shaped flowers in a range of colors: white, pink, lavender, and purple. It has also been hybridized to make semidouble and fully double spurless forms. Another native species is the common eastern columbine (*A. canadensis*). The eastern columbine has a wide natural range and therefore many variations, but it is usually smaller statured than *A. chrysantha*. Also, flowers are smaller, somewhat pendant, and two-toned red with yellow held in open sprays. When grown with the yellow columbine, the two will cross-pollinate freely, producing offspring with large orange and yellow blooms.

Even before its long season of winter and spring bloom, the velvety shamrock leaves of wood sorrel add immeasurably to the cool-season garden.

Related to the columbine but less widely known is the yellow meadow rue (*Thalictrum speciosissimum*, syn. *T. flavum*). Of course, with a name like that, how can anyone be expected to ask for it at nurseries? Nevertheless, this is one of the few meadow rues that likes the hot-weather climates. It carries much-dissected, ferny foliage in the fall, and it looks even richer in texture than the columbine. Meadow rue leaves tolerate frost and freeze during winter while adding immeasurable beauty to garden vignettes in sun or shade.

As new leaves emerge and fill out the lacy mounds in early spring, they are often touched with hints of rose and bronze hues. Later, as the robust inflorescence bolts from its center, the plant takes on a new dimension and structural appeal. Meadow rue's flowers are small, sulfur-yellow tufts, densely arranged at the tip of the stalk, like cheery exclamation points for the garden. Though the flower is not as beautiful as some other species of *Thalictrum*, the yellow meadow rue makes up for it with incredible vigor as well as the ability to grow in a wide range of soils and sites. Yellow meadow rue is the perfect addition to shady plantings of cast-iron plant (*Aspidistera elatior*), holly fern (*Cyrtomium falcatum*), and lilyturf (*Liriope*). It is also great pondside in wet soil with sedges, or grown with beargrass (*Nolina*) in dry shade.

Wood sorrel (*Oxalis crassipes*) has leaves that more closely resemble clover than ferns, but it still imparts a genteel look to any plant combination. Actually arising from a small, bulblike structure, the wood sorrel is active above ground so long that it is easy to classify it as a perennial instead of a bulb. Plants break dormancy early in fall if moisture is sufficient, and they even produce a flower or two before the winter. Cold weather has little effect on the downy, shamrocklike foliage other than to make the leaves fold down tightly and take on a reddish cast over the usual emerald green. A cold spell near 0° F can temporarily erase the foliage, but plants quickly rebound with new growth immediately upon warmer weather's return.

Pink evening primrose makes an elegant consort for this pastel blue century plant (*Agave scabra*), and will simply go dormant with the searing summer heat.

For months in spring, wood sorrel produces showers of dainty, rose-pink, funnel-shaped flowers that swirl shut until the sunshine coaxes them open. The diminutive size of individual flowers is offset by the sheer volume of blooms produced, occurring until hot weather forces plants to retreat. The bright pink flowers are displayed best with a foreground of silver or white, such as *Lamium maculatum* 'White Nancy' or variegated English ivy (*Hedera helix* 'Glacier'). Bronze-leaf *Ajuga reptans* offers a somber color contrast, and *Ajuga* 'Burgundy Glow' adds a color echo with the touches of pink in its marbled foliage. A white form of wood sorrel is also available but is somewhat less vigorous than the more common pink. It is valuable in darker venues where the white flowers are more visible at a distance.

Other species of *Oxalis* grace southern gardens during the cool season, but most are happy to avoid freezing weather. *Oxalis braziliensis* sports compact, dark green leaves with wine-colored flowers similar to the wood sorrel. It slowly increases over the years to form a dense, low mat of foliage studded with richly hued blooms. The Wild Weed of the West, the Bermuda buttercup (*O. pes-caprae*), is the scourge of many a California garden, where it is just too darn successful. I have seen entire yards consumed in a sea of soft yellow, nodding blooms and light green, cloverlike leaves. It *is* a pretty sight, but not a pleasant thought if you want to grow anything else. In the South, cold winter weather seems to keep it in check (along with the torrid summer weather, I would suspect), so it is nothing to be feared away from the West Coast.

Some of Texas's finest wildflowers are summer-dormant perennials that revel in the cool weather of winter, bloom in spring, and sleep in the heat. Lady Bird Johnson's favorite, the pink evening primrose (*Oenothera speciosa*), survives underground as simple undifferentiated roots (some as thick as a pencil, and sometimes only as big around as a pencil lead). Fall growth produces thrifty, dark green rosettes punctuating lawns and beds. Any section of root will sprout vegetative growth if severed from the parent plant, so the plant is all too easy to spread around. The flattened rosettes slowly increase in size and number, until there seems to be a frightful lot of the little five-inch foliage stars.

Plants quickly bolt and form buds when the weather warms, as stems stretch to ten inches tall—and they seem to be coming out of the woodwork. Fears are allayed, however, when the first buds open to reveal two-inch, poppylike bowls of soft pastel pink with darker veins and yellow boss of anthers in the center. Flowers are produced in waves but steadily gain momentum through the weeks of bloom. The color and form of the pink evening primrose are easily complemented by bluebonnets, a motif found along Texas highways. However, due to the aggressive, invasive nature of this flower, it is best used in landscapes, in large-scale schemes, or with shrub borders where the competitive threat is mitigated. I imagine that a dry landscape of cool-blue desert spoon (*Dasylirion wheeleri*) and frosty century plant (*Agave americana*) would look stunning in a sea of pastel pink evening primrose.

One of our true native buttercups, *Ranunculus macranthus*, grows from a tight, clawlike root structure similar to the dried Persian ranunculus bulbs found in nurseries (this particular ranunculus, however, is not available as a dormant bulb). In leaf, the native buttercup is a far more handsome plant than its cultivated counterpart. The compound foliage is a deeply lobed, light green with dark stains scattered amid the leaves. Rosettes over a foot across are common, and the plants thrive in damp ground. During winter, the foliage of *R. macranthus* consorts splendidly with variegated grassy-leafed sweet flag (*Acorus gramineus* 'Variegatus'), *Arum italicum* 'Pictum', and bronze *Ajuga reptans* 'Atropurpurea'. Springtime yields the added bonus of satiny yellow, semidouble buttercups in large clusters. Do allow this plant to go to seed and spread, as it is a real gem.

Yet another native perennial of the American plains with a winter-growing disposition is the downy or fragrant phlox (*P. pilosa*). Numerous tiny starts sprout from massing underground rootlets in fall, each stem bearing a series of small, simple, slightly hairy leaves (that's the downy part). As winter progresses, the mound of tiny stems grows in height and density, forming a lush green carpet when allowed to take over larger spaces. This perennial is a team player; it allows any and all companionship from spring bulbs and other flowers that choose to peek through the foliage.

In the midst of the midspring melee, *Phlox pilosa* forms large heads of five-petaled flowers in various shades of pink. The perfume from these exuberant blossoms rises from their lowly position to the lucky nose of anyone in the garden (that's the fragrant part), but I prefer to get on my knees to indulge in the delicious scent up close. Fragrant phlox is perfect naturalized in lawns, as a companion to spring bulbs, or integrated into garden beds as a unifying element. I am still awaiting the day when there is too much of it in my garden.

While most gardens go barren for half the year, people living in the southern region need not give up the delicious interplay of foliage form and texture during winter. Also, the bonus of colorful springtime flowers is guaranteed with little effort. By including some of the summer-dormant, cool-season perennials in beds and borders, it is possible to enjoy the benefits of living where one can garden 12 months of the year.

Soft pink heads of fragrant phlox mingle with the richly colored blooms of wood sorrel. Both can sleep through the worst conditions of summer.

Chapter 5

Foliage in the Winter Garden

As touched upon in the previous chapter, the winter sunbelt garden need not be bereft of foliage color and structure. Nearly every gardener desires the flashy colors of flowers, but we must restrain ourselves from becoming myopically "floracentric" during winter. Beauty can be found in the frost-tinted leaves of red, burgundy, and bronze that mingle with the jade and emerald evergreens.

Silver, gray, blue, and even purple foliage is also part of the scene during frosty weather. And architectural form and other structural interest of leaf and limb can add a subtle depth or sophistication to our gardens in winter. Some additions of bold foliage go a long way in creating focal points and interesting contrast of color and form. Cardoon (*Cynara cardunculus*) is a giant artichoke relative that grows well during winter in the warmer two-thirds of the South. The enormous silver leaves are deeply lobed and even rather spiny when older. They arrange themselves concentrically around the plant's base so as to give the effect of a large gray fountain. I seem to always underestimate the final size that a mature cardoon can attain when I plant the one-gallon plants in fall. Late spring finds me removing an errant 30-inch leaf or two that has reached over, menacingly shading some other valuable plants (regular artichokes offer the same look for the more timid gardener). Still, I wouldn't be without cardoons in the garden even if they are seemingly not team players when mature.

Planting cool-season vegetables is an easy way to include colorful, bold foliage in the winter garden. Red-leaf lettuce comes in an almost endless array of hues and textures. Bronze is most common, but dark and medium red and even pink lettuce selections can be found, and the seed is easy to start. Although most of my salads come from the vegetable garden, I always transplant some seedlings into small pots so that I can decide later where to include them in the beds and landscape. Rosette forms of developing lettuce heads are an unending source of beauty and interest as they consort with linear bulb foliage and cool-season flowers. Fortunately, their size is easily managed; the fresh leaves go to the kitchen instead of the compost.

Red mustard is even more cold tolerant than lettuce, and for those with very cold spells during winter, it is the best choice. 'Osaka Red' has large, rounded, garnet leaves that erupt up and out of beds and borders, giving more dimension to plantings than lettuce. The richly colored leaves are further complemented in spring by the tall, airy stalks of yellow flowers. Like the bronze-red leaves of lettuce, garnet-colored mustard leaves are fabulous companions for blue or white flowers as well as yellow and orange blooms.

Larger than mustard, Swiss chard produces big, oval, jade leaves on long stems; certain varieties bear scarlet,

OVERLEAF: Common flowering kale in an uncommon setting: no rows or masses, a solitary kale highlights a simple planting with *Lamium* 'White Nancy'.

RIGHT: Gentle giant, cardoon is a sculpture unto itself, creating a lovely foil for Byzantine glads and mealy blue sage.

yellow, coral, pink, or orange leaf stems (petioles) and veins. Swiss chard is a robust plant that deserves space in beds and borders, where it transforms the ordinary into the extraordinary. Even if planted amid lowly liriope, Swiss chard is an exciting focal point. Its lush, juicy profusion of leaves always draws the eyes of visitors to the garden. I am particularly fond of the luxuriant leaves of red Swiss chard juxtaposed with Iceland poppies. Chard does not always give up the ghost during summer (I've seen plants live all summer long here in Texas), so it is necessary to terminate it if other warm-season plants share the space. No problem for me, as chard is one of my favorite leafy vegetables for eating.

Out of the red and bronze leafy vegetables and into the cool pastels, everyone is familiar with the white and purple ornamental kales (*Brassica oleracea* cultivars). There is, however, no reason to stop there within such a diverse and cold-hardy group. The ornamental cabbages offer similar structure (without the ruffles on leaf margins) with the added bonus of soft pink or rose center coloration. Even more interesting and decorative are the beautiful forms of edible kale, which sport gorgeous foliage on robust, cold-hardy plants. 'Red Russian' has huge scalloped leaves of patina blue that develop a plum-colored cast in cold weather, and 'Red Bor' produces tight heads of crisp, frilly purple leaves that turn violet-amethyst with frost. Best of all, these glamorous kales are as satisfying as vegetables in the kitchen as they are in the garden. Thus they can be plucked to make room for other plants without regret.

There is just no comparison, though, to the overall mystic beauty of the common red cabbage. Unlike the rich purple heads found in the produce aisle of your grocery store, red cabbage plants produce pastel, gunmetal-blue leaves in an open, concentric arrangement that is not as heavy-handed as the ornamental kales and cabbages. Planted next to variegated society garlic (*Tulbaghia violacea* 'Variegata') with a frothy mélange of white alyssum, lavender and primrose-yellow pansies, and bluebonnets, this ugly duckling from the vegetable patch becomes a swan in my garden.

Golden feverfew (*Tanacetum parthenium* 'Aureum') doesn't have a large leaf, but tight, feathery, chartreuse foliage that breaks the monotony of green leaves as well as sharply contrasting with bronze and burgundy tones. Golden feverfew stays quite contained even when it puts forth branches of tiny white daisies in late spring. Although it is naturally a perennial, golden feverfew sometimes dies out in the Lower South during summer. This cold-hardy plant does make a very colorful and useful annual in winter.

Another source of chartreuse foliage in the sunbelt garden comes from the decidedly perennial golden oregano (*Origanum vulgare* 'Aureum'). Golden oregano produces tidy, thick mats of mottled green and golden leaves that add to the foliage tapestry of the garden throughout the year. Like the golden feverfew, golden oregano is a great foil for

Edible kale 'Red Bor' is even more beautiful than the ornamental varieties, with the added bonus of tasting delicious.

orange or purple flowers, and it combines well with burgundy, bronze, and blue foliage. In order to survive in summer, the oregano needs a spot that still receives sun after the trees leaf out again in spring.

Fortunately, silver-leafed sages (*Artemisia spp.*) are perfectly cold hardy and persist in the winter season. *Artemisia* 'Powis Castle' is hands down the best sage for hot, humid climates (it does well in dry areas, too). A shrub, rather than an herbaceous perennial, 'Powis Castle' needs to be kept in check in all but very large settings, as it can easily spread seven or eight feet across in the South. With a little pinching and pruning, 'Powis Castle' has a home in small gardens, mingling nicely with both summer and winter flowers. During the cool season, grow pink larkspur and lilac *Hesperis steveniana* in the place where summer-blooming, pastel blue plumbago lies dormant, for year-round complement to the *Artemisia's* silver filigree foliage.

Lamb's ears (*Stachys byzantina,* syn. *lanata*) is another perennial that keeps a good wintertime appearance in most of the sunbelt. In fact, lamb's ears seems to like the cooler weather better than the heat, which it only tolerates (the variety 'Helen von Stein' is the best in torrid Gulf Coast climates). The delightfully soft and inviting furry leaves of lamb's ears make a great foil for delicate pinks as well as shocking magenta flowers. It maintains a low profile (in fact, variety 'Silver Carpet' never sends up the two-foot-tall bloom stalks, so is always low) and works well with shorter winter annuals like alyssum, violas, Swan River daisy, and *Chrysanthemum multicaule*.

The common and readily available dusty miller (*Senecio maritima*) is very cold-hardy and quite dependable during winters in the southern latitudes. The thick, felty, silver leaves are deeply incised so as to give the plant a delicate appearance (but don't be fooled; it has an ironclad constitution). Dusty miller makes a great addition to pastel plantings of 'Imperial Pink Shades' pansies, and it highlights the satiny flowers of *Godetia amoena*. If dusty miller's bright yellow flowers on tall stems don't fit the picture, just clip them off, and more of the almost white foliage will sprout.

One of my favorite silver-foliage accents in the winter garden is *Lamium maculatum* (cultivars 'White Nancy', 'Pink Pewter', and 'Beacon Silver'). The low, sprawling plants have simple spade-shaped leaves, which are mostly silvery-white with green margins. A reliable perennial for shady areas, *Lamium* persists, dependably, in the Upper South and West Coast (where nighttime temperatures are somewhat cooler). My garden seems to be on the cusp of the Upper and Lower South since *Lamium* sometimes only barely survives the punishment of summer.

Even when *Lamium* is used as an annual, a gardener can get lots of mileage out of it during winter. Plants tolerate the sun in cool weather, and if they receive shade when trees leaf out in spring, they look good until the dog days of summer (that's when they crater out in my garden, at least). Low-growing, shade tolerant, and freeze hardy, *Lamium* cannot be beat. The cultivar 'White Nancy' seems to be the most vigorous grower, producing terminal clusters of white, hooded flowers in spring. I plant 'White Nancy' with pink-flowered wood sorrel (*Oxalis crassipes*) and strawberry begonia (*Saxifraga stolonifera*) for an easy-care foliage tapestry in winter. In spring, the profuse, pink wood sorrel flowers overflow onto the shimmering silver foliage.

If you are more inclined toward cool, powder-blue foliage in your garden, it can be found in a variety of shapes and sizes. Bold, inflexible pads of some prickly pear cactus (*Opuntia violacea* and *O. macrocentra*) offer substantial form and color for sunny, well-drained sites. In fact, when drought-stressed and exposed to cold, these cacti will even develop a rich, purple cast. (In my rather wet climate, this is best achieved by growing them in pots.) Either way, the prickly pears lend valuable color to the garden during winter.

That same pastel blue can be found in a couple of other desert denizens. Century plants (*Agave americana, A. parryi, A. scabra*, and

The silver filigree foliage of *Artemisia* 'Powis Castle' contrasts the brightly colored blooms of Clarkia and is wonderful with pastel flowers.

Architectural blue sotol (seen here with desert verbena) creates delightful combinations with floral consorts in winter or summer. (Photo by Charles Mann.)

A. palmeri) offer a rigid architectural form that can be impressive (even overwhelming, if the largest are planted). The radially symmetrical, "floral" form of agaves is delightful as a powder-blue foil for winter annuals like California poppies, African daisies, or China pinks.

The blue desert spoon, or sotol (*Dasylirion wheeleri*), gives a more yielding option for soft blue, structural form. Looking all the world like a pastel blue sea urchin, the desert spoon consists of many thin but rigid leaves, gently twisting and radially arranged about a central core. The open, airy aspect of this sun-lover is complemented by ethereal wands of pastel *Clarkia elegans* and pink Drummond's phlox.

Cool blue foliage on a smaller scale can be achieved with the blue-gray leaves of certain perennial *Dianthus* species. (In particular, *Dianthus sylvestris* and *D. gratianapolitanus* 'Bath's Pink' survive the worst heat and humidity.) These mat-forming perennials enjoy average garden conditions with at least a half day of sun and decent drainage. Throughout winter the low-growing (only two to three inches high) plants make a tidy ground cover and an excellent complement for pink, lavender, and soft yellow pansies. In spring these *Dianthus* sprout thin, four-inch stems bearing charming pink, clove-scented flowers.

Some evergreen, woody plants that take the heat all summer also give the added bonus of exciting winter coloration during the cool season. Foliage hues can be rust, red, or bronze, and intensity is usually based on temperature and exposure to the winter sun (the colder and sunnier, the better). Some plants, needing only a chill to produce good winter color, may even be cut to the ground by a hard freeze. These are best used in milder climates if winter color is desired.

Heavenly bamboo (*Nandina domestica*) is so common and overused in the warm regions that I may be chastised for mentioning it at all in this book. However, it can be used artfully in the garden, and it is very resilient as well (I would put *Nandina* in the "can't kill it with a club" category). The foliage on most cultivars turns autumn red or brick red after the first chill winds of winter, and it stays that way until new growth is ready to emerge in spring. Many varieties will also sport large sprays of bright red berries. In the garden, the best use of the shorter heavenly bamboo is to contrast the darkened foliage of winter with white narcissi (like 'Avalanche' or 'Grand Primo') or summer snowflakes (*Leucojum aestivum*).

Dwarf forms of *Nandina domestica* (and there are many) offer the same winter color at a lower level in the garden, where blue, purple, or yellow violas consort with the foliage. Sweet alyssum, white China pinks, and kale also mix well with the rusty red leaves of compact heavenly bamboo. The form 'Nana Purpurea' stays markedly short but seems less graceful when compared to the others. However, this variety turns fiery red in winter's cold, and the vivid foliage contrasts nicely with the silver, golden, blue, and green leaves of other plants in the garden. Despite its redundant use as a foundation planting, where these dwarf *Nandina* are lined up like soldiers against a wall, a single specimen of 'Nana Purpurea' makes a colorful addition to the winter garden.

The evergreen barberry, *Berberis x gladwynensis* 'William Penn', is quite content in sunbelt gardens, enduring all the extremes that come with the territory. In winter, cold weather turns the leaves a lovely coppery bronze. The color persists until spring's warmth returns. I am particularly fond of dark blue pansies (like 'Crystal Bowl Deep Blue') and Spanish bluebells (*Hyacinthoides hispanica*) as accompaniment for the bronze foliage of 'William Penn'.

One heat-loving shrublet that really dresses up for winter is the Arizona plumbago (*P. scandens*). This shade plant is best appreciated in gardens where hard freezes never visit but chill winds still blow (freezing temperatures will kill it to the ground). When winter comes, the smooth, simple leaves of Arizona plumbago become a rich garnet-maroon, persisting until spring. Jade-green *Liriope* planted beneath makes a semiprecious combination for shady areas in winter.

Maintaining stems and foliage only in milder climates, red bird of paradise shrub (*Caesalpinia pulcherrima*) delivers an encore to its stunning summertime performance. In winter, wine-colored seedpods top the feathery leaves, which have turned various shades of maroon and gold. Red bird of paradise can be beautiful on its own or in concert with the subdued colors of other desert vegetation. For some reason, maintenance norms include chopping these otherwise elegant shrubs in half in the fall; this is an unnecessary practice at best that robs one of further enjoyment into winter.

Whereas winter gardens in the North celebrate the evergreen of some plants that enliven a dreary landscape, sunbelt gardens can reflect a rainbow of colors from foliage alone during the cool season. Gardeners can enjoy the precious metals of silver, gold, pewter, and bronze interwoven with soft blues, chartreuse, garnet, and purples. This creates a colorful winter garden rich in textures, where choice plantings of bulbs and annuals play off of these many-hued foils as endless combinations are imagined.

CHAPTER 6

Cool-Season Container Gardening

There are many reasons to include planted containers and pots in the winter garden. For some people with very limited space in which to garden, pots offer the only venues for flowers at any season. Others may find that as the sun drifts lower in the southern sky during fall and winter, most of the garden is in shadows, and pots allow one to focus flower power where the sun still shines.

Where damaging cold weather is a possibility (however statistically remote or reliable), container gardening ensures that one's especially tender treasures need not perish when the icy winds blow. Pots of frost-tender flowers like Ixia, Freesia, Babiana, Schizanthus, Nemesia, and Clarkia can revel outdoors in perfect growing conditions on my patio, yet still be protected from the invariable freeze by moving them to cover once or twice a season. The containers spend most of their time enjoying the sunshine out on the pot patio, and when the threat of damaging cold passes, I can sit back to watch the show of flowers.

Practicalities aside, there are aesthetic motivations for growing cool-season flowers in containers. Pots add structure, color, depth, and dimension to the garden that would be difficult to find otherwise. Containers of endless shapes and sizes become bold focal points in the garden, lending weight and substance as anchors in beds and on courtyards, terraces, and patios. The color of the containers, be they naturally neutral or boldly brilliant, creates an additional source of interest and definition for any garden. Pots elevate flowers and foliage above the common two-dimensional confines of the average

garden, transforming it into a rich, extraordinary space. Often an architectural specimen plant with great structural interest can be showcased in the perfect container such that the two attain a sculptural quality. These stars take center stage in any garden.

Growing flowers in pots also allows the gardener to create specialized growing conditions for plants needing different soil than that found in the garden. Especially when the cultural requirements for certain plants call for impeccable drainage, or none at all (bog gardens are easy in pots), containers allow for a simple solution. I find it easier to fill containers with flowers during the cool season, when heat and drought are not constant watering adversaries. Pot culture adds a feeling of sophistication to the sunbelt winter garden as common florist cinerarias, cyclamen, primulas, and kale rise to new heights. This enables the gardener to imbue any corner with splashes of color and mingling textures.

One more notable trait of container plantings at any season of the year is that it's so much easier to achieve an aura of completion when planting in such confines compared to the seemingly endless nature of the rest of the garden. It may take weeks, months, or even years to

OVERLEAF: Kitty Lucy visits the pot patio.

BELOW: Poor man's orchids revel in Arizona desert winters.

RIGHT: Freesia and Nemesia at home by the stone terrace.

complete particular beds or other areas in the garden, but one can combine flowers and foliage in a pot and have a finished product in an hour. Especially in winter, when the bodacious effusion of the summer garden may be waning, colorful pots add invaluable interest.

Almost anything can be grown in containers, but I like to focus on rare foliage plants, bulbs, and annual flowers in my winter pots. These can be mixed and matched in any fashion, sometimes combining certain flowers and foliage in a single pot and other times growing solitary specimens, or masses of a single flower. Mixed-color annuals such as jewel-toned *Nemesia* or pastel *Godetia* make lovely blends all on their own. I also enjoy the stunning simplicity created when one color of flower is massed in a container.

Some of my potted desert denizens, which are solo performers in summer, take on the accompaniment of winter annuals during the cool season. The lavender daisy (*Macheranthera tanacetifolia*) enjoys the same well-drained soil as my potted prickly pear cactus (*Opuntia macrocentra*). Both can be left out in the cold without much worry, and the winter and spring blooms of the daisy embellish the purple-blushed cactus pads as well as its apricot-yellow flowers. Some of my pots contain such large century plants, cacti, and desert spoons that it would be difficult to add to them. In this instance it seems easiest to sprinkle a few seeds into the gravel on top of the pots. Also, an additional container or two of African daisies (*Dimorphotheca* or *Osteospermum*) give the collection an amazing punch. Still other containers with tropical rock figs or tender succulents get facelifts when winter annuals are added to the scene. In such cases, I invariably plant the cool-season bulbs and annuals that also need protection from frost.

If you want a knockout performance from container gardens, it is essential to remember regular feeding and timely watering. Even new

potting soil has limited nutrients available, and frequent waterings quickly leach that resource away. Older, previously used potting soil will almost certainly be devoid of much in the way of available nutrients. Because most annuals and bulbs are indeed heavy feeders, it is vital to give these plants everything they want. I use a balanced, water-soluble fertilizer and soak the entire soil mass (foliar feeding is insubstantial at best). Do also remember that growth and flower production take water, and wilted plants can't grow or bloom much. Watering the pots when the flowers need it is key. Water the soil deeply rather than casually sprinkling the leaves.

If you live in an area frequented by frost or hard freeze during winter, it's a good idea to decide from the start if you are willing to protect tender flowers from such inclement weather or if cold-hardy choices are more appropriate. Knowing that some or all of your pots are able to endure the cold allows you to give attention to lighting a fire and making some hot cocoa. I, unfortunately, choose to live dangerously: I grow quite a few frost-sensitive, cool-season bulbs and annuals in pots that invariably need to be covered or brought to safety during the cold northers. Those treasures are well worth the effort in my opinion, although sometimes with the extra worry during a harsh cold spell, I'll mix a bit of brandy in with the hot cocoa.

Even if the rest of the garden tends to be quiet during the winter months, it is always possible to indulge in just a little cool-season floral fun with containers. Winter gardening in pots is the best way to start exploring the beauties of the cool season in the sunbelt states. Cultivating the many winter-growing annuals and bulbs in pots allows the timid gardener to commit to a project of any size without the concern of taking on an entire bed. However, once one enjoys the fruits of such labors, it will be easier to conceive of expanding into the whole garden.

LEFT: Hybrid tulips, mere annuals for most in the sunbelt, nevertheless make stunning containers.

ABOVE: Potted hybrid freesias with *Nemophila maculata* growing at the base.

PART II
Southeastern
SUMMER GARDENING

ABUNDANT FORESTS NATURALLY COVER MOST OF THE TERRAIN in the American Southeast, evidence of the ample moisture needed to grow large trees and sustain woodland ecosystems. The rich diversity of tree species has its epicenter in the southern Appalachian mountains and radiates throughout the rest of the South, with an astounding array of hardwoods and pines mixing together in a sylvan mosaic covering the humid Southeast.

Water is the pervasive governing force that makes it all possible. Reliable rainfall and humid air define the quantity and quality of vegetation growing from east Texas through the South to the Atlantic Coast. Not only are the native forests extensive, but the trees themselves grow to be quite large. Understory woody plants abound in the form of small trees, shrubs, vines, and even palms, and beneath their canopy are still more herbaceous plants, all in competition not for moisture but for light.

Where trees abound, sunlight is at a premium. The meadow clearings and open savannas give refuge to sun-loving perennials and grasses, which also can be found along the forest margins created by roads cut through the trees. The meadows are home to many of the native perennial wildflowers that have become garden mainstays. Coneflowers, asters, goldenrods, butterfly weeds, and sunflowers are just some of the native southeast flowers now at home in our sunny borders.

SOMETHING ABOUT SOUTHEAST SOILS

The soils throughout the Southeast tend to be acidic (low pH) compared to the alkaline soils of the arid West. Some pockets of calcareous soil are scattered about the humid sunbelt states, but these are exceptions more than the rule. Also, the soil structure is predominantly sandy in texture, although areas of clay soil infrequently occur. The acidic, sandy soil conditions favor a vast quantity of different garden plants. The soil can be easily cultivated as is or improved by the addition of organic matter. Embellishment with compost or humus creates the quintessential garden soil that most shrubs, perennials, and grasses enjoy. High heat and humidity do, however, speed the decomposition of organic matter in southern garden soils, necessitating annual additions of compost. (Just imagine how much dead leaf and plant debris there would be by the end of a growing season in a dense forest or rich meadow.)

In regions of high rainfall and persistent humidity, it is important to consider soil drainage. Areas of wet soil should be filled with plants that *like* it that way. Cannas, hibiscus, swamp butterfly weed, elephant ears, grasses and their kin, crinum, and ginger lilies are examples of just some of the many plants that can make the most of a poorly drained site. Bog gardens are a natural in the moist Southeast, where gardeners can capitalize on an area of wet soil in a variety of manners. Rich soil affords the lush growth and luxuriant canna-banana look of the tropics, or the simplicity of sedges, rushes, and grasses, short or tall. Lean wet soils favor the unique, exotic-looking carnivorous plants (sundews, pitcher plants, and Venus flytraps) that are increasingly rare and threatened in native habitats. Water gardens, ponds, and pool plantings are also easy to maintain in a humid environment where the bold foliage of moisture-loving plants revels in such conditions.

Where plant choices dictate the need for increased drainage, raised beds are the answer. Although gardeners across America embrace the raised flower bed as some sort of misguided horticultural ideal, nowhere is it more essential for producing a broadened range of growing conditions than in the torrid Southeast. Especially for those gardening in flat country where there are no hills allowing excess water to flow away from the roots, there is a need to create small hills within the garden itself. These well-drained beds are microenvironments that make all the difference in the world when growing plants not adapted to wet feet.

Raised beds can be simply built up from native soil, with or without the addition of organic matter. They can also be constructed of coarse sand or even gravel (scree) for exceedingly fast drainage. Certainly for gardeners wanting to try an extensive variety of plants, it makes sense to have a wide range of soil conditions with which to experiment. This allows us, in the tradition of Goldilocks gardening, to find the site where moisture and drainage are just right for any particular plant.

IT'S THE HUMIDITY, STUPID

The most noteworthy condition affecting summer garden success in the South is humidity. Moisture is always present to fuel summer showers and keep gardeners

mopping their brows. Everyone talks about the torrid conditions. There is an odd one-upmanship throughout the Southeast regarding which locale has the worst humidity. Residents of Houston, New Orleans, Mobile, and Charleston will argue among themselves over who suffers the most humidity. The differences are beyond me, so I will not choose sides in this debate. I do, however, propose that such fervent loyalist competition would be better demonstrated by seeing who could grow the biggest crinum or make the best mint julep.

One thing is certain: The Gulf Coast is more humid than areas further inland and north. As a result, the Lower South has to play by a different set of gardening rules than the Upper South, where folks can successfully grow more temperate fare. Torrid tropical nights dominate the Gulf Coast for half the year, and the ever warm air stifles plants unable to tolerate it. Subtropical plants thrive in these conditions (just set your

Something tells me we're not in Kansas anymore. Indeed it's Tony Avent's display garden at Plant Delights Nursery near Raleigh.

95

houseplants out for the summer and see) while temperate perennials only struggle or fail miserably. Therefore, I will in this chapter present a mixed bag of the best heat-tolerant, temperate perennials and subtropical garden perennials capable of surviving winter in USDA Zones 7 and 8.

THE LOOK OF THE GARDEN

The most striking thing about summer perennial gardens in hot, humid climates is the size that plants attain. Ample moisture, warm nights, and a long growing season conspire to produce towering giants out of what would be modest-sized perennials in northern gardens. It is important to maintain a sense of scale when gardening under such circumstances, and to allow plants the required room to grow to their full potential. This doesn't mean that you shouldn't garden if you have only a small space, but it implies that discerning choices must be made when selecting perennials for the diminutive garden lest the finished product in August look like an oversized hair ball.

I am often frustrated by the space limitations of my own small garden, which doesn't offer the large sunny nook required for a monstrous clump of Joe Pye weed or plume poppy. I dream of annexing my neighbor's unused sunny lawn while I manage to squeeze in only a few of the cannas, ornamental grasses, and ginger lilies one can choose from. The variegated cane grass (*Arundo donax* 'Versicolor') and black bamboo must be whittled back on a yearly basis so that they don't spread beyond my means. Still, I love my garden's summertime jungle ambiance of lush exotic growth.

Friends and relatives, remembering the genteel Dr. Jekyll (or is that Gertrude Jekyll?) appearance of the garden in winter and spring, are rather shocked by summer's Mr. Hyde persona. Some people just don't trust a plant that can shoot up from the ground to ten feet tall in only a few months, although a small tree or large shrub that size is obliquely nonthreatening. This may be why many gardeners in the kudzu-choked South prefer the safe, static predictability of tedious quantities of sheared shrubbery. Although such gardens are considered sublime by some, I just like plants too much to be content with nothing but clipped boxwoods and hollies. I prefer the dynamic and dramatic exuberance of a variety of perennials, grasses, and flowering shrubs with all their different forms, textures, and sizes. Above all, I enjoy the color and fragrance of flowers and the animated birds and butterflies drawn to them. Lucky for gardeners in the Southeast, all can be attained and maintained with a little flare if you dare to garden on the wild side.

LEFT: Pitcher plants and smaller sundews compose this beautiful vignette of a carnivorous plant bog.

ABOVE: Towering Joe Pye weed, variegated maiden grass, and Russian sage are magical together, but this combination takes up a lot of space.

CHAPTER 7

PERENNIALS FOR SUMMER BLOOM

The moist Southeast is the perfect home for herbaceous perennials, which grow from rootstock and rosettes at ground level to become towering stalks of glorious bloom. There is usually plenty of water—the driving force for leaf, stem, root, and flower development—during the growing season to support such extravagant growth. Sunshine, of course, fuels the growth of all green plants, and nutrients in the soil facilitate the process of photosynthesis. But this all hinges on the supply of water available.

I am particularly fond of herbaceous perennials that can be cut to a quick at the end of the season and thus open up the beds for a parade of cool-season bloom. Bulbs and winter annuals easily fill in the void created when retiring summer-blooming perennials are cut back for winter. Then, there is only slow, modest growth at the crown of such plants, and they don't require more space until ready to reclaim their vast territory in the summer sun. Some heat-loving flowering perennials maintain a high profile during winter months, but these are exceptions to the rule. As a result, there are many opportunities for winter gardening with cool-season annuals and bulbs in southeastern gardens.

Some of the best perennials for summertime bloom in southeast gardens follow. For ease of location, I have grouped some of the selections in terms of the many members of a particular genus, as well as collections of varied flowers.

VERBENAS

Let's begin with the many varieties of garden verbena (*Verbena canadensis*) now available. An indestructible nature, low-creeping habit (six to eight inches high), and long bloom time (spring to fall) combine with a menagerie of white, pinks, lavenders, and purples (more colors and cultivars appear each year), making this one of the premier perennials for hot sunny gardens, where it softens edges and mingles with everything else at the front of the bed. Garden verbena is the perfect costar for beds burgeoning with summertime prima donnas, adding color harmonies and contrasts for many other perennials.

The popular *Verbena canadensis* cultivar 'Homestead' is almost too vigorous for small spaces, as it will sprawl out to cover large areas in a single season. Though not always a team player when planted with smaller perennials, 'Homestead' produces rich royal-purple flowers with such abandon as to be forgiven its lapse in manners. It combines well with taller perennials such as golden black-eyed Susan (*Rudbeckia fulgida*), orange butterfly weed (*Asclepias tuberosa*), and red lipstick sage (*Salvia darcyi*). 'Homestead' also generously cloaks the ground at the feet of orange or yellow daylilies, red roses, and white Mexican petunias with a dense layer of healthy, dark green leaves that make the perfect foil for abundant purple blooms.

For those who need something brighter, there is brilliant magenta *Verbena canadensis* 'Batesville Rose'. This selection exhibits the same blossoming exuberance as 'Homestead' without the extra vegetative growth that can conquer a whole bed. The gorgeous chartreuse foliage of golden sweet potato (*Ipomoea batatas* 'Margarita') is stunning combined with the flowers of 'Batesville Rose'; including peach-colored *Portulaca* 'Mango' makes it delicious.

Several selections and hybrids of *Verbena canadensis* have graced our gardens with lavender, light violet, and bluish-purple flowers on sturdy free-blooming plants. 'Abbeville', 'Blue Princess', 'Lilac Time', and 'Greystone Daphne' are some of the named varieties available to those in search of cool summer colors. These verbenas are splendid mixed with silver *Artemisia* 'Powis Castle' or *Stachys* 'Helen von Stein'. Steely blue Indian grass (*Sorghastrum nutans* 'Sioux Blue') and white garden phlox (*P. paniculata* 'David') or sky-blue cape plumbago (*P. auriculata*) complete the refreshing scene.

Verbena 'Sissinghurst' (sometimes classed as *V. tenera*) is hands down the best pink form available for hot-weather gardens. Lower and tighter in growth habit than the others, it nevertheless puts on a nonstop show of pastel, coral-pink flowers. 'Sissinghurst' is simply wonderful skirting the powder-blue grassy foliage of little bluestem (*Schizachyrium scoparium*) or the similarly hued desert spoon or sotol (*Dasylirion wheeleri*), while being echoed by the blooms of *Salvia coccinea* 'Coral Nymph'.

White *Verbena canadensis* (named 'Snowflurry', 'Alba', or simply 'White') is another summer garden workhorse, producing a myriad of pristine blooms from spring to fall. The perfect accompaniment to almost any color scheme, this verbena especially makes a sound addition to the all-white moon garden. Imagine the neat compact mounds surrounding the white forms of garden phlox, coneflower, swamp milkweed, ginger lily, butterfly bush, tropical sage, and moonflower. When it's hot outside, why not design the garden for night?

Tall verbena (*V. bonariensis*) is a distinctly different creature altogether. Its four-foot-tall, thin, erect stems carry aloft a multitude of bright lavender flower heads, yet the plant has scant foliage. This plant's translucent habit confounds some gardeners but can be used to advantage if one doesn't always relegate tall verbena to the back of the border, where it may not have enough substance. Definitely more than one plant of tall verbena should be planted in any area for maximum impact from this delicate-looking perennial. It's ideal with big grasses and boisterous cannas.

MILKWEEDS

The milkweeds (*Asclepias spp.*) can't seem to escape slanderous nomenclature, but they are definitely not weedy in the garden. The mildly two-toned, tangerine-orange flowers of the butterfly weed (*Asclepias tuberosa*) are a midsummer blessing for gardeners and butterflies alike. The plant is indispensable for attracting our favorite friends to the garden, and it requires only full sun and good drainage. The one- to two-foot-tall plants are quite innocuous until the color show begins, when it might be good to have the compact clumps couched between purple *Verbena canadensis* 'Homestead' and white appleblossom grass butterflies (*Gaura lindheimeri*). After blooming, butterfly weed and other milkweeds produce lovely, swollen, erect pods that split open in autumn to release seeds, each with their own silky parachute.

Swamp milkweed (*Asclepias incarnata*) is quite happy in regular garden settings, but it doesn't mind wet feet if you have such a site in the sun. The sturdy three- to four-foot-tall plants have simple leaves that are arranged on the stem so as to give the plant a geometric, architectural look. When two-inch clusters of pastel pink blossoms begin to show, the swamp milkweed comes into its own—though it still benefits from a supporting cast, as it is somewhat naked at the base. Blue-flowered bog sage (*Salvia uliginosa*) and *Canna glauca* help the pink swamp milkweed and its white form 'Ice Ballet' look their best.

**OPPOSITE: Canna 'Durban',
containerized and set in the
pond, needs the sedate green
foliage of palm grass (Setaria
palmifolia) to temper its
fiery image.**

Mexican milkweed (*Asclepias curassavica*) is grown as a hot-weather annual and even a cut flower, but for those who garden in sultry Gulf Coast climates it is a trustworthy perennial. For the glorious monarch butterfly, which feeds as larvae upon the foliage and sips nectar from the red and yellow blooms as adults, this plant is home. Like the swamp milkweed, this cousin from south of the border grows tall and somewhat knock-kneed and should not be forced to grow alone. Purple Mexican petunia (*Ruellia brittoniana*) and maiden grass (*Miscanthus sinensis*) are likely consorts for the flamboyant bicolored flowers. An all-yellow selection, 'Silky Gold', allows this delightful gem into the gardens of those who eschew the garish colors found in the wild form, where it can gently mingle with tall verbena and the white cultivar of *Ruellia*.

SUN-LOVING PERENNIALS FOR MOIST SOIL

Blackberry lily (*Belamcanda chinensis*) is, despite its deceptive common name, actually a member of the iris family. Vigorous, healthy fans of leaves arise from a small rhizome that expands only slowly over time and grows to two feet tall before blooming. The valuable foliage is then embellished by open, branched flower stalks rising above the leaves, producing a succession of orange-and-red-spotted, six-petaled blooms. (Hybrids called candy lilies expand the color range to yellow and purples.) The effect is like slow-motion fireworks, but the show doesn't stop there. Swollen seedpods develop through late summer and split open in fall to reveal berrylike clusters of shiny black seeds. These readily germinate the following spring, increasing the size of *Belamcanda* colonies.

The world of cannas is both daunting and exciting. In their long history of cultivation they have been loved, then despised, and now loved again. Those gardeners who never hated cannas can now come out of the closet and proclaim their affection. Certainly no plants are as easy to grow in the subtropical heat as these, and they yield both luxuriant foliage and exotic flowers. The rhizomes of cannas are quite hardy underground, being able to survive winter's chill throughout most of the South. These adaptable perennials can be grown as aquatics submerged in water, or in the lush bog garden, or in regular soil of most beds and borders. In all cases, cannas enjoy rich soil with lots of food to fuel their rapid and exuberant growth.

Two of the most colorful new hybrids that are the vanguard of the canna renaissance have multicolored leaves of purple-red dramatically striped with green and yellow veins. The foliage alone is outrageous, but these five- to six-foot-tall hybrids produce large, colorful blooms as well. *Canna* 'Durban' is topped with fiery orange-red blooms that I don't usually enjoy until my head has been baked in the summer heat for a few months—after that I love it. *Canna* 'Phaison' (also known as 'Tropicanna'™) produces flowers that are a clear, brilliant orange.

Another new hybrid with similar foliage but a dwarf habit (just three to four feet tall) is *Canna* 'Pink Sunburst'. As the name suggests, this cultivar produces salmon-pink flowers—perfect for gardeners who can keep a cool head during summer. An older hybrid, *Canna* 'Pretoria', is also called the Bengal Tiger canna due to its bold green-and-yellow-striped foliage. This elegant beauty erupts with clear tangerine-orange blooms that are perfect with *Salvia x* 'Indigo Spires'.

In contrast to the flamboyant foliage and flowers of the dashing new hybrids, some wonderful species of cannas have a more subtle beauty. Unsurpassed vigor and a greater resistance to pests are another reason to try them. *Canna indica* 'Purpurea' (a.k.a. *Canna* 'Intrigue') is perhaps the best bronze-leafed canna around. Unlike most other forms that lose their reddish cast as heat and age take their toll, leaves of *C. indica* 'Purpurea' keep their rich color on seven-foot-tall stems that are crowned with small, glowing orange flowers and inflated green seedpods. Another valuable species, *Canna glauca*, sports the most delightful blue-green leaves, which impart an unusual cooling effect in the garden. In addition, *C. glauca* has soft yellow blooms that perfectly complement the foliage; the cultivar 'Panache' blooms with a parade of salmon flowers.

Ginger lilies (*Hedychium spp.*) also enjoy torrid summer weather and rise from tuberous underground roots to grace southern gardens with exotic tropical foliage and the panache of gorgeous blooms, yet they are not nearly as commonly seen. The original butterfly ginger (*Hedychium coronarium*) forms a clump of canelike stems with medium green, six-inch-long, pointed leaves striking out in an opposite fashion, looking similar to a ladder. From the green conelike structure that forms on top of the six-foot-tall plants emerge glistening butterfly-shaped blossoms, white with creamy yellow brush, that are two to three inches wide. Each flower lasts just a day, but each day finds new blooms opening, each powerfully fragrant with a honeysuckle perfume. New hybrids of this treasure expand the color range into yellow, gold, and peachy tones, all of which are gloriously scented.

The ginger lilies need not be relegated to the tropicalismo style of canna-banana gardens (although they are a shoe-in there) but also make excellent accent plants along with temperate-looking Joe Pye weed, garden phlox, tall verbena, anise sage, and ironweed. Within a shallow depression bed in my garden I have *Hedychium* 'Gold Flame' backed by *Canna* 'Phaison', and joining *Asclepias curassavica* 'Silky Gold' and *Ruellia brittoniana* 'Alba', with chartreuse *Ipomoea batatas* 'Margarita' cloaking the ground at their feet. All enjoy the extra moisture captured by the sunken setting.

LEFT: Canna 'Pink Sunburst', grown here with *Persicaria* 'Firetail', is beautiful in foliage even without the bonus of bloom.

ABOVE: Butterfly ginger, like all ginger lilies, thrives in rich soil and benefits from consistent watering and fertilization.

The dark mysterious foliage of *Canna indica* 'Purpurea' contrasts the cream-edged leaves of Abutilon 'Souvenier de Bonn' and complements the purple flowers of *Solanum rantonnetii*.

Other equally valuable species of ginger lilies include the delta ginger (*Hedychium greenii*), which sports slightly darker green leaves with a maroon cast to the undersides and coral-red blooms. It is especially fond of a bit of shade and consistent soil moisture and is a delightful companion to coral honeysuckle (*Lonicera sempervirens*). *Hedychium coccineum* is particularly vigorous, and it flushes with blossoms all at once rather than a few at a time. The variable, reddish to pink flowers open with protruding stamens, which give the entire six-inch-long spike the look of a bottle brush.

MALLOWS

Reveling in the same conditions as cannas and ginger lilies (moist soil and sunshine), the mallows (*Hibiscus spp.*) also add a touch of the tropics to the summer garden. The heat-loving perennials are, in addition, quite cold tolerant, as they escape winter's chill by retreating to the ground, only to return the next summer when they bolt up to six or seven feet tall. All have blooms similar to the iconoclastic blossom of the tropics—the shrubby *Hibiscus rosa-sinensis*, with a whorl of golden anthers and stigma protruding from the center of five broad, rounded petals.

Scarlet mallow (*H. coccineus*) is an elegant albeit giant perennial that easily can reach seven feet tall and three feet wide in a season. The glossy maplelike leaves add great textural dimension to the garden on their own, and the six-inch-long, shocking-red blooms are indeed a crowning glory. Scarlet mallow makes a steamy ménage à trois with Canna 'Pretoria' and Mexican firebush (*Hamelia patens*). Southern rose mallow (*H. moscheutos*) grows shorter and wider than the previous species, filling out a space up to six feet tall and four feet wide. The simple elliptical leaves offer a coarse texture but are quickly overshadowed by huge billowy blossoms in soft pink, white, or white with a crimson eye (my favorite). The buxom blooms are easily ten inches across, yet some hybridizers, needing something larger, have bred varieties with even bigger flowers on compact plants. Personally, I find flowers the size of Frisbees to be downright hard to integrate into the rest of the garden, if not scary, and prefer to plant the wild types. Southern rose mallow looks best with the more subtle beauty of variegated maiden grass (*Miscanthus sinensis* 'Cosmopolitan') and bog sage (*Salvia uliginosa*).

JIMSON WEED

Jimson weed (*Datura inoxia*) is another source of larger-than-life flowers, but grown on a water budget. The tropical-looking, large leaves suggest that this plant, too, likes to live in wet soil, but it is quite happy in well-drained conditions. As an economical measure to save water, *Datura* opens its huge, pleated, trumpet-shaped blooms at sunset

The hauntingly beautiful jimson weed is remarkably easy to grow, but full sun is a must.

(quite an eye-catching event occurring in just minutes), giving it another common name, moonflower. This captivating perennial, immortalized by Georgia O'Keeffe in her collection of botanical paintings, can stand alone in the garden as well as sit center stage, accompanied by costars such as butterfly weed, blazing star (*Liatris squarrulosa*), appleblossom grass (*Guara lindheimeri*), and little bluestem grass.

CONEFLOWERS, AMERICAN CLASSICS

Nothing exemplifies the summer cottage garden like the quaint, glowing faces of black-eyed Susans and coneflowers. The wonderful *Rudbeckia* species have been the most valuable American commodity to be exported to the rest of the world since jazz. Europeans have even taken a good thing and made it better through judicious selection, so that we can now be proud of wonderful native American perennials with hard-to-pronounce German names. There are many to choose from, but some are exceptionally heat tolerant and thrive even on the Gulf Coast.

The most popular selection of perennial black-eyed Susan across the United States is *Rudbeckia fulgida* var. *sullivantii* 'Goldsturm'. This slowly

RIGHT: Rudbeckias are as American as jazz and thrive throughout Dixieland. Pictured here is *Rudbeckia triloba*.

increasing perennial makes neat clumps of dark green leaves that form a nice ground cover in mild winter climates. 'Goldsturm' shifts gear from low-profile perennial to a high-profile garden glory in midsummer, when three-inch golden blooms open on top of compact, 18-inch-tall stems. The flowers stay in bloom for over a month while they enjoy the camaraderie of *Salvia x* 'Indigo Spires', purple *Verbena* 'Homestead', and white *Phlox paniculata* 'David'.

Shining coneflower is now definitively hallmarked by one outstanding selection. *Rudbeckia nitida* 'Herbstsonne' seems to be the only form of this native wildflower available in the nursery trade, although one would hardly classify a seven- to eight-foot-tall giant as simply a wildflower. While other flowers catch our attention in spring and early summer, sturdy stems sporting large, lobed leaves slowly rise to substantial heights in the border where 'Herbstsonne' grows. After branching and putting on an additional three-foot length of stems, buds open, revealing lemon-yellow, drooping petals surrounding bright green central cones. This towering giant needs associates of equal caliber, so 'Herbstsonne' is best planted with Joe Pye weed or scarlet mallow, tall cannas, and gigantic ornamental grasses.

Three-lobed brown-eyed Susan (*Rudbeckia triloba*) is one of my favorite perennials, but it is unfortunately a short-lived one. It grows almost like a long-lived biennial as compact, unassuming rosettes begin to bolt and rise into three-foot-tall clumps of multibranched stems. The one-inch flowers are small in comparison to other *Rudbeckia*, but they are produced in such a profusion during late summer and early fall as to more than compensate for their slight size. The cloud of golden-yellow flowers with brown centers blooms for months and complements a host of other perennials in sunny and shady beds, too, since three-lobed brown-eyed Susan tolerates shade. *Rudbeckia triloba* self-sows about the garden, so though individuals may not persist for long, there will always be some of these valuable late-summer flowers around.

I was first enamored with cabbage-leaf coneflower (*Rudbeckia maxima*) when I saw the mound of bold, glaucous foliage in winter. The large, rounded leaves form neat clumps that enliven the winter garden, contrasting with linear foliage of narcissus and Dutch iris. In summer, naked scapes bolt up to heights of five to seven feet, topped by a few large sunny blossoms that seem to hover with the butterflies in the garden. Although it rises to great heights, plant *Rudbeckia maxima* in the front of the border with ruby-foliaged cardinal flower, where it can be appreciated all year. Other "see-through" plants, like tall verbena and fountain grass, make good company.

SMALLER PERENNIALS FOR MOIST SOIL

Cardinal flower (*Lobelia cardinalis*) is as much a part of the southeast landscape as its namesake feathered friend. The bronze-red leaves form distinctive rosettes during

winter, which later bolt and rise to three-foot-tall stems studded by burgundy foliage and crowned with a parade of brilliant red, open-faced, tubular flowers. As cardinal flower enjoys moist soil, it is best planted with rushes, sedges, or dwarf sweet flag (*Acorus gramineus*), which also thrive in such a site. A white-flowered form of the cardinal flower (it has green leaves) and a pink-flowered selection are also available for those who find red to be too hot.

Blue lobelia (*L. siphilitica*) is a robust perennial with much the same habit as its red cousin, but on more vigorous plants that quickly become larger colonies. It also likes a moist site and blooms midsummer with tall spires of blue flowers with white throats. Best of all, *Lobelia siphilitica* has thrown its genetic hat into the hybridizer's gene pool along with *L. cardinalis* and *Mexican L. fulgens* to produce assorted new vigorous garden perennials with an incredible range of colors. These vibrant summer flowers now expand the realm of red into burgundy and rose, and go beyond, to purples and pinks. *Rudbeckia* 'Goldsturm', blackberry lily, and garlic chives (*Allium tuberosum*) complement them delightfully.

Also at home in moist soil conditions is the knotweed relative *Persicaria amplexicaule* 'Firetail', but this perennial is not invasive like its kin. Clump-forming 'Firetail' has five-inch-long, arrowhead-shaped leaves that give the plant substance early on as well as while in bloom. Three-foot-tall, thin, naked stalks carry tight ruby-red spikes that are three inches long and last for many weeks in summer. Long-blooming 'Firetail' makes an excellent consort for *Phlox paniculata*, *Rudbeckia* 'Goldsturm', hybrid *Lobelia*, or *Hemerocallis fulva* (or all, together). It can tolerate drier soil when offered shade, but its real limitation seems to be the torrid heat of the Gulf Coast, so it is best used in the Upper South.

FOLIAGE FLAIR AND STRUCTURE

One of the few perennials grown predominantly for colorful foliage, painter's palette (*Tovara virginiana* syn. *Persicaria virginiana*) is wonderfully subtle. The triangularly shaped leaves on somewhat arching, two-foot-tall stems are marbled with creamy white and shades of pink on a light green background. Summer finds dainty flower sprays resembling tiny, red coral beads loosely strung on thin wire, which hover above the foliage. Painter's palette prefers some shade and consistent moisture, and it increases by underground roots becoming a hefty mass. It fits into woodland settings or can be planted in a more exotic venue with cannas and elephant ears (*Colocasia*).

With a lower stature but more rambunctious demeanor, chameleon leaf (*Houttuynia cordata*) is a foliage plant of the first order. This native of Indochina has an incredible range of heat and cold tolerance, and it wants only water. The heart-shaped leaves are a kaleidoscope of color, marbled in green, yellow, and carmine (with good sun). Best color is seen when chameleon leaf is grown in full sun in bog conditions, but because it is wont to travel it may be prudent to sink the plant into the ground within the bounds of a pot. In drier, shady places *Houttuynia* is less colorful but also less aggressive. Any plant able to rise above the six-inch-tall chameleon leaf can cohabitate successfully.

A perennial grown not only for its bold, glaucous foliage but also for its imposing stature is the plume poppy (*Macalaya cordifolia*). This is one of those perennials that can scare the less adventurous gardener by its ability to reach mammoth proportions—ten feet or more—in a few months, increasing the size of its clumps through underground stems. The six- to eight-inch-long, olive-green leaves are decoratively lobed with a unique white underside. At its pinnacle of growth the plume poppy is crowned with the panache of coppery, cloudlike blooms. Tolerant of a wide range of soil conditions, this plant really needs lots of room in the sun, where it is complemented by large ornamental grasses.

Of all the plants with the unfortunate common name of "weed," none is perhaps more deserved than the native pokeweed (*Phytolacca americana*). To many this strapping perennial is just that, but to others it is a magnificent plant. Thick, juicy stems rise to create a small treelike vision with large, simple leaves and red stems. The three- to five-foot-tall plants have insignificant flowers but later produce quantities of wine-colored berries in pendant chains. Because pokeweed thrives in moisture-retentive soil and full sun, it would be grandly Gothic to mass blackberry lilies, with their own parade of jet-black seeds come late summer, and dark-leafed *Alternanthera dentata* 'Ruby' or black coleus in the foreground.

SALVIAS

The genus *Salvia* includes so many species that are garden-worthy in the Southeast that it is hard to choose only a few of the best. It should also be mentioned that the sages included in Part 3 of this book (plants for the arid Southwest) also perform well in more humid climates.

The anise sage (*Salvia guaranitica*) is a sturdy, clumping perennial that can easily grow to become a

Towering red spires of hybrid lobelias are a welcome sight to hummingbirds, while ghostly hosta blooms lure nocturnal moths.

Chameleon leaf is quite aggressive in moist soil and sun, but it makes a compatible ground cover under robust elephant ears, crinums, and spider lilies.

three- to four-foot-tall by two-foot-wide mass of bright green stems cloaked by spade-shaped leaves and topped by spikes of blue flowers all summer. The selection 'Argentine Skies' has delightful sky-blue flowers, and the variety 'Brazil' has flowers of an electric, dark blue color. A particularly striking form of anise sage, 'Black and Blue', has the same dark blue flowers and the bonus of a black calyx holding it to the stem. Anise sage is not too choosy about soil moisture and tolerates a wide range of conditions. In drier sites the vivid blues are fabulous with the acid yellow of *Patrinia scabiosifolia* and bright pink *Phlox paniculata* 'Robert Poore', whereas in a moisture-rich venue scarlet mallow and Mexican milkweed are great partners.

Mexican bush sage (*Salvia leucantha*) makes a three-foot-tall, rounded mound through most of summer, with narrow olive-green stems clasping white stems. In late summer and into fall, the plants produce tall spikes densely laden with fuzzy white and purple flowers. A selection named 'Midnight' sports solid purple flowers and makes itself known in the garden. *Lantana montevidensis* hybrids of white, cream, yellow, or orange make lively consorts, along with variegated maiden grass (*Miscanthus sinensis*

'Morning Light'). I like the all-purple Mexican bush sage backed by the three-lobed brown-eyed Susan (*Rudbeckia triloba*).

Salvia x 'Indigo Spires' is the product of crossing two species of sage (*Salvia farinacea* and *S. longispicata*), and it looks rather like one of its parents, the blue mealy sage, on steroids. Nevertheless, this vigorous hybrid is a workhorse producing nonstop color in the garden through summer and into fall. The rather lax, spreading stems are topped by long, undulating spikes of dark blue flowers as the stems then branch out for further growth and blooms. By late summer, plants easily attain four feet tall and wide, and the ten-inch, twisting flower spikes lend a wonderful sense of movement to the garden. Cooler weather intensifies the color of the blossoms to a deep indigo, and the plants bloom until frost. In my garden I let 'Indigo Spires' cavort shamelessly with the yellow-striped foliage of *Canna* 'Pretoria' and the arching coppery inflorescences of shrimp plant (*Justicia brandegeana*).

The stoloniferous, spreading habit of bog sage (*Salvia uliginosa*), coupled with its tongue-twisting botanical name, scares some people away from this otherwise wonderful perennial. Thin stems bedecked with small oval leaves branch out to form a large but airy plant up to five or six feet tall and wide. Small blue flowers with white centers are endlessly produced on long wiry spikes all over the plant, creating a blue, misty veil in the garden. Bog sage loves wet sites but also revels in average garden conditions. In a moist spot let it romp with the multicolored foliage and orange blossoms of *Canna* 'Phaison' and zebra grass (*Miscanthus sinensis* 'Zebrinus').

Pitcher sage (*Salvia pitcheri*), a plains native, is quite happy in dry, sunny sites, where it grows to four or five feet tall but maintains a narrow profile. The thin foliage seems a disguise when the large spikes of showy blue flowers arrive in late summer. Each day sees new flowers popping out of the branched floral spikes at random so that they are never densely flowered, but the show persists for many weeks. This perennial seems born to play among robust ornamental grasses like *Panicum, Miscanthus,* and *Pennisetum,* which offer late-summer tawny blooms that complement the sky blue of the sage.

A tender perennial at best, the burgundy sage (*Salvia vanhoutii*) is certainly worth replanting after harsh winters erase it from my garden. In Gulf Coast gardens it performs with greater long-term reliability, and it can't be beat for nonstop color throughout the hot weather. The plants can easily get to five feet tall with dark green, spade-shaped leaves loosely clothing the openly branched stems. Rich, velvety, maroon blooms appear from the embrace of same-colored bracts arranged densely on flower spikes, and even the developing crook-necked inflorescence is dazzling. This sage loves the good life and needs rich, moist soil for best performance. In my garden the colors of the burgundy sage are echoed by the wine-colored trunk and leaf stems of Abyssinian banana (*Ensete vetricosum* 'Maurelii') and maroon-centered pink flowers of *Ruellia* 'Chi Chi'.

Bog sage, paired with Canna 'Phaison', is adored by English and European gardeners for its stalwart nature and long blooming season.

SUBTLE BUT STURDY

Certainly more compact and less flamboyant is the respectable perennial *Sedum telephium* (now *Hylotelephium telephium*) 'Autumn Joy'. This 18-inch to 2-foot-tall succulent forms tidy, long-lived clumps with multiple stems garnered with pastel green, rounded leaves. In summer, each stem is topped by clusters of flower buds that look like a small head of broccoli. Although the flowers bloom a muted, fleshy pink, the show is just beginning, as the flower heads continue to mature and darken into a deep russet-red color over time. 'Autumn Joy' is great in average garden conditions but tolerates extremes of wet and dry soil and even some shade with little impact on its reliable performance. *Rudbeckia* 'Goldsturm' and dwarf fountain grass (*Pennisetum alopecuroides*) make a lovely, subtle trio with 'Autumn Joy'.

Another modest-sized perennial for southeast summer bloom is garlic chives (*Allium tuberosum*). This often overlooked gem is in the "can't kill it with a club" category and should be pursued by those who need guaranteed garden success. The strongly aromatic, bright green, straplike foliage is simply sublime, and the foot-tall plants blend easily into a variety of settings. In summer, 18-inch-tall stems bearing two-inch spherical clusters of tiny white stars grace the garden and can even be cut and brought inside. It is a splendid partner for Sedum 'Autumn Joy'. Plants multiply by rhizomatous clumping and through seeding about (the seedpods are also charming in the fall garden), but I don't have too many in my garden as of yet. The white flowers and simple grassy foliage go with just about everything, so I just keep moving the extras about to other parts of my small garden.

GULF COAST GLORIES

Although some valuable *Ruellia* species are native to the United States, the Mexican *Ruellia brittoniana* is hands down more robust and floriferous. The wild form grows three to four feet tall, with a somewhat lanky profile that doesn't seem to have quite enough of the dark green, long, elliptical leaves to cover all its stems. It produces continuous crops of one- to two-inch, funnel-form, lavender-blue flowers, which nicely complement the dark foliage but can become lost at a distance. The white-flowered form is equally floriferous, and the blooms show better in the garden since they are not hiding amid dark green leaves like the former. The cultivar 'Chi Chi' has narrower leaves and smaller flowers of soft pastel pink with a maroon eye. All of these forms of the Mexican petunia, as it is called, will spread about by underground stems and seed wherever they are happy (in parts of Zone 7 the site must be protected), but I don't consider them a problem in the garden. Mostly, the awkward legginess of these tall perennials needs to be tempered by choosing the right partners to plant with them, like ornamental grasses.

Cousin to the renegade purple loosestrife, cigar plant (*Cuphea ignea*) is also happy growing in moist soil but shows no predilection for invading wetlands. This compact subtropical perennial is only winter hardy along the Gulf Coast, but it is welcomed as a heat-loving annual further north. The thin, branching stems bear dark green, diamond-shaped leaves and a constant parade of one-inch, orange, tubular flowers with darkened tips. Recently introduced cultivars extend the cigar plant color range to include soft pink and a white form for those who don't love orange. *Hybrid Cuphea x* 'David Verity' is a vigorous orange-blooming cigar plant that grows to two feet and is reliably hardy in my Zone 8 garden. It enjoys a seasonally wet site in the heavy clay soil of my informal sedge meadow, where the abundant orange flowers are joined by purple heart (*Setcreasea pallida*) and clumps of white rain lilies (*Zephyranthes candida*).

An old standby in gardens of the Deep South, shrimp plant (*Justicia brandegeana*) looks as odd as its common name suggests. Loosely clad with simple, velvety leaves, sprawling stems grow up and out, forming a slowly increasing clump three to four feet wide. Throughout summer there is a generous production of arching, three-inch

Tight clumps of white-flowered garlic chives bloom in concert with pink garden phlox and spider flower. Few plants could not combine with these gems.

115

Compact *Justicia* x 'Fruit Salad' (top) is perfect for container plantings such as this one, where apple-red flowers poking from banana-yellow bracts make delicious additions.

spikes of overlapping, copper-colored bracts looking like prawns. The small, white, split-faced flowers that appear from under each scalelike bract do little to change the overall crustacean image, as the plant might belong in the garden of Dr. Moreau. I like coppery shrimp plant grown with the patina-blue foliage of Lindheimer's muhly or other such ornamental grass, which can become a blue sea for the animated blooms. A selection with butter-yellow bracts and white flowers does much to give this perennial a much-needed makeover, creating a more palatable choice for mainstream gardeners.

Other species of shrimp plants for the hot summer garden, *Justicia fulva* and *J. tomentosa*, have orange and reddish bracts, range in size from two to five feet tall, and thrive even in southwest gardens. But the best choice is a spunky little hybrid called *Justicia* x 'Fruit Salad'. This super-compact (rarely over a foot tall) plant has just enough velvety leaves to keep it alive and is otherwise covered with erect spikes of soft yellow bracts from which small apple-red flowers randomly sprout. Like other shrimp plants, it thrives in sun or shade, tolerates wet and dry soils, and is perfect for pots and small gardens. While other perennials may become towering monsters during long Gulf Coast summers, 'Fruit Salad' stays small and makes a charming partner for white caladiums and pastel yellow Ganges primrose (*Assystasia gangetica*).

In the same tropical *Acanthus* family as Mexican petunia and shrimp plant, Persian shield (*Strobilanthes dyerianus*) is indispensable for hot-weather foliage color interest in sun or shade. The branched, two-foot-tall plants are clad in five-inch elliptic leaves that are iridescent silver and purple upon a dark green background, with solid purple undersides. Persian shield is an elegant departure from the monotonous summer green of subtropical gardens. It is winter hardy up to the lower parts of Zone 8, but well worth the effort of taking some easy-to-root cuttings at the end of fall in colder climes. In my garden, Persian shield embellishes the reds of tropical sage flowers and chili piquin fruits in shade, and in the sun, with international flair, it highlights yellow Mexican milkweed 'Silky Gold' and white Mexican petunia.

Though the occasional wealthy seafood restaurateur may enjoy flowers shaped like cigars and shrimp, many Gulf Coast residents no doubt long for "normal-looking" garden fare. In response, I offer the friendly face of a daisy. The Transvaal daisy (*Gerbera jamesonii*) is a wonderful subtropical perennial good through the lower half of Zone 8, where it faithfully blooms spring to fall. They ask only for some shade (eastern exposure seems to be divine) and good drainage. It must be noted that a great deal of selection and hybridization has gone into producing huge flowers, with an effusion of petals on compact stems in a wide range of colors. Sadly, these are without much vigor once they leave the climate-controlled world of the greenhouse. It is best to pursue the old-fashioned cultivars that bear a closer resemblance to the durable wild form. These have narrow-petaled flowers on tall stems in a reduced range of colors: red to coral, pink, and white. Transvaal daisies mingle with hardy ageratum and garlic chives in perfect harmony.

PRETTY IN PINK, AND WHITE

Tall garden phlox (*P. paniculata*) is a mainstay of summer gardens in the North, and fortunately some forms of it are heat tolerant enough and mildew-resistant enough for gardens in the Deep South. The clumping plants are formed of straight tall stems, clad in narrow elliptic leaves, rising to three or four feet with little fanfare until they bloom. Then each stem is crowned by a large (six or seven inches), tight panicle of fragrant, small, five-petaled flowers looking like rounded stars. *Phlox paniculata* cultivars 'David' and 'Mt. Fuji' are two of the best plants, with clean white flowers that go well with most everything in the garden from *Asclepias* to *Zinnia*. Variety 'Robert Poore' is taller than most cultivars, with bright pinkish-lavender flowers that absolutely glow. The color is just like that of the old-fashioned garden phlox, which also does quite well in heat and humidity. It is easiest to contrast the brilliant blooms of 'Robert Poore' with yellows of *Patrinia* or *Rudbeckias*, and then tempered by the subdued bronze foliage of burgundy fountain grass.

It is the unusual nature of its small dragon's-head flowers to pivot on the spike and be moved about on a whim that gives the obedient plant (*Physostegia virginiana*) its name. Certainly its behavior in the garden indicates otherwise, as the wayward perennial happily migrates about by underground stems and forms gypsylike colonies on moist ground. The rigid, two- to three-foot-tall stems terminate in spikes of soft pink blooms that look good nestled at the feet of China rose 'Old Blush' and fountain grass (*Pennisetum spp.*). The variety 'Vivid' is a brighter-than-usual pinkish-mauve that would look good with equally vivacious,

The metallic purple leaves of Persian shield are as versatile to design with as the plant is adaptable in the garden. Here yellow Ganges primrose mingles with it in partial sun.

variegated dwarf bamboo (*Pleioblastus variegatus*) in the foreground—both would be somewhat tamed in light shade with drier soil.

Another garden perennial that has flowers suggesting reptilian connections is the native turtle head (*Chelone glabra, C. lyonii,* and *C. obliqua*). The slowly expanding clumps of this moisture-loving perennial are a delight in the garden compared to roving masses of stoloniferous plants. Three-inch-long, toothed, oval leaves are trouble-free, but they bring the turtle head no notice until late-summer flowers take the stage with sturdy spikes of bright purplish-pink or creamy white flowers. The one-inch blooms shyly peek out from the flowering stalk yet never seem to open, so that individual blossoms indeed resemble a turtle's head. This is a flower that will always get attention for its unique appearance rather than for lavish displays of color. It is worth growing for its ease and trouble-free nature.

Bright lavender-pink flowers of tall garden phlox 'Robert Poore' may seem shocking to our eyes, but butterflies find them attractive.

CLASSIC FARE

Hostas and daylilies are also some of the most common perennials in northern gardens, and for some folks these are the first ones learned. The mind-numbing selection of hybrids and cultivars that both of these perennials have to offer could easily fill a book—and do fill several catalogs devoted to such obsessions. But in the hot and humid Deep South, the possibilities quickly become limited to just a few. Still, there are some hostas and daylilies for those who need such old standbys in their southern gardens.

The best bet for success with plantain lilies in a torrid climate is the species *Hosta plantaginea* and some of its cultivars. This broad-leafed perennial loves consistently moist ground in part sun or shade, but it should not really be considered a bog plant as it does not like to stand in water. The oval, light green, shiny leaves are quite large and form an umbrellalike clump up to two feet wide—stunning in its own right. But the best part about this plantain lily is the August treat of large, waxy, white, bell-shaped flowers that fill the garden with a divine perfume. The hybrids of *Hosta plantaginea* include 'Honeybells', with fragrant pale lavender flowers, and the particularly robust, white-bloomed 'Royal Standard'.

Most daylilies that can survive in southern gardens are late spring bloomers, but the old tawny daylily (*Hemerocallis fulva*) really thrives in the heat of summer. In fact, escaped, naturalized populations of the tawny daylily can be seen throughout the Southeast, and this is certainly one of the first plants to have passed across the fence from one gardener to another. The two- to three-foot-tall, creased, arching linear foliage makes handsome clumps in the garden, where it can effectively cloak the naked legs of other taller perennials. In early summer the large, rusty orange flowers open, one day at a time, upon tall leafless stalks thrusting from the foliage clumps. The color is somewhat muddy, but the tawny daylily flowers can be highlighted by mixing in blue *Salvia*, golden-yellow *Rudbeckia*, or white flowers for companions. An ancient Japanese double form of *Hemerocallis fulva* called 'Kwanso' brings a thousand-year-old history as well as resilient beauty into the garden.

Plantain lily 'Honeybells' (foreground) prefers rich moist soil and light shade, like the impatiens surrounding it in this North Carolina garden.

AMERICAN BEAUTIES

We have several wonderful native species of *Eupatorium* in the United States, but two in particular are unsurpassed for hot summer blooms. Joe Pye weed (*Eupatorium fistulosum*) is by far the most famous of these New World perennials, although I'm not entirely sure who Mr. Pye was. This hardy perennial, however, is far from obscure in any garden setting, where it makes a huge impact. From the ground up in spring, thick stalks quickly rise to 10 or 12 feet with whorls of narrow, dark green leaves, making an imposing feature on their own. In the heat of summer each stalk is crowned by a flattened, wide (12 to 18 inches), lacy inflorescence of small dusty mauve flowers and buds. Joe Pye weed is both subtle and substantial, but the small, individual flowers don't bear close inspection except by the hosts of butterflies drawn to the irresistible blooms. Other members of the land of the giants, such as *Rudbeckia* 'Herbstsonne', *Canna indica, Hedychium coronarium,* and *Ricinus communis* (castor bean), make suitable partners for this towering perennial.

As large as Joe Pye weed, hardy ageratum (*Eupatorium coelestinum,* a.k.a. *Conoclinium coelestinum*) is demure. But this modest-sized perennial is tough as nails and able to survive in less-than-ideal, dry sites. From invasive, creeping underground stems rises a small thicket of narrow, erect shoots. The 15- to 20-inch-tall stems sport simple, elliptical, clasping leaves and are topped by semibranched flower heads with lavender-blue, cottony blooms. The flowers look very much like the annual ageratum sold as a bedding plant, but this one doesn't die at the end of the season. Hardy ageratum makes a great filler plant when its invasive habit is used to knit together other perennials and grasses in the garden. Its tolerance of drought and shade allows it to prosper with three-lobed brown-eyed Susan and tropical sage under the canopy of trees.

Related to *Eupatorium*, ironweed (*Vernonia noveboracensis*) is an underused perennial for the sunny border. Rumor has it the common name is derived from the tough-as-nails rootstocks, which are almost impossible to dig up. I wouldn't know for sure, since I've only planted ironweed and have never wanted to remove this slowly clumping, well-mannered flower from any garden. The sturdy stems never need staking, and they rise to five or six feet tall without much cause for notice from the simple, narrow leaves. The rich violet-purple, buttonlike flower clusters that form at the apex of this plant really capture one's attention, however. I like to grow ironweed with other tall, robust perennials like scarlet mallow, orange canna, and lemon-yellow shining coneflower, contrasting both floral forms and colors.

LAST BUT NOT LEAST

Unique structure and flower color make up for *Patrinia scabiosifolia*'s difficult name. The plant is easy to grow in good soil with sun.

Patrinia scabiosifolia is relatively new to the cultured garden scene and as yet has no common name by which to recognize it except for 'golden lace'. The foliage of the tightly clumping perennial is deeply lobed and resembles that of pincushion flower (*Scabiosa*), only a little bit rougher. Tall stems bolt from the compact basal growth in summer (five to six feet) and transform *Patrinia* into an elegant, albeit unusual, beauty with loose, airy clusters of minute sulfur-yellow flowers. After flowers fade, the ripening seed heads carry on the glowing color, and even the stems take on a bright yellow glow. *Patrinia* loves sun and good garden soil, and it looks great with dark blue *Salvia* guaranitica or light blue *Salvia pitcheri*. The addition of *Verbena bonariensis* and *Panicum virgatum* 'Heavy Metal' completes the picture.

Stokes' aster (*Stokesia laevis*) is a delightfully compact perennial for southeast gardens, especially when compared to the towering giants that prosper during long, hot summers. Dark green, straplike leaves make relaxed, neat little mounds only four inches tall and about a foot wide—perfect for the front of the border. Stokes' aster revels in consistently moist soil and sunshine but will tolerate some shade and drought. The big, pastel blue, three-inch daisy flowers are layered with many fluffy inner petals, like a southern belle's petticoats, and arise from the foliage on slightly branched, one- to two-foot-tall stalks. They make great cut flowers and are only flawed by the fact that they just don't stay in bloom long enough (only three to four weeks). Lavender *Verbena canadensis* and burgundy-leafed wood sorrel (*Oxalis regnellii* 'Triangularis') make unequaled companions for sky-blue *Stokesia laevis*.

Recent discoveries of new color variants of the Stokes' aster have brought this native perennial into the spotlight. Cultivar 'Mary Gregory' has soft butter-yellow blooms that are quite a break from the usual color and make a rare treat planted aside the amethyst leaves of purple heart (*Setcreasea pallida*) and citrine variegated sweet flag (*Acorus gramineus* 'Ogon'). Variety 'Purple Parasols' sports dark blue flowers, later maturing to deep violet-purple, while 'Omega Skyrocket' blooms blue, but boldly, on three-foot-tall stems that allow for deeper placement in beds and borders. Of course, there is also a white-flowered form of Stokes' aster.

With a procession of bloom from late spring through fall, many gayfeathers (*Liatris spp.*) are native to the United States. The plants command attention with their unique spiked form yet demand little care or space, making gayfeathers perfect for the small garden. Dotted gayfeather (*Liatrus squarrosa*) is a late-summer treasure best planted in sun and well-drained soil so that its vertical ascent won't be compromised by floppy behavior. The two- to three-foot-tall stalks are marked by tight round clusters of light lavender blooms discreetly spaced at intervals so that the fuzzy flowers appear dotted up and down the stem. Dwarf gayfeather (*Liatrus microcephala*) sprouts many demure, 12- to 18-inch flower stalks smothered from top to bottom with bright lavender, textured blooms. It likes well-drained soil, too, and makes a dainty accent for the front of the bed.

The mainstay of the summer garden, perennials are best used in combinations that complement and contrast form, color, and texture. Shrubs, ornamental grasses, and annuals are all valuable partners that share center stage as they collaborate with summer-blooming perennials. With consideration to proper siting and willingness to combine varied plants together for synergistic impact, perennials make spectacular displays in southeast gardens.

The many species of gayfeathers are still underused in our gardens and have the status of "wildflowers" instead of valuable perennials. Pictured here is dwarf gayfeather.

CHAPTER 8

SOUTHEASTERN SUMMER SHRUBS

Shrubs and small trees that bloom during hot weather are the linchpins of the summer garden, adding unparalleled structure, depth, and dimension. As with broadleaf evergreens, palms, and bamboo, it is best to design around these pillars of the garden when planning the larger landscape, thus allowing for the favorable placement of associate perennials and grasses.

Ideal planning situations, however, rarely present themselves, and we are sometimes faced with the eleventh-hour addition of some "must-have" wonderful woody plant that will force us to rethink the rest of the garden's equation of proportion, space, color, and texture. It is much easier to introduce a new perennial to the scene than a new small tree or shrub, which will slowly grow into its position of prominence over time, pushing a few other lesser plants out of the picture each year. Because I have but a small space in which to garden, I lean toward the compact shrubs and have to appreciate the larger specimens in other people's gardens.

Of course, the spring-blooming trees and shrubs that dominate southeastern gardens are famous. The camellias, azaleas, magnolias, redbuds, and dogwoods are also notably content to sit out summer in the shade of taller trees while they ready themselves for next spring's bloom. The American Southeast is covered by trees and other woody plants, so most of our native shrubs are shade-lovers. Natives like plumleaf azalea, beautyberry, and oakleaf hydrangea enjoy an understory habitat, but most of our summer-flowering garden fare are exotic bushes and small trees from distant lands.

Most of the flowering trees and shrubs of summer prefer life in the hot sun. Some will tolerate partial shade, but generous bloom will always come from these woody plants situated in good sun.

CRAPE MYRTLES OF ALL SIZES

The queen tree of the southeast garden in summer must be the crape myrtle (*Lagerstroemia indica*). Although some southerners are riding a wave of antiroyalist sentiment and spurn the ubiquitous tree as being too common, for many, crape myrtles are the hallmark of summer. During the hottest months, the brightly colored, crinkled petals surround golden-yellow floral centers, and then do double duty as confetti scattered frivolously on the ground below. Without the festive clusters of one-inch blossoms in brilliant shades of watermelon red, purple, lavender, pink, or white, one might think crape myrtles to be simple, elegant trees. Their branches and trunks exhibit clean, graceful lines, and the smooth, peeling bark makes a wondrous multicolored pattern resembling an oil painting. In addition, the small, neat leaves can add flaming orange and reds to the fall palette. Of course, keeping the foliage

OVERLEAF: Lavender-blue spikes of chaste tree are a refreshing sight on hot summer days.

ABOVE: A grand 'Redheart' rose of Sharon dominates the display garden of Kim Hawks at Niche Gardens Nursery near Chapel Hill.

healthy-looking and free from powdery mildew requires full sun, good air circulation, and the judicious selection of the best cultivar for your area.

Larger specimens of crape myrtles can reach 15 or even 20 feet in height, which means you may get to inspect the intricate bark patterns while your neighbors enjoy the colorful splash of flowers. For some gardens, a tree of this size is perfect, but most times disgruntled and uninformed home owners will chop the hapless tree in half to create a shorter version with resulting flowers in easy view. These mutilated trees, along with those that are annually "coat-racked" in a ritual of bad pruning designed to "make more blooms," are grotesque shadows of their former elegant selves (and it should be noted that while larger flower clusters are produced by the coppiced specimens, there is no net gain of blooms compared to unpruned individuals that create more numerous, but smaller, clusters). It is better to select the right cultivar in the first place, not only based on the flower color but also on the ultimate mature size it is to attain.

Some midsized crape myrtles top out at 6 to 12 feet in height, depending on soil and site. Dark red 'Cherokee' and rich purple 'Catawba' are both in this size range, as is the white clone 'Glendora White'. Pink forms in this class include bright 'Seminole', pastel 'Near East', and bicolored 'Peppermint Lace'. These are best positioned in the garden among large evergreens like hollies and bamboos, where their summer color can be fully appreciated and their bare aspect in winter is balanced by lush green foliage.

Selections of crape myrtle reaching only four or five feet in height are better suited for particularly small gardens. I've had some luck with these but notice that powdery mildew is their Achilles' heel. If they are to be planted, give them only the best site with full sun and free space about the branches, and fertilize them at least twice a year. The well-fed plant is a healthy plant, less prone to disease. The incredibly small, so-called crape myrtlettes grow only a foot tall and are supposed to be good for pots and bedding out, but I'd just as soon use a world of other annuals and tender perennials for such duty.

LARGE SHRUBS TO SMALL TREES

Where I live in Texas, the chaste tree (*Vitex agnus-castus*) is so commonly used and well adjusted to the climate that one might think it to be a native; however, the drought-tolerant small trees are actually from the Mediterranean region. Unlike our 15-foot-tall, multitrunked, umbrella-shaped trees, *Vitex* is for many other people just a shrub of varying sizes (in the cold winter climates of Nebraska and Oklahoma it is grown as an herbaceous summer-blooming perennial). The aromatic, gray-green, maplelike leaves are a valuable asset in their own right, but most people grow the chaste tree for its strong, vertical spikes of tiny lavender-blue flowers. The plants bloom in early summer, and then again in late summer in my neck of the woods; others may experience a summer-long procession of flowers. Pink- and white-flowered forms are also available.

The rose of Sharon shrub is actually a tough-as-nails hibiscus (*Hibiscus syriacus*). The bush- to tree-sized plants require no pampering, but they enjoy the good life with the refinement of a little pruning in winter, when the plants are dormant. Specimens can be kept small so as to fit into the garden scheme as just another pawn, or they can be encouraged to reign supreme. The rather plain, slightly lobed foliage makes a nice green foil to set off the three-inch mallow flowers of white, red, pink, or lilac. I am fond of the simple, single forms, which look like charming but stout little hibiscus flowers of the tropics, whereas the double forms look uncultured and tawdry. 'Redheart', white with dark red center, is one of the toughest and yet still quite a beauty. 'Diana' is the largest flowered form and a refreshing pristine white, around which it is very easy to design the rest of the garden colors. 'Blue Bird' is a delicious pastel lilac with deep violet eye that just begs to be surrounded by other flowers with hues of lavender, amethyst, and sky blue.

My favorite China rose is 'Old Blush'—if you can grow this rose, then do it!—but don't plant it alone without companions.

The rose 'Altissimo' takes up more of the small bed than I had allotted; each winter I reduce its sturdy frame to keep it in check.

While most rhododendrons and azaleas (also botanically known as *Rhododendron*) are the darlings of southeast spring gardens, there is one maverick that marches to the beat of a different drummer. The plumleaf azalea (*Rhododendron prunifolium*), a southeast native, is an enchanting small tree that thrives in dark forest understory. In midsummer these sites are illuminated by a flaming floral display. The tiered, thin branching of the mature 10- to 12-foot-tall trees gives the plumleaf azalea an oriental air, but even young specimens possess a unique, attractive habit. Flowers open in terminal clusters like reddish-orange parasols composed of a loose circle of outward-facing bells. This informal shrub/small tree is perfect for shady areas where it can bloom with the white-flowered oakleaf hydrangea, ferns, and plantain lilies.

ROSES

No discussion about gardening is complete without mentioning roses. Yet I know in advance that not everyone will be happy with just a limited mention of a few choice plants. I heartily encourage anyone who wants to wade into roses more than just ankle deep to read one of the several books or catalogs packed with information about them. Most roses bloom in late spring, but that is not reason enough to mention them in this book, and others are remontent (blooming again in the fall), which still doesn't cover the midsummer season. I'd like to showcase a few of the roses that share their flowers after the fanfare of spring fades, performing admirably throughout hot summer weather.

Hybrid tea roses are not my favorite plants—I consider them too stiff and ungainly—but their voluptuous flowers are some of the most welcome sights in the garden or in a vase. These bushes do very well in torrid climates, however, and can't be ignored. They should, however, be well tucked into beds and borders where other perennials and short ornamental grasses can cloak their wretched-looking, naked stems. I would also encourage every gardener to go beyond the monotonous prescription of the ages, the barren rose bed—or "rose ghetto," as my friends like to call them. Yes, a little air circulation is a good thing, but I have found that hybrid teas do quite well in my humid garden with all sorts of perennial and annual company (and they look so much better with friends). I have five hybrid tea roses in my small garden, along with a Bourbon, ramblers, a China, several floribundas, a Polyantha, and the little sport called 'Happenstance'. Of course I have a 'Peace' rose—it is unavoidable—but I like the single forms like 'Dainty Bess', 'Mrs. Oakley Fisher', and 'Altissimo' better. In my garden they are combined with desert spoon (*Dasylirion*) and yuccas in a truly Texas twist. Even in 100° F heat, these single forms of hybrid tea flowers last for a week. However, cutting and bringing them inside to air-conditioning extends the life of any summer rose.

The class of roses called the Polyanthas offers plants of both modest size and graceful habit. The flowers are much smaller and less complex than the hybrid teas, usually without the divine scent, but their quaint little double blooms are tirelessly produced in sizable clusters. Polyantha roses are great for pots and the fronts of beds, where they can be enjoyed up close. The pastel pink cultivar 'The Fairy' is tough as nails despite its beguiling charm. 'Summer Snow' is a cool white that coordinates easily with most garden color schemes, but 'Margo Koster', with its peachy tones, is my personal favorite. An antique rose called 'Caldwell Pink' (possibly a Polyantha) wins the award for being the best hot-summer bloomer. After an early spring blight of mildew, the foliage stays clean and healthy for the rest of the season, even turning a rich orange shade in fall. Flowers are small, lavender-pink, and densely packed with petals, occurring in clusters, nonstop. Baking against a south wall at my mother-in-law's house, three-foot-tall 'Caldwell Pink' keeps the strange company of Russian sage, hardy aloes, society garlic, and Mexican bear grass.

I don't think anything can compare with the China roses. They are flowering shrubs unparalleled. These sturdy but glamorous woody plants have a full bushlike habit that can, though rarely, get to the size of a small tree. The foliage is clean and healthy, and the two-inch simple flowers are produced without effort from spring to fall (indeed, in mild winters the China roses never stop blooming). 'Old Blush' is my favorite with its rich pink, semidouble blooms and golden centers produced lavishly throughout the year. It is so undemanding, yet very rewarding, and is the backbone of many an old southern garden. 'Old Blush' looks great with blue-leafed ornamental grasses (*Muhlenbergia lindheimeri, Panicum* 'Prairie Sky', or *Sorghastrum* 'Sioux Blue') and silver *Artemisia* 'Powis Castle', as well as white-flowered *Guara lindheimeri* and pink *Echinacea purpurea*.

The vigorous China rose 'Mutabilis' has slightly larger single blooms changing from butter yellow to pink and then darker rose. It really is quite a sight in full bloom, but the carnival colors are best framed by the subtle foliage of burgundy-leafed Japanese barberry (*Berberis thunbergii* 'Atropurpurea') and yellow-striped zebra grass (*Miscanthus sinensis* 'Zebrinus'). I must admit, though, in the Deep South I'd love to see a robust 'Mutabilis' entertaining the intimate embrace of sky-blue plumbago (*P. auriculata*) as the latter rambles and weaves throughout the branches of the rose. For those without pastel lives, China rose variety 'Louis Phillippe' offers clusters of crimson double blooms on a bush with a cast-iron constitution. It is simply splendid next to the dark green leaves of hollies, and including the late-season *Ilex* berries results in a dazzling combo come Christmas, when 'Louis Phillippe' is still in bloom.

MIDSIZED SHRUBS

Hydrangeas love the Southeast. Their large clusters of smaller, paperlike blooms have an old-fashioned charm that some gardeners see as being a bit too old. Largest of these plants is *Hydrangea paniculata* 'Grandiflora', which can grow to be a large bush (almost a small tree). Grapefruit-sized heads, dense with creamy white flowers, adorn the plants for months in summer, and the aging, fading blossoms maintain interest,

This large decades-old specimen of *Hydrangea paniculata* 'Grandiflora' dominates this garden space grandly, yet a small young plant will still please.

changing into pastel green and finally brown. This shrub prefers consistent soil moisture and revels in good garden conditions where it freely associates with other vivacious garden perennials. The universal white blooms of this hydrangea are easy to mix with most other colors. The *Hydrangea arborescens* cultivar 'Annabelle' is a smaller plant, but it has larger, dome-shaped flower heads and makes an excellent cut or dried flower of white, green, or brown (depending on when it is harvested). This hydrangea can be cut to the ground annually in winter so as to keep it in bounds for the smaller garden, but it will still slowly spread by suckering stems.

Our American native son, the oakleaf hydrangea (*H. quercifolia*), is an elegant bush for four-season interest. Bold, whitened stems outlined with peeling, brown, papery bark and topped with fat buds give the oakleaf hydrangea a delightful winter aspect. Big lobed leaves lend a luxuriant, exotic touch to the garden, and the pronounced, oval clusters of glistening white that top the stems in summer illuminate any shaded venue. Fall finds the oak-shaped foliage following further mimicry by turning rich shades of orange and maroon. The selection 'Snow Queen' is the finest form available of this already wonderful shrub. Tropical sage (*Salvia coccinea*) in the wild scarlet form or white cultivar 'Snow Nymph' makes a great consort for this garden centerpiece.

Nothing says "the South" to me quite as much as the sweet perfume of the waxy white gardenia (*G. jasminoide s*). Its three-inch-long, simple leaves are dark green and glossy, and it is a handsome shrub when kept free of aphids and whiteflies. Gardenias love a rich acid soil with plenty of food and moisture, and a position in full sun for the best flowering (they should also be positioned close enough for frequent sniffing). The most common double-flowered varieties of gardenia include 'Mystery' and 'August Beauty', with the latter producing a greater number of slightly smaller flowers. Their moderate cold hardiness seems to depend more on the plant's ability to slow its growth and harden off before a freeze than the actual low-temperature event. My garden seems to get no more than a day of tempered fall weather before the first blast of arctic air hits, so I am forced to add extra protection in the form of a sheet or two. I'm looking forward to trying the fragrant, single-flowered cultivar 'Cline's Hardy' to see if it is better able to take the quick transition to cold.

The name alone makes butterfly bush (*Buddleia davidii*) everyone's favorite—who wouldn't want to attract butterflies to the garden? These shrubs are really quite tough despite the impression given in bloom, with long, arching tresses of tiny, sweetly scented flowers. The five- to six-foot-tall, vase-shaped plants are clad in simple, narrow, green or gray leaves, depending on cultivar, and tend to dwell in obscurity until they start to blossom. When in bloom, butterfly bush looks like a fireworks display, as the tiny yellow-centered flowers of white, pink, lavender, purple, or violet open from the base toward the tip of each cluster. Entire clusters of brown spent flowers detract from

Red-purple tresses of bloom explode from this butterfly bush and beautifully contrast the blue mist spirea.

129

Gray foliage and lavender flowers make butterfly bush 'Lochinch' perfect for people with pastel sensibilities.

the shrub's beauty, but they can be removed to keep the plants looking fresh. The hybrid 'Lochinch' has silvery gray leaves and lavender blooms that make the perfect tireless companion for Hibiscus syriacus 'Bluebird'. Large spikes of bright, clear pink flowers on 'Pink Delight' contrast nicely with its gray-green foliage, making it an apt partner for China rose 'Old Blush'. I like the dark purple petals and orange eye of compact 'Nanhoensis' and grow it next to fall-blooming royal sage (*Salvia regla*) so the season can end with a splash of scarlet-orange and purple, replete with attendant hummingbirds and butterflies.

The American beautyberry (*Callicarpa americana*) is not grown for its flowers, which are small and insignificant, but for its brilliant metallic-violet berries that cluster along the long branches. Since the color display starts in midsummer and lasts through fall, the up-to-six-foot beautyberry makes an excellent addition to any hot-summer garden's color scheme. A native of the southeastern woodlands, this open, rambling bush tolerates shade, but it also performs admirably in sun. The unusual color of the berries is nicely harmonized by an underplanting of purple heart (*Setcreasea pallida*) and complemented by the white-fading-to-green blooms of 'Annabelle' hydrangeas.

Someone purchasing a new, containerized specimen of abelia (*Abelia x grandiflora*) from a nursery might expect the tidy, clipped bush to remain demurely compact after being planted in the garden. However, once left to its own devices, abelia soon shakes off the image imposed by fastidious shearing and sends out tall, arching stalks (much to the chagrin of anyone expecting a permanent meaty ball of green). Abelias are graceful, informal shrubs with thin, delicately arching stems decked with small, dark green, glossy leaves tinged with bronze. Throughout summer the five- to six-foot-tall shrubs subtly burst into flower as the branch tips bear clusters of small, white, tubular bells nestled in winged calyces. Even after the flowers fall, small rounded clusters of reddish floral bases persist. Smaller cultivars of abelia, such as the diminutive-leafed 'Sherwoodii', make it easier to fit this ideal shrub into small gardens like mine. 'Edward Goucher' also attains half the usual size, except with soft pink flowers. The variegated form, 'Sunrise', is also more petite and has beautiful leaves streaked with white, yellow, and pink. *Abelia chinensis*, one of the parents of the commonly grown hybrid abelia, is a dandy in its own right. This vigorous, six-foot-tall shrub with relaxed branching is in constant summer bloom, and the clusters of white flowers act like veritable butterfly magnets.

Although the Japanese barberry blooms in early spring with tiny yellow blossoms, the red-leafed forms of this tough-as-nails shrub (*Berberis thunbergii* 'Atropurpurea') are indispensable for foliage color in the summer garden. The densely packed, small,

Caryopteris 'Worcester Gold' **is captivating even before flowering, and its compact size is a boon for the small garden.**

burgundy leaves make a valuable foil for flowers of all colors, whether they are pastels or fiery reds, yellows, and oranges. As long as it is grown with at least half a day's sun, these barberry leaves will keep their wine-red color. Best of all, the bush is delightfully midsized, maturing at about five feet, and there are even smaller cultivars to choose from. The three- to four-foot-tall 'Rose Glow' sparkles with variegated new growth marbled in cream and pink, eventually maturing to the sedate burgundy. Smaller still is 'Crimson Pygmy', at two feet, able to fit into the smallest sunny garden and break the summer's monotony of green.

SMALL SHRUBS

In the Upper South, at least, the blue mist spirea (*Caryopteris x clandonensis*) makes a drought-tolerant small shrub for summer bloom in sun. The small, toothed leaves are very aromatic but rather unappealing unless the yellow-foliage form, 'Worcester Gold', is grown. Then the small bush adds quite a spark of color even before the advent of lavender-blue, wispy flowers whorled about foot-tall, thin stems crowning

The smoky haze of Russian sage flowers is elegantly opposed by the crisp starched appearance of garlic chives.

the plant. The green-leafed varieties also grow to about three or four feet and bloom in varying shades of blue, with 'Dark Knight' producing the deepest shade of indigo amid a gray-green foil. 'Longwood Blue' is distinctly later blooming than other cultivars, with green foliage. In a well-drained, sunny site, *Caryopteris* is great with *Liatris* and *Agastache rupestris*.

Another minor shrub best suited for the Upper South is Russian sage (*Perovskia atriplici-folia*). In colder climates this plant is listed as a sub-shrub since it grows as an herbaceous perennial despite its woody nature. But in milder climates Russian sage maintains a winter countenance, its bare branches covered with a ghostly white haze. This shrublet must have full sun and well-drained soil to make a pleasant mound of aromatic, ferny, silver-gray foliage. For months in summer, Russian sage carries large, loose branches of tiny, smoky lavender flowers above its head. Being a modest-sized plant, Russian sage mixes well with white garden phlox, purple coneflower, and *Guara lindheimeri* 'Siskiyu Pink'.

Mexican oregano (*Poliomentha longiflora*) is another aromatic, drought-tolerant shrublet that blooms in summer, but this three-foot-tall plant thrives in the torrid Lower South. More surprising still, Mexican oregano likes light shade. The brittle-stemmed shrublet bears small, oval leaves that can be used for cooking purposes just like its culinary namesake. Terminal spikes of long-tubed, soft pink, salvialike flowers make quite a show through late summer in lightly shaded, well-drained sites. New selection 'Bustamante' sports pastel lilac blooms, but either would be splendid in the company of blue-flowered cape plumbago and variegated dwarf bamboo.

TROPICAL SPECIALTIES

Just as there are some plants ill suited for the Deep South that prosper farther north, so the opposite is true. The steamy Gulf Coast supports some wonderful small trees and shrubs that fail in colder zones. Angel's trumpet (*Brugmansia* spp. and hybrids) is one such glory of the subtropical garden that can make others envious of such "difficult" growing conditions. Thick, juicy but woody stems to 15 feet tall carry large, oval, green leaves and an abundance of huge, pendant, trumpet-shaped flowers. In addition, the big ten-inch blossoms become sweetly fragrant at nightfall, seductively perfuming the entire garden until just past sunrise. Of course these plants like moisture, and rich, fertile soil keeps the garden's angels in trumpets from spring to fall. In such a site cannas and bananas make good companions.

The white angel's trumpet (*Brugmansia suaveolens*) is a classic that is hard to beat, but there are pink- and peach-colored hybrids that are also compelling. In my Zone 8 garden I grow the yellow-peach hybrid *Brugmansia x candida* 'Charles Grimaldi' in a low spot where the heavy clay soil gains and holds ample moisture, while a raised bed in

Potted aloe foliage calms the dazzling display of this pink hybrid angel's trumpet.

front is home to the lovely Mexican blue palm (*Brahea armata*). Even though the annual cold of winter takes the angel's trumpet to the ground, the plant returns with warm weather to grow into another eight-foot treasure by midsummer. In a milder Gulf Coast climate I might not lose this small tree at all, but I enjoy the chance to grow a cool-season crop of sweet peas, larkspur, and opium poppies in the sunny space temporarily vacated by the *Brugmansia*.

Within the same nightshade family is another wonderful group of subtropical bushes perfect for Deep South gardens: *Cestrum*. The most familiar of this interesting genus of shrubs is the night-blooming jessamine (*Cestrum nocturnum*). It is a rather common-looking, somewhat scraggly bush with simple, dark green, shiny leaves and well-camouflaged floral clusters of tiny green trumpets. After dark these tiny star-shaped trumpets open to emit one of nature's most potent perfume potions. The high-frequency fragrance is unusually enchanting to me, but some people might disagree. The plant is tender to frost, but a cross with *Cestrum diurnum* is quite hardy in my Zone 8 garden. *Cestrum x nocturnum-diurnum* is a robust six-foot-tall shrub with simple glossy leaves, producing multitudes of apricot, star-shaped trumpets (unscented) in terminal clusters from spring to fall. The shrub

Tropical Turk's cap and palmetto form this informal but elegant screen in a Florida garden.

RIGHT: Inflorescences of firespike punctuate the flamboyant white blossoms of tropical hibiscus.

quickly recovers from a very hard freeze and doesn't even lose a leaf at 20° F. The less hardy *Cestrum auranticum* is a smaller bush with similar habit and darker, mango-colored blooms from spring to fall. Pink-flowered *Cestrum elegans* is a six- to eight-foot-tall shrub with velvety leaves, blooming both in spring and late summer with grapelike clusters of blossoms that hang from the tips of branches. It prefers a frost-free lifestyle.

An odd-looking relative of the hibiscus, Turk's cap, or sleeping hibiscus (*Malvaviscus arboreus*), is a wonderful shade-tolerant shrub for Gulf Coast gardens, where it will bloom year-round. Dark green leaves are a pleasant foil for the bright red, semipendant flowers (also sometimes found in white and pink forms), which resemble tight buds of tropical hibiscus blossoms. Although this tender shrub is from Mexico, it also evolved up the coast into Texas and beyond, where the smaller, hardier variety of Turk's cap grows under the name *M. arboreus v. drummondii*. This plant acts like an herbaceous perennial in areas of heavy frost, such as my garden, but like a woody shrub in warmer zones. I remember my first glimpse of hardy Turk's cap in my youth, growing wild with dwarf palmetto (*Sabal minor*) under a pine forest canopy in east Texas. I still love the two plants mingling together in the garden.

The tropical genus *Clerodendron* contains several small trees and shrubs adapted to southeastern garden conditions. The harlequin glorybower (*Clerodendron trichotomum*) is a wonderful, summer-flowering, small tree for the Southeast. Usually multitrunked, specimens mature at about 15 feet, looking like compact little catalpa trees with their exceptionally big leaves. Midsummer finds large clusters of tiny, white, star-shaped flowers held by dark pink calyces, with the added bonus of an enchantingly sweet fragrance. Shiny, dark blue fruits, clinging to the pink bracts, replace the fallen blossoms and continue color into autumn. The best flowering is in full sun when given consistent moisture, but I grow my specimen under the afternoon shade of a pecan since our summers can be dry.

Cashmere bouquet (*Clerodendon bungei*) is a massing, suckering shrub that grows permanently woody or can return from cold weather from the ground each spring when faced with a severe freeze. Its unbranched, erect stems are loosely clad with large, spade-shaped leaves and are crowned by four- to six-inch, domelike clusters of tiny mauve flowers and darker buds. It is easily mixed with perennials and ornamental grasses and, in fact, looks much better for it. Tall verbena, Persian shield, and garlic chives do well with the roving companionship of cashmere bouquet. *Clerodendron speciosissimum* is a red-flowered, tropical African cousin with the same suckering habit.

Mexican firebush's stalwart constitution and coppery foliage make up for a lack of grandiose blooms.

In mild winter climates it makes a great summer-flowering shrub, but in my garden I am testing its ability to return faithfully from winter's chill as a reliable perennial for hot-weather bloom. *Clerodendron ugandense*, with its late summer sprays of two-toned blue, butterfly flowers, is another candidate for such treatment at home in the bed with peach-colored angel's trumpet (*Brugmansia*).

The Mexican firebush (*Hamelia patens*) is yet another example of a tropical tree/shrub that acts as a perennial when exposed to colder winter weather. In mild winter climates this plant is a permanent fixture of the garden, enjoying all the heat that a summer can produce. The three-inch-long, simple leaves have a nice coppery hue that works well with the continual clusters of small, orange, tubular flowers and looks great with bamboo muhly (*Muhlenbergia dumosa*) and scarlet mallow. In my Zone 8 garden, the firebush returns after winter's cold has cut it to the ground, and it grows easily to six feet tall by the end of a hot Texas summer. Yet further north, this heat-loving shrub is grown like any other summer annual since even young plants bloom in earnest, complete with coppery-orange leaves.

Firespike (*Odontonema strictum*) is another tropical shrub that acts as an herbaceous perennial for me, since it is reliably root hardy and quickly grows when the hottest weather returns (as it always does). Better still, firespike loves heavy clay soil and shade, both of which I have in spades. The dark green, glossy leaves are simple and make a great foil for the intense red blooms. The tubular flowers are rather small, but collectively they make a large inflorescence that wandering hummingbirds can't miss. Gulf Coast gardeners can enjoy firespike with shrubby tropical hibiscus (*H. rosa-sinensis*) or Turk's cap, while those who endure more cold in winter can grow it along with the herbaceous perennial counterparts of these. In either case, the company of dwarf palmetto (*Sabal minor*) complements the zesty firespike.

Flowering maples (*Abutilon spp.* and hybrids) are relatives of cotton and hibiscus that make sturdy, colorful, shrubby additions to the southeast gardens where winter temperatures are mild or protection is given. Large, yellow and green bicolored leaves are the hallmark of *Abutilon pictum*, the cultivar 'Gold Dust' being almost exclusively used. The irregular checkered pattern of yellow-smattered, maplelike, lobed foliage is displayed on tall singular stems; occasional orange, bell-like flowers add interest. Frequent pinching encourages a shorter, wider, and more branched form. A dwarf, well-branched form of *A. pictum* called 'Thompsoni' gives the same look, with half-sized leaves and flowers on smaller plants appearing more shrublike. The *Abutilon* variety 'Souvenier de Bonn' is also tall and lanky, but it has dark green leaves bearing cream-colored margins and the same orange bells, making a dramatic statement in the garden. It seems to be the variegated form of a vigorous green-leafed *Abutilon* known as 'Marion Stewart'. These thrive in sun or semishade with moist soil, and readily return in my Zone 8 garden from freezing weather with gusto (along the Gulf Coast they may remain permanently above ground). They make marvelous additions to plantings of bronze-leaf canna, ginger lily, and grasses.

Those abutilons (*Abutilon x speciosum,* a.k.a. *Abutilon x hybridum*) grown for their colorful blossoms, the "flowering" maples, are a diverse lot resulting from years of zealous breeding by enthusiastic hybridizers. Well-branched shrubby plants growing up to four or even six feet tall (depending on mild winters or not) with three- to four-inch, dark green, lobed leaves, display a delightful array of two- and three-inch-wide, dangling bells in a range of colors. The enchanting white, pink, red, burgundy, yellow, peach, or orange blooms resemble antebellum hoop petticoats, except that it's okay to look up into the centers of these to enjoy the golden floral centers. Hybrid flowering maples bloom through the heat of summer into fall as long as they have rich moist soil, and depending on the severity of winter the plants continue to gain in size each year (temperatures lower than 20° F will take them to the ground). Bearing smaller, more elongated leaves, the species *Abutilon megapotamicum* and its hybrids are adorned with small, bell-like blooms half the size of the other Abutilon hybrids, but usually in greater profusion. These plants also show a greater tolerance to cold weather.

Small trees and shrubs lend essential permanence and structure to gardens. Along with palms, bamboos, and large grasses, they form the "bones" of gardens large and small. Thoughtful placement, however, is imperative to their longtime performance as well as to our long-term satisfaction. Around these dependable woody plants the rest of the garden evolves as we add foliage and flowers to knit the whole together. ✵

Compact colorful *Abutilon* 'Thompsoni' is excellent for small gardens and containers. Like all flowering maples it prefers rich moist soil.

CHAPTER 9

Palms, Grasses, and Bamboos

Foliage is fundamental to successful garden design. The colors and textures that different leaves add to many completed plant combinations cannot be underestimated. Flowers are enhanced when viewed with the subtle foil of various greens, blues, golds, bronze, or white variegated leaves. The bold, evergreen, architectural forms of palms; the ethereal, billowy, linear foliage of grasses;

and the strong, erect stems and willowy leaves of bamboo all add dimension and depth to the garden. When mixed with other flowering plants, these textures break up the monotony of sticks resulting from the exclusive use of perennials and shrubs. Indeed, palms, grasses, and bamboos infuse the garden with subtle mystery and embellish the flowers among which they are planted. Many of these plants revel in the Southeast but sulk in other climates, giving the southern gardens that include their diverse foliage a rich and unique appearance.

PALMS AND BANANAS

Live oaks and southern pines dominate the landscape of the South. With the exception of some coastal cities and most of southern Florida, one does not see the bold silhouette of palm trees as a feature that defines the area. Yet palms are native to the Southeast—although these are generally smaller understory plants that make up the diverse forest ecosystems of the region. One of the larger imported species of palms has made its way into the hearts and homes of many: the Bermuda palmetto (*Sabal bermudana*), which is found along old town streets and in turn-of-the-century gardens. This stout fellow gives the illusion of the tropics but is hardy enough to face down freezing weather (Zone 8) that sometimes frequents subtropical coastal cities. Like all Sabal species, the fan-shaped leaves of this palm are large, olive-green, leathery, and slightly folded in the center. Mature specimens are usually 15 to 20 feet tall, but young specimens of this slow-growing palm are very garden-worthy.

More common in my own part of Texas is the Mexican palmetto (*Sabal mexicana*). Indigenous to the eastern part of Mexico along the Gulf, north up into the lowlands, and along the lower coast of the Lone Star State, this drought-tolerant palm has been brought further north into gardens and seaside towns. The Mexican palmetto's tight, ball-like crown of foliage is distinctly different from other fan palms planted locally. It is the most resilient of the larger palms found in the region, enduring the capricious winter weather that rolls down the Great Plains to the coast (Zone 8). Although there are nice specimens in the town where I live, I was not lucky enough to inherit one with my house. It could have made a most lovely heart of the garden, setting the stage for all to follow.

OVERLEAF: Though not true palms, bananas lend similar architecture to the garden. *Abyssinian* banana cultivar, 'Maurelii' is choice.

ABOVE: Mexican palmetto cavorts with red castor bean and banana in a delightful combination of exotic foliage.

Similar to the Bermuda and Mexican palmettos, but not quite as versatile, is the Florida palmetto (*Sabal palmetto*). Called palmetto and cabbage palm, it is also a dense-growing tree of some stature and is able to survive freezing Zone 8 weather. This is the state tree of South Carolina and the mascot of Charleston, where its compact form graces city streets and it is the logo for many local products. The Florida palmetto likes wet feet, however, and resents drought; it shows the most cold hardiness when well watered. It is ideal in the moist, acid, sandy conditions common in its native Southeast—sites that could be a limitation for other evergreens. Clever nursery growers are currently selecting specimens from the northernmost part of the Florida palmetto's range in North Carolina so as to propagate the toughest individuals for a wide range of future gardens.

Hardly a tree, the shrubby dwarf palmetto (*Sabal minor*) is a widely spread native of the Southeast, where it happily lives in the shade of larger trees. In an unusual adaptation, this dyslexic plant actually grows its trunk down deep into the soil several feet instead of up toward the sun. Most likely developed as a way to survive fire, this makes the dwarf palmetto unusually cold hardy (to Zone 7), and specimens can bounce back from sub-zero weather. Without an obvious trunk, the large, stiff, dark green fans thrust up out of the soil, making a lovely foliage display. Large, arching sprays of flowers and then berrylike fruits decorate the dwarf palmetto in summer and fall. Capitalizing on its shade tolerance, I've tucked my dwarf palmetto into a darkened corner where its foliage contrasts with the leaves of holly fern, dwarf sweetflag, sedge, and crinum.

The saw palmetto (*Seranoa repens*) is also a forest underling, although it occupies a smaller natural range than the shrubby dwarf palmetto. The saw palmetto has distinctly different foliage from its *Sabal* kin: The leaves are small, pleated, rounded fans with jagged teeth running along both sides of the leaf stem. Both light green and pastel blue forms occur in the wild, although the blue-leafed saw palmetto has more garden potential. These plants do form trunks, but they snake around on the ground, sometimes forming formidable clumps, and rarely rise more than several feet tall. Their low profile makes the saw palmetto resistant to cold (Zone 8) as well as easy to use in the garden. The powder-blue fans cloaking the base of pink or white rose mallow and peach-toned ginger lilies make a breathtaking sight.

My favorite palm for the Southeast is the hardy, compact native called needle palm (*Rhapidiophyllum hystrix*). This short-trunked species grows to only six feet tall, after which it begins to send up pups to form a clump of stems. This won't happen overnight, however, and the slow-growing needle palm is perfectly proportioned for the small garden. Dark green, fan-shaped leaves arranged horizontally about the crown give even young needle palms a balanced appearance. The densely hairy, beehive-looking trunk is armed with a formidable array of dark, four-inch-long spines, which I respectfully avoid in autumn while clearing away accumulated dead leaves with a stick. This understory plant shows remarkable shade tolerance but also prospers in full sun. Needle palms are delightfully cold hardy (to Zone 6), reportedly surviving −12° F without a scratch! My specimen stands counterpoint to a fountain, which is the focal point for half of the garden.

Although actually an ancient gymnosperm (cone-bearing pine relative), the sago palm (*Cycas revoluta*) looks like a delicate, low-growing palm and thrives in the hot Southeast. The rigid, cardboardlike leaves look quite delicate and feathery, but one touch of the shiny jade foliage will show you just how tough a plant this is. This slow grower likes full sun but tolerates some shade, and it can eventually develop a trunk up to eight feet tall. Most garden specimens will likely be much shorter, with the three- to four-foot leaves whorled in a nestlike pattern. Sago palms are generally classed as frost

Powder-blue foliage of saw palmetto complements the plumbago flowers and contrasts with yellow croton leaves in this Florida garden. This palm is worthy of greater use in sunbelt gardens.

This young specimen of needle palm in my garden is a joy in every season. It anchors the fountain just off the stone terrace.

hardy but freeze-tender (Zone 9), yet plenty of large, healthy individuals thrive in local Zone 8 landscapes. Alabaster leaves of caladium and white-flowered periwinkle show off the dark, feathered foliage of sago palm during summer.

With tall trunks and dense crowns of long, wide leaves, it is hard to think of bananas as being anything but palms. Despite their morphological similarities, however, banana plants are large juicy-stemmed herbs without any woody tissue in their leaves or trunks. Being structurally composed almost exclusively of water, bananas need consistent moisture to grow well, and they prefer water-retentive soils. Frequently seen throughout the South, the common banana (*Musa paradisiaca* var. *sapientum*) is usually grown for its foliage—lush mops of large, bright green tropical leaves atop 10- to 15-foot stems. Winter will usually frost the leaves or freeze the plants entirely to the ground, but as with cannas, new shoots emerge and grow like gangbusters in warm weather. In milder winter climates near the coast, these plants may flower after a year or two and finally produce small tasty fruits. A much smaller version sporting maroon-splotched leaves with solid burgundy undersides, the blood banana (*Musa zebrina*) produces the same exotic look in a much smaller space. These five-foot-tall tropical perennials make tidy, multistemmed clumps over time and revel in rich moist soil with good light. They are unfortunately more tender than the common banana and benefit from a winter mulch in my zone.

I am particularly happy with the cold hardiness of the heat-loving Abyssinian banana (*Ensete vetricosum* 'Maurelii'), a robust, nonclumping plant with rosy trunk and leaf stems. This stout fellow makes up in resilience what it lacks in gracefulness. Though winter's cold will clip the five-foot-long, lush tropical leaves, the stem is superbly insulated and resists freezing even when the soil surface crusts with ice after prolonged cold. In my specimen's auspicious shadow grow wine-colored *Salvia vanhoutii*, pink *Ruellia* 'Chi Chi', and *Saccharum* 'Pele's Smoke', all of which thrive in the moist, rich conditions.

ORNAMENTAL GRASSES

Many wonderful ornamental grasses, both native and exotic, are delightfully easy to grow in hot and humid weather. Their airy, cloudlike forms and delicate linear foliage contrast smartly with the leaves of other plants and add whimsical movement to the garden. Most of these grasses, however, are quite substantial; some are giants. Their use in beds and borders is limited by their size, and like everything else that I might want, I sadly can't fit all of them in my small garden. Sometimes I find it easier to place these botanical fountains of foliage in the middle of the lawn, where they can grow unencumbered and make pleasing sculptures. What makes most ornamental grasses so attractive is not just their aesthetic qualities but the ease with which one can grow these heat-loving, cast-iron plants in the South. These selections exhibit variable drought tolerance but will definitely thrive with constant moisture. With few exceptions, the only key ingredient in the culture of grasses is sunshine—the more, the better.

By far the largest of the ornamental grasses is the formidable giant reed (*Arundo donax*), which can shoot up to 15 feet high, 2-foot plumes topping the plants at the end of summer. This plant loves moisture and can be found

The columnar form of 'Heavy Metal' switchgrass draws the eye up from the yellow lantana toward pendant lavender blooms of the crape myrtle beyond.

commonly in bar ditches along roadsides, where they make junglelike thickets. The variegated form of the giant reed (*A. donax* 'Versicolor'), however, makes an excellent addition to the garden. Spring's growth is especially vibrant, with each wide, lax leaf prominently striped with creamy white. This color becomes muted in the heat of summer, when the two-inch-thick canes tower overhead, but the overall form is still pleasing. Mild winters will not harm the standing stems, but I cut them to the ground each year to favor the superlative new growth. Slowly creeping underground stems can be contained in the smaller garden either actively (I dig up parts of the thick rhizomes every other year) or passively through containment with barriers.

Another large grass not for the faint of heart is hardy sugar cane (*Saccharum arundinaceum*). This ten-foot-tall ornamental has strong narrow stems with long, thin, gray-green leaves, each bearing a whitened stripe in the middle. Late fall finds the towering plants crowned with large, airy, pinkish plumes that keep the grass attractive into winter. Unlike the giant reed grass, which looks good as a narrow clump, hardy sugar cane is best used in large gardens where adequate space can be given to developed ten-foot-wide clumps. In such venues the large grass complements palms, small trees, shrubs, and hefty perennials like plume poppy and Joe Pye weed.

Although sugar cane is a common crop in some southeastern states, the bronze-leafed sugar cane (*Saccharum officinarum* 'Pele's Smoke') is exceptionally ornamental. This heat-loving grass quickly rises six to eight feet tall from tight clumps that constantly produce new leafy shoots, giving a multitiered appearance. Both the wide, curved leaves and shiny, thick canes (heavy with water and sugar) are a richly colored reddish-bronze. Like all sugar cane, it is happy in rich soil with ample moisture. Its

Inland sea oats, one of the smaller ornamental grasses and shade tolerant, sways over the marbled leaves of painter's palette.

sophisticated foliage adds drama to the monotonous green of summer and is stunning against the yellow-striped leaves of *Canna* 'Pretoria' punctuated by the spikes of *Salvia* x 'Indigo Spires'. 'Pele's Smoke' is cold hardy only in milder areas, so I mulch my specimen to guarantee its survival during Zone 8 winters and then cut the stalks to gnaw on the sweet cane.

Switchgrass (*Panicum virgatum*) was an underappreciated diamond in the rough until beautiful, blue-leafed forms were selected that made this plains native irresistible to gardeners and landscapers alike. This modest-sized, clump-forming grass is loose but tidy, producing a soft, billowy, cloudlike effect in the garden even before the summer blooms anoint the plants with open, airy panicles like a mist of tiny auburn beads on thin wires. 'Cloud Nine' is the gentle giant form of this usually four-foot-tall grass. It grows twice as large, with a soft gray-green foliage cast and huge, airy seed heads making a wonderful veil through which to view autumn. Variety 'Heavy Metal' makes a particularly narrow, erect, columnar clump with its steely blue leaves rigidly ascendant, in contrast to the normally lax, drooping effect of most switchgrass. It is particularly nice with gayfeather, tall verbena, and other vertical accents. The bluest foliage yet found in a switchgrass is the powder-blue 'Prairie Sky', which also has the normal, more open habit and flowing foliage texture. 'Prairie Sky' switchgrass contrasts comfortably with tall summer-blooming perennials and shrubs like China rose 'Old Blush' or *Abelia* 'Edward Goucher'. Where temperatures begin to cool in early autumn, many switch-grass cultivars take on a reddish-auburn cast that further enhances their position in the garden, but this is most pronounced up north.

Indian grass (*Sorghastrum nutans*) is another native clump-former of the Great Plains with an iron-clad constitution, making it perfect for garden use. The selection 'Sioux Blue' has pastel blue leaves a half-inch wide that radiate out in a wide, three-foot, mounding clump. Dense, feathery floral spikes of lustrous gold, turning to cinnamon, are prominently displayed on tall stems in an open manner. Pink *Salvia greggii* and *Salvia microphylla* make fine long-blooming companions to enjoy the delicate embrace of 'Sioux Blue'.

One of my favorite native grasses, inland sea oats (*Chasmanthium latifolium*), is also one of the few that is shade tolerant. From an early tussock of dense green foliage sprout strongly vertical, narrow stems bearing flattened leaf blades. Into early summer, the two-foot-tall compact clumps look like tidy little bamboos and impart a refined texture to informal perennial plantings. Summer finds stalks adorned with arching sprays of bright green, pendant, flattened floral spikes resembling oats. As the season progresses the seed heads ripen and turn to brown, but they are no less beautiful in the garden. However, this grass's tendency to seed about in beds leads me to harvest the stalks for indoor arrangements, where they can cause no trouble. Oakleaf hydrangea and scarlet tropical sage make a lovely ménage à trois for the shade with inland sea oats.

Maiden grass (*Miscanthus sinensis*) seems to have single-handedly led the ornamental grass movement in this country, becoming one of the most popular and widely planted hardy ornamental grasses. The dense clumps of vertical stems form pillarlike stands, with gently curving foliage arching out from the top in all directions. Depending on the cultivar, late summer and fall find the four- to six-foot-tall grass crowned with silky, branched, fingerlike floral spikes, which become fluffy white plumes as they mature. Although some clones are able to handle drought, maiden grass prefers full sun and constant moisture. These plants have a lovely tawny winter aspect even while dormant, but they should be cut clear to the ground in early spring to allow for new growth.

Slender maiden grass (*Miscanthus sinensis* 'Gracillimus') is not as flashy as some of its variegated kin, but it is as tough as it is elegant. The erect fount of foliage is quite

Slender maiden grass adorns a stairway with grace, contrasting the form of the American beautyberry opposite.

White arching leaves of variegated maiden grass create a stunning focal point while echoing the color and form of the nodding Abyssinian gladiolus flowers.

drought tolerant, perhaps due to its thin, wispy leaves, which contrast nicely with other textures in the garden. The reddish-brown plumes of summer make this ornamental grass a delight well into autumn. *Miscanthus* variety 'Sarabande' is an improved form of the slender maiden grass with incredibly fine foliage. More compact at four feet tall, *Miscanthus* 'Morning Light' has delicately variegated, narrow leaves, giving it a subtle frosted appearance. Its crimson blooms in summer make it particularly wonderful planted next to the blue wands of *Salvia uliginosa* and lacy yellow *Patrinia scabiosifolia*.

Wide leaves distinguish the other variegated forms of maiden grass. *Miscanthus* 'Zebrinus' has three-quarter-inch-wide leaf blades generously punctuated by horizontal bands of creamy yellow. From a distance the five- to six-foot-tall clumps, spangled with yellow, make a dramatic statement in the garden, and they are particularly effective when contrasting the bold bronze foliage of bananas or castor beans (*Ricinus communis*). The white-striped *Miscanthus* 'Variegatus' is a durable old standby that interjects an effusive white foliage fountain into the static surroundings of summer's green leaves. It plays center stage in white borders and moonlit gardens, but I like to contrast the linear texture and light color with cannas, red-leaf barberry, and dark purple butterfly bush. Other cultivars of maiden grass with bold variegated foliage include 'Cabaret' and 'Cosmopolitan', both of which hold their inch-wide leaves in a pronounced horizontal pattern, lending a nice tiered effect. These are tall plants (to seven feet) in good soil conditions, lending a commanding presence in the summer garden.

A different species, *Miscanthus transmorrisonensis* is an evergreen ornamental grass that does not die back at the end of the season like its close kin. Although the tawny foliage and stalks of regular maiden grass in winter have a subtle look all their own, it is quite nice to enjoy the refreshing green leaves of evergreen *Miscanthus*. The plants are both shorter and wider than *M. sinensis*, forming three- to four-foot-tall domes of narrow, arching, jade-green foliage that seems to cascade around the edges.

Fall sees the plants crowned with the fingerlike blooms found on other maiden grass, a look that is carried through winter. My specimen of evergreen maiden grass is planted in a low spot of the lawn, where it revels in heavy clay that is sometimes inundated by heavy rains. It makes a fine-textured turnstile in the garden year-round.

Hardy fountain grass (*Pennisetum orientale*) is a compact bunch grass growing to only about a foot tall and wide. The unassuming green leaves are embellished early in the season with pinkish-tan, feathery plumes rising above the foliage. It is perfect for containers and smaller beds, where larger ornamental grasses would overwhelm their neighbors. The giant form of *P. orientale* called 'Tall Tails' is not diminutive at all, however. This is not a problem if your garden has room for another five- to six-foot-tall grass. 'Tall Tails' loves heat and produces masses of long, arching, foxtail-like plumes that are tan with just a blush of pink. Slightly shorter, at four feet, is the fountain grass hybrid that I'm inclined to call "kick ass grass" because of its incredible performance, *Pennisetum orientale x incomptom*. This relative newcomer blooms nonstop throughout summer and fall, with long, ropy plumes that start out creamy white with a touch of pink, aging to clean white—quite dramatic with *Salvia* x 'Indigo Spires'. Background lighting does wonders for this and all the fountain grasses.

Sedges, grasslike plants with an equally durable disposition, expand the range of reliable perennial elements with linear foliage. Umbrella sedge (*Cyperus alternifolius*) is an old garden plant in the South, and due to its spreading, creeping habit it is one rarely purchased, as friends and neighbors have passed it around for ages. Four-foot-tall, narrow columns rise from dense rhizomes, making a forest of naked green stems that are each topped with an umbrellalike circle of flat leaves. Like most of its kin, the umbrella sedge loves wet soil, even growing well in bogs, but it is quite able to withstand drought. Its profile is echoed by tall verbena, and elephant ears offer bold contrast in moist sites.

The genus *Carex* contains a whole world of grasslike plants that range from dense tufts quite suitable for lawn substitutes, to larger clumps still perfect for the smaller garden. Palm sedge (*Carex muskingumensis*) makes modest thickets of diminutive, jade-green, foot-tall "palms." Actually, each little tree is a stem that has a whorl of leaf blades spiraling up at the top. This odd character is particularly happy in shaded conditions but also tolerates sun when in wet soil. Since it is winter dormant, palm sedge time-shares bed space with the cool-season wood sorrel (*Oxalis crassipes*), which in turn sleeps under the shadow of tiny palm groves in summer. Selection 'Oehme' is a variegated sport of the palm sedge with gilt edges.

Japanese sedge (*Carex morrowii*) grows as a one- to two-foot-wide, relaxed mop of languid, narrow leaves. This evergreen sedge is tidy,

"Kick ass grass" bloomed for months and still looked good when the blue pitcher sage came into flower at summer's end.

Narrow grasslike leaves of golden bamboo nod above the broader foliage of low-growing Kuma bamboo.

even if informal, and is usually found in a wide range of both white and yellow variegated forms. Happiness for the Japanese sedge is moist soil and partial shade, but the resilient plant tolerates wetter or drier and sunnier or darker conditions heroically. The most common form, 'Aureo Variegata', is striped with golden yellow, but one can also purchase selections of Japanese sedge with white edging, such as 'Ice Dance' and the fine-leafed 'Silk Tassel'. All are easy to grow and easy to blend into the garden in a variety of settings.

White star sedge (*Dichromena latifolia*) is a small, innocuous grassy clump until summer, when it produces two-foot-tall stalks with glistening white floral heads surrounded by starlike bracts. This sun-loving plant can survive standing water and then bake dry in the clay soil of my garden during summer, but it does look better without the torture of extremes. It is a perfect addition to a bog garden and is smashing planted with the black-leafed elephant ear (*Colocasia esculenta* 'Black Magic').

BAMBOOS

Bamboos are grasses in the truest sense, but their distinct differences from the other ornamental grasses both in morphology and use in the garden lead me to describe them in a separate section. These woody-stemmed grasses range from tall species that make formidable clumps, occupying a similar niche in the garden as shrubs or small trees, to low-growing, thin specimens that make excellent ground cover.

The taller bamboos offer a unique substance and architecture not found in other woody plants, yet they are not static, for they lithely dance and sway in the slightest breeze. The shorter forms are found with beautiful yellow or white variegated foliage that is lovely on its own but also harmonizes with many other colors and textures in shaded or sunny venues. Most, but not all, bamboos increase through underground stems, which run a distance of a few inches to a few feet before throwing up a new vertical stalk. This habit, and no doubt the myths of monstrous behavior (I have never seen bamboo knock down a house or consume small children), have conspired to scare gardeners away from these wonderful evergreen grasses. Nevertheless, the slender, graceful stalks of bamboo offer a subtle beauty that is hard to find elsewhere and is therefore worth the small amount of trouble to achieve.

There are two ways to stem the tide of invasive forms of bamboo: active containment and passive containment (in my garden I do both). Passive containment means planting the bamboos inside of a sturdy barrier, which keeps the underground stems going in circles while one can enjoy the beauty of the graceful leafy stalks. Active containment means the gardener will eliminate unwanted new stalks as they appear each spring, which is as easy as kicking the vulnerable young shoots when they first appear. Although landscapes are, by definition, low-maintenance and noninteractive plantings on one's property, unconfined bamboo would be somewhat threatening. However, in a garden where the gardener is out and about regularly, it is easy to nip the spread of invasive bamboos in the bud, and the tender six-inch shoots also make a tasty vegetable for the table.

One of the most common bamboos, the golden bamboo (*Phyllostachys aureas*), has been rather overplanted in the past and left to its own devices, so that its 10- to 15-foot-tall canes have taken over entire backyards (and perhaps even consumed a pet or two). It is still valuable because of its tough-as-nails vitality, and when kept in check, it makes a durable addition to the mélange of small trees and shrubs in the garden. The erect amber stems contrast subtly with the bright green, willowy foliage to create a unique contribution of oriental elegance. My passively contained specimen has given me valuable year-round privacy as it sits on the property line, shielding the garden from prying eyes.

Black bamboo (*Phyllostachys nigra*) is less commonly seen in gardens, although its legendary hardiness suggests that it would thrive as far north as Zone 6 without winter damage. The 10- to 20-foot-tall stalks are green the first year, then age to a dark ebony with white bands at the nodes, making a sublime contrast with the green lance-shaped leaves. At a distance black bamboo serves its purpose as an addition to the other woody plants in the garden, but it does bear close inspection so that one can enjoy the sophisticated appearance of the aged stalks. White *Salvia coccinea* 'Snow Nymph' would make a lively summer consort. The *P. nigra* variety 'Henon' has stems that mature to a ghostly white rather than the usual black.

Rare but valuable *Phyllostachys bambusoides* sends up narrow culms to 10 or 12 feet with outward-spraying branches. Individual stalks tend to arch and sway in the slightest breeze as the widely spread foliage makes an excellent sail. The variety 'Castillonis' has beautiful buff-yellow stems with bright green marks on the flat side of each branch junction. This distinct coloration fades with the years, so older stalks should be thinned out to expose the smart-looking young culms.

The clumping bamboos are generally not as hardy as other bamboos, but they usually perform well in the Deep South. *Bambusa multiplex* is one such treasure that makes ten-foot-tall botanical fountains of willowy foliage against strong lines of slightly arching stems. The variety 'Alphonse Karr' has particularly showy stems, boldly striped with green and golden yellow, and enjoys the same sunny sites and moist soil as kahili ginger, making an excellent pair. The Mexican weeping bamboo (*Otatea acuminata*) is distant kin at best, but it has a similar aspect, with just a bit more

Framed by ponytail palms, golden yellow stems of bamboo 'Alphonse Karr' enjoy the limelight in John Greenlee's garden.

of a pendulous nature to its arching stems. Its lush yet languid form makes a delightful contrast to the too-rigid profiles of many shrubs and small trees. It is nicely echoed by the relaxed sprawl of butterfly bush.

The large, spear-shaped leaves of Kuma bamboo (*Sasa veitchii*) are an unusual departure for bamboos and look especially odd on such short (two-foot-tall) plants. This spreader thrives in shade and seems quite indestructible, at least in the Upper South, as it muscles its way through the soil. It shares space well when the competition can rise above the dense foliage, so anything growing four feet or taller won't mind Kuma bamboo at its feet. In winter the wide leaves are neatly trimmed with straw-colored edging while the centers remain their usual jade green. Heavenly bamboo (*Nandina domestica*) makes a wonderful complement in any season.

The dwarf bamboos unfortunately suffer from nomenclatural confusion with a single plant alternately labeled as *Pleioblastus*, *Arundinaria*, and *Semiarundinaria*, depending on whom is asked. These wonderful little plants don't seem at all confused when in the garden, however, and make themselves at home in a variety of settings. Having asked several expert growers about a few of my favorites, I am no more certain about their names than I was at first, but I do know that I like them.

The golden leaf bamboo (*Pleioblastus auricoma*, syn. *Arundinaria viridistriata*) is a compact, running plant composed of rather large yellow leaves striped with green, held neatly on thin, wiry stems. Growing only two to three feet tall, this is the perfect choice for small gardens and even large containers. Though the evergreen foliage is valuable in winter, cutting the plant down to the ground every few years will encourage brilliant new growth in spring. Golden leaf bamboo gently contrasts with the glowing red stems of coral bark Japanese maple (*Acer palmatum* 'Senkaki') and echoes the yellow-splashed foliage of gold dust aucuba (*A. japonica*) in shady sites. It also interacts well with fiery cardinal flower (*Lobelia cardinalis*), Mexican milkweed (*Asclepias curassavica*), and purple Persian shield (*Strobilanthes dyerianus*) in moist, sunny sites.

Variegated dwarf bamboo (*Pleioblastus variegatus*), another modest-sized plant, bears smaller leaves arranged in dense tufts on wiry stems up to two feet tall. The foliage reveals refreshing strokes of green and white, with no two leaves alike. Also tolerant of shade, this colonizing ground cover will slowly spread into sculptured mounds of green and white that show quite well in darker corners of the garden. Try it as a consort for oakleaf hydrangea, as the latter can rise above the rambunctious fray.

Variegated dwarf bamboo is less than a foot tall, but rises to the challenge of prospering in difficult, dry shady sites.

Pygmy bamboo (*Pleioblastus pygmaea*, a.k.a. *Arundinaria* and *Sasa pygmaea*) is the smallest of these woody grasses—only a foot in height—but it is still a vigorous colonizer with creeping underground stems. The yellow variegated form is particularly beautiful and makes a compatible ground cover in sun or shade. Since all but the smallest plants can rise above its petite canopy of foliage, pygmy bamboo is hardly a bamboo to fear. In fact, I rather like when pygmy bamboo runs and interjects its small sprays of tiny yellow-striped leaves into neighboring foliage and flowers.

Without the diverse and dramatic addition of foliage, a garden is but a collection of flowers. The bold leaves of palms and bananas and linear texture of grasses and bamboos all conspire to transform southeast gardens into masterpieces that reflect an American style of horticulture. These plants are treasures that gardeners in cool climates would envy, and we are lucky to use them.

CHAPTER 10

Vines for Southeastern Gardens

In an environment where tall trees dominate the landscape and, more specifically, our gardens, one might not see the need for adding climbing vines to the cacophony of twigs and branches reaching for the light. Certainly in the land of kudzu, gardens might somehow appear more tamed with the exclusion of those vining plants that portend a threat, however elusive it may be.

Yet small gardens and courtyards with barren walls or fences need some delicate raiment, and larger landscapes with old buildings or big fences need cover, too. In these situations, vines come to the rescue, cloaking unsightly edifices with class.

I love flowering vines because they mold themselves to the shapes of the structures on which they climb, softening the hardscape with their verdant touch. They transform static fixtures, adding an elegant beauty and height to the garden that is hard to find elsewhere. More often than not I'm looking for sturdy new structures for flowering vines to clamber upon and am creating trellis-sculptures for that very purpose. Delicate vines that weave their tapestries of foliage and flowers into supporting small trees or shrubs are the epitome of elegance. I even think that the barren skeleton of a small, dead tree will do nicely in a pinch—the transformation of death into life, once cloaked again with leaves and flowers, is inspiring. However, some vines can be quite aggressive and need an exceptionally large run, so I will mention only a few of the "scary" species, with ample mention of the more delicate, smaller individuals.

In a land of ample summer moisture, annual vines are able to grow and bloom, performing so well as to be reliable mainstays in southeast gardens, and are therefore also included. These plants may need to be planted every year, though some seed themselves and return on their own. At any rate, annual vines are valuable, colorful additions to summer gardens in hot climates, and they may prove the safest for gardeners new to flowering vines or easily intimidated by the threat of kudzu.

It's hard to believe that an evergreen vine, bravely sending out clusters of flowers in February despite cold weather, would also be blooming during the dog days of summer. However, the remarkable, native coral honeysuckle (*Lonicera sempervirens*) is such a plant, and it has a gentle demeanor very different from its Japanese cousins, who've gained a reputation for being too aggressive. The oval, clasping, olive-green leaves make a great foil for the two-inch, coral-red, tubular flowers that are clustered on branch tips up and down the vine. Coral honeysuckle is cold hardy and drought tolerant once established, and it also tolerates shade, though it blooms best in full sun. Hummingbirds love to sup at the coral-red blossoms, which is reason enough to plant this

OVERLEAF: Coral honeysuckle is everything one could want from a hardy vine.

ABOVE: Potato jasmine is gorgeous but, alas, has no scent.

honeysuckle near a patio or veranda. The selection 'Alabama Crimson' is particularly floriferous, although it is hard to imagine that a plant like coral honeysuckle can be improved upon. Luminescent yellow clones of this vine are also available, allowing it into gardens where the red may be considered vulgar.

Mexican flame vine (*Senecio confusus*) is a heat-loving, compact vine that is evergreen in mild climates but reliably returns from a hard freeze to grace the garden in midsummer and fall. Thick, twining stems bearing three-inch, simple, toothed leaves spiral up supports quickly in hot weather while tips of lateral branches produce small clusters of large blooms. The two-inch, vivid orange daisies with reflexed petals and tangerine centers age to a darker shade before fading altogether, but new buds and blossoms continue for a parade of color that lasts for months. Mexican flame vine is a richly hued plant for sassy color schemes, but it can also be toned down with the addition of gold, bronze, and red foliage in the foreground.

Another summer-flowering vine for lovers of the color orange is the hardy, deciduous trumpet creeper (*Campsis radicans*) and its hybrids. Wild trumpet creepers easily surge to the tops of telephone poles in the Southeast, with a flaring crown dripping with dense clusters of large scarlet-orange trumpets—quite an improvement over the ubiquitous barren poles pervading the countryside. Nonetheless, it indicates a monstrous grower that has limitations in garden settings. Without an ugly telephone pole needing a makeover, it is best to grow the tamed hybrid trumpet creeper, *Campsis x tagliabuana* 'Madame Galen', with restrained growth and large clusters of scarlet-tinted, orange, wide-faced trumpets. The Chinese trumpet creeper (*C. grandiflora*) also shows a less aggressive habit with clusters of magnificent apricot, five-petaled, funnel-shaped flowers. Best of all is the *C. radicans cultivar* 'Flava', which proffers lovely flowers of pastel yellow-peach on gentle plants. In my garden, it grows on the fence behind similarly colored angel's trumpet (*Brugmansia* 'Charles Grimaldi').

Compared to orange flowers, white is easier for most people to integrate into gardens (although I love the two colors together), and the large, pendant clusters of white stars with yellow eyes that adorn potato jasmine (*Solanum jasminoides*) are everyone's favorite. This vine spirals and clambers its thin stems with great enthusiasm but rarely acts overwhelming. The simple foliage is able to withstand a light frost, but it defoliates when temperatures hit the mid-twenties. Colder temperatures take the potato jasmine to the ground, but it recovers (in Zone 8), and because the vine in time stretches upward to 20 feet with flowers and foliage out of view, I see this as a good thing. The golden variegated form of potato jasmine is particularly beautiful, but it doesn't show the same vigor in heat or ability to respond after freezing and so is best planted in mild climates.

In the stifling heat of sultry summers along the Gulf Coast, the star potato vine (*Solanum seaforthianum*) blooms stoically, producing large, dangling clusters of light purple, starlike flowers with yellow centers. These are followed by small red berries, hanging in a similar fashion amid deeply lobed, pinnate foliage. The drought-tolerant vine is seemingly a modest grower, keeping it manageably small in my garden, but can get to 20 feet in tropical Florida, where it knows no frost. It may not return from a hard freeze, so I protect my specimen. Star potato vine grows by clambering and trailing about, only holding on by an occasional clasping leaf stem, so it is ideal to train up into a small tree or shrub.

Although the annual forms of morning glory (*Ipomoea tricolor* and *I. purpurea*) are easily grown in the South, a perennial relative called blue dawn flower (*Ipomoea indica*, syn. *I. acuminata*) loves the heat. The heart-shaped leaves are sometimes lobed, and the hairy, twining stems eagerly seek out any support on which to climb and conquer. Blue dawn flower produces three- to four-inch-wide, dark purple-blue funnels like any other morning glory, only they turn violet-pink as they age through the day. They are charming blossoms on a dangerous plant—the blue dawn flower would climb and sprawl to 30 feet if possible. Large expanses of ugly chain-link fence come to mind, but any suitable run in full sun makes a perfect home for this rambunctious perennial vine; just keep it out of the small garden. It easily freezes to the ground but returns with a vengeance in spring, reclaiming all lost territory and then some. I'd be inclined to plant orange trumpet creeper alongside blue dawn flower and let the two fight it out with dazzling results.

Not all vines climb, and the sweet potato vine (*Ipomoea batatas*) demonstrates that and more—not all vines need to bloom in order to add summer color. Sweet potato vines love heat and humidity and just

Star potato vine absolutely loves torrid heat, as long as there is ample water for growth. When everything else looks tired, this one is in its prime.

grow better the hotter it gets. Trailing stems run along the ground and through and over other garden associates, adding their splashy foliage color and texture to the garden, and the plants happily set tubers (the "sweet taters"), which usually return after a Zone 8 winter. Tip cuttings root easily and ensure next year's plants.

The first ornamental sweet potato to hit the scene was *I. batatas* 'Blackie'. With deeply lobed, eggplant-colored leaves and a desire to run at length, to ten feet or more, this plant is a designer's dream. 'Blackie' weaves in and out of other low foliage and flowers, tying the summer garden together harmoniously with a rich, dark color accent. More recently two other cultivars of sweet potato have shown themselves to be equally valuable. The chartreuse, heart-shaped leaves of *I. batatas* 'Margarita' are every bit as intoxicating as their namesake. In full sun the foliage even takes on a golden cast, but it is also a much more dense grower than 'Blackie', as 'Margarita' produces many-branched stems that march forward and *over* any low-growing plantings in their way as it unfurls a glowing carpet of color. Caution must be used in placing this plant in the garden, as it will bowl over everything less than a foot in height and spreads out across the ground up to six feet from the base. More compact and lower-growing with smaller, arrowhead-shaped leaves of many colors is *I. batatas* 'Pink Frost'. This three-inch-high plant has leaves marbled in green, white, and pink with surprisingly the best color and no scorching in full sun. 'Pink Frost' is perfect for filling in between perennials and grasses during summer in difficult sites since it is little troubled by anything but cold. All cultivars of sweet potato spill delightfully over the sides of containers.

Tropical relatives of the morning glories include the haunting moon vine (*Calonyction aculeatum*), whose large, white, funnel-form blooms enchantingly unfurl each evening during summer into fall. The moon vine loves heat, and few other places can grow this vine like the hot, humid Southeast. Twining stems with large heart-shaped leaves eagerly smother supports narrow enough to succumb to the vine's embrace, with thickest growth and abundant bloom produced in full sun and rich, moist (even wet) soil. Planting this moonlight magic outside the bedroom window guarantees countless opportunities for viewing the ghostly blossoms.

Most amenable of the sweet potato vines, 'Pink Frost' weaves a lovely brocade among other flowers without being overbearing.

Mina lobata is another annual vine kin to the morning glory but unfortunately rarely seen. The foliage is deeply lobed (looking like a fleur-de-lis) and the spikes of flowers are very unusual—short, erect chains of small, bullet-shaped blooms the color of a sunset. *Mina* is a delicate vine that is hardly overwhelming and needs to be planted in groups in order to achieve some impact. It looks great growing into and onto other shrubs, perennials, or grasses. The thin, twining stems make themselves at home without being an imposition on their host, imparting stalks of yellow, orange, and scarlet flowers like colorful little banners. It is also fun to plant *Mina lobata* at the base of a rose trellis for a splash of summer blooms against the green and coppery foliage.

The tropical black-eyed Susan vine (*Thunbergia alata*) is similarly intolerant of frost and so is grown as an annual. This modest-sized vine does enjoy the heat, though, and is thoroughly enjoyable where summers are long and hot. The pointed, arrowhead-shaped leaves are small and neat, making a dense, dark green foil for the short, wide-faced, golden trumpets with dark eyes. Recently hybrids have expanded the range into soft yellow and creamy white blooms, with or without the dark center, all of which are worth growing. The black-eyed Susan vine will only ascend to about four feet in a season but does so with relish, forming a dense cover for whatever trellis or support on which it is set. Its compact size makes it the perfect vine for intimate spaces.

Clock vine (*Thunbergia gregorii*) is another tropical that resents hard freezes and is best used as a glamorous exotic annual. A summer's worth of growth can produce 15 feet of twining stems, velvety arrowhead leaves, and large, vivid orange flowers. Like its cousin, the clock vine's flowers are wide-faced trumpets, but they lack a dark center. Clock vine is a frivolous addition to the garden inasmuch as the plants are hard to come by where I live, but I am driven to plant the bright orange flowers on the same trellis as

Orange clock vine, topped by the multicolored blooms of *Mina lobata*, is brilliance incarnate.

In an interesting twist, plants are grown on the outside of this container, spotlighting passionflower.

the purple hyacinth bean and let them play together for the summer.

The sky vine (*Thunbergia grandiflora*) is a heat-loving tropical perennial that is able to return heroically from temperatures in the teens and grow again the next season. Sky vine has large, glossy, arrowhead-shaped leaves on pencil-thick, twining stems that rise to six feet tall in my garden by late April. By fall the vines get to be 15 feet and more (and in Florida they don't stop there), so I'm glad to have the winter weather check their growth. The large hanging clusters of three-inch-wide, blue trumpets are an awesome sight and make it well worth growing the rather large climber. On a sunny pergola or large arbor, the sky vine can cavort with the pink-flowered coral vine (*Antigonon leptopus*), whose lacy tresses will hang down and mingle with the large blue trumpets.

Many forms of passionflower (*Passiflora spp.*), with their lobed leaves and exotic flowers, can be planted in the Southeast. Our native species, the maypop (*Passiflora incarnata*), is a resilient, drought- and cold-hardy vine that sprawls and climbs by long, coiled tendrils in its search for sunshine. The three-inch flowers are intricate but exhibit faded blue color, and the plant has a propensity to sucker about. The hybrid 'Incense' is a cross between the maypop and an Argentine species, and it has large, showy flowers in rich purple shades. This hybrid is vigorous and cold hardy like its American parent, but sadly, it suckers like the maypop. Another hybrid, *Passiflora x alatocaerulea*, has large, three- to four-inch, fragrant flowers of lavender and white petals with a darker, frilled "crown." This less hardy vine is also much more restrained. One of its parents, the Brazilian species *P. caerulea*, is an evergreen vine hardy to the mid-teens that sports large blue flowers. Because all of these passionflowers climb by means of thin, coiling tendrils, supports must be fine textured enough for them to grab hold, but I still prefer the transformation that occurs when one climbs onto a sedate evergreen, holly, or photinia.

Hyacinth bean (*Dolichos lablab*) is a heat-loving annual vine that is so successful in the South that it always reseeds itself without fail. For people who want a lot of color with little fuss, this is the vine to plant. Spiraling dark stems carry purple-veined, jade-green, trifoliate leaves with a purple undercast, making hyacinth bean attractive from the start. Through summer the handsome vines are also punctuated with short spikes of small, violet-pink, pealike flowers followed by three- to four-inch-long, brilliant royal-purple pods. Hyacinth bean tolerates some shade but develops the best color in full sun. Its annual nature makes it perfect for creating welcome summer shade over a patio or terrace and dying off in winter, when the warm sunshine is desired. A few seeds will always fall to the ground for next year's plant.

The thick, glossy, dark green leaves of pink mandevilla (*M. splendens,* syn. *Dipladenia*) enchant everyone who sees this tropical vine. Pastel pink, five-petaled flowers with soft yellow throats, blooming in spite of the hottest weather imaginable, amaze even me—how does the plant manage to look so good? More common is the hybrid *Mandevilla x amabilis* 'Alice du Pont', which is sparsely clad with foliage that is larger and more textured than the species. The hybrid's blooms are also larger—four inches across—and are a bright rose pink. Mandevillas have a thick, tuberous root that gives them the ability to forgive the forgetful waterer, and they even return from a freeze. For best results, plant them in well-drained soil in the hottest spot possible in good sun.

One could hardly ignore climbing roses, as some do bloom through the summer months. In particular, the climbing form of China rose 'Old Blush' is a real treat for a large, sturdy support. The ambling canes easily sprawl 15 feet and more with occasional showers of wonderful semidouble pink roses. The considerable weight of this plant's woody stems dictate a sturdy support so that one can always enjoy this long-term investment. The climbing form of floribunda rose 'Iceberg' is also a dandy. Although nothing can surpass the spectacular spring display of large, glistening white, semidouble blooms, the midsummer performance of this climbing rose is heroic. The pure white flowers held in small clusters are nothing if not refreshing to look at on hot summer days. This climber is ideal for an arch, as long as it is solidly built.

More than trees or shrubs, vines seem to be the link between earth and sky in the garden. Due to their ability to embrace other plants and structures, flowering vines weave a certain sort of magic as they reach for heaven while showering us with color.

CHAPTER 11

SUMMER BULBS

Bulbs, corms, and tubers are outstanding survival tools for plants living in hot, dry climates, where growth and flowering are cool-season events and the organs are used for dormancy through a season without moisture. This is not the case for summer-flowering bulbs (also tubers and corms), which grow and bloom in the hot season. Storage organs help the summer growers survive winter's cold or accompanying dry season, but the plants flourish in the hot, humid Southeast, adding foliage and floral pizzazz to our gardens. A few of these are winter-growing bulbs that then take a summer siesta only to awaken during the hottest months, erupting into bloom without any foliage.

Though most of these treasures are grown for their exquisite bloom, some are cultivated for handsome foliage alone. All of these summer bulbs thrive in garden conditions where they can be counted on as perennials, but some do profit from prudent intervention and sound horticultural practice. Without exception, the summer-growing bulbs are heavy feeders and prefer some extra fertilization during growth. Many of these summer bulbs are perfect for pot culture and make handsome accents for the patio or courtyard garden.

BULBS FOR SHADE

Orchid pansies (*Achimenes*) are longtime favorites in the South, although lately they have been on the decline (perhaps due to a lack of nursery interest in purveying them). These shade- and moisture-loving tropical perennials form fragile, scaled rhizomes from which they return in early summer after the weather gets hot. Short-stemmed, mounding plants with small, velvety leaves soon produce large, wide-faced, tubular flowers, two to three inches across, in shades of blue, purple, pink, and white. Currently, hybrids are found in bulb catalogs (don't be discouraged by the size of the tiny rhizomes), but these come from the various, still-valuable species from south of the border. The blue *Achimenes longiflora* and purple *A. grandiflora* 'Atropurpurea' are two sturdy perennials that can still be found in older gardens, with a variety called 'Purple King' reportedly enduring 0° F in Tennessee. Grown in moist shade with white caladiums and orange impatiens, the blue or purple orchid pansies would make any northerner long for sultry summers and mint juleps. Alas, foraging squirrels take their toll of the apparently tasty rhizomes and should be discouraged.

The large genus *Oxalis* includes both summer-growing and winter-growing species, so gardens can support the quaint shamrock foliage of these wood sorrels year-round. Purple leaf wood sorrel (*Oxalis regnellii* 'Triangularis') has proven itself throughout the South both in its ability to survive cold winters and in its stoic performance during hot, humid summers. The dainty

OVERLEAF: Purple leaf wood sorrel is a perfect consort for a multitude of plants.

ABOVE: Used creatively, caladiums can again be exciting additions to garden plantings.

plants grow in compact mounds of burgundy-purple leaves, reaching only six or eight inches in height. Even in shady conditions the foliage does not lose its vibrant color, and delicate, nodding, pale pink flowers provide a wistful accent. The fragile tubers of purple leaf wood sorrel look like those of *Achimenes* and are dishearteningly small, but they will grow in any moist soil with at least partial shade. To achieve a cool-looking combination for the front of the border, plant purple leaf wood sorrel amid variegated liriope or spider plant (*Chlorophytum*) with white-flowered *Achimenes* or impatiens.

The fancy-leafed hybrid caladiums (*Caladium x hortulanum*) are successful, heat-loving tropical aroids that have become a bit of a cliché in the South as bedding plants. However, that is a matter of aesthetics, and certainly the vigorous plants deserve a home, if not a better integrated use in southern gardens. The six- to eight-inch, heart-shaped, patterned leaves of caladiums are usually marbled in white, red, or pink, with dozens of new hybrids to join the old standbys. These are tropical plants, however, and resent anything other than hot weather. So, as with peppers and impatiens, wait until the weather is settled and the ground is warm before planting (cool weather stunts their growth).

Along the Gulf Coast, caladiums can persist and the sturdy cultivars (especially lance-leafed hybrids) or species can perennialize, but they need soil with good drainage to avoid winter rot. In the colder parts of the Southeast, caladiums can be dug and stored in the fall, although I, like many other gardeners, prefer to purchase new bulbs each spring. Best results come from bulbs grown in moist, rich soil in partial shade, and it doesn't hurt to fertilize them during the growing season, as they are heavy feeders. The bold, patterned foliage of caladiums is often enough for some, but I love to mix it with other colors and textures, integrating the dynamic leaves into other planting schemes. The red-leaf forms, for instance, are stunning when grown with the yellow variegated dwarf sweet flag and ferns, whereas the white-leaf forms may illuminate an all-white composition of variegated liriope, white impatiens, and begonias.

ELEPHANT EARS, CRINUMS, AND SPIDER LILIES

Related to the demure caladium is the robust elephant ear (*Colocasia esculenta*), which is also at home in the hot, humid Southeast. Usually found in its original velvety green form, with the potential to grow up to six feet tall and with four-foot leaves, the elephant ear has seen some improvements lately. Black-leafed cultivars 'Jet Black Wonder' and 'Black Magic' are truly remarkable and boldly go in the garden where no elephant ear has gone before. Along with the black-veined cultivar 'Illustris', these plants are focal points in the summer garden and are exciting with white or yellow variegated foliage like maiden grass or *Canna* 'Pretoria'. It is a bog plant, however, and should be grown with lots of water if one wants to achieve a giant. If garden space is limited, a smaller plant can be cultivated by giving it less water and less food (elephant ears, too, are heavy feeders).

Another note in the garden melody known as "The Song of the South" is the crinum lily. Though not a true lily, the genus *Crinum* has several species and many hybrids that have made their permanent homes in the land of cotton. These long-lived plants with bulbs the size of a man's thigh are permanent features of southern gardens; they often outlive the homes around which they were planted. The swarthy clumps of whorled straplike foliage make crinums bold features in the garden even when not in bloom, but it is the flowers that most people imagine when they think of these plants. Most crinums bloom before the dog days of summer, and also sometimes in response to the late rains of September, acting like giant rain lilies. Mostly, though, crinum flowers open in the evening to perfume the night, and then fade in the heat of the day.

A few crinums can be relied upon to flower in midsummer and yet tolerate the colder winters that face everyone away from the Gulf Coast. In all of crinumdom they are only the tip of the iceberg, but they are the best bet for most gardeners in the Southeast. With lush, semi-evergreen mops of long, curving, blue-green leaves, the Orange River lily (*Crinum bulbispermum*) makes itself known before the advent of blooms in early spring. Each of the naked stalks adorning a clump of these bulbs is crowned with a dozen white or pink trumpets heralding the spring season but flowering in summer as well. The old white 'Alba' blooms over a period

'Black Magic' elephant ear is deserving of a place in the sun, provided that there is also rich soil and lots of water.

of four or five months, seeing it into midsummer. Its floriferous, hardy constitution, along with a propensity to set seed, has led the Orange River lily to parent many hybrid crinums with good summer bloom.

Hybrid *Crinum x powellii* is the result of crossing *C. bulbispermum* and *C. moorei*. It is beautiful, floriferous, and sturdy—one of the perfect crinums for all the South. In particular, *C. x powellii* 'Alba', a white cultivar, is a sure winner with exceptional resilience in sun

Vibrant red spider lilies rise above the fray of *Plectranthus* foliage near my needle palm— what a pleasant surprise!

or shade. The cultivar 'Cecil Howdyshel' blooms a rich pink and can produce a parade of flowers lasting many months. Either form of this hybrid crinum is worthy of being the centerpiece of a summer garden. When possible, the lush clumps of leaves should have some contrasting counterpoint of foliage, either bold or ferny, to celebrate the crinum's form.

A cross between two separate but similar genera of South African bulbs has resulted in one of the most heat-tolerant summer beauties imaginable. The winter-growing, summer-blooming *Amaryllis belladonna* and *Crinum moorei* (or even *Crinum x powellii*) have parented tough, summer-flowering bulbs sometimes called crinadonnas, or botanically speaking, *x Amarcrinum*. The various clones range in color from raspberry to an almost-white blush pink, with an equal variance in fragrance (some are divine). Unlike most crinums, the bulbs of *x Amarcrinum* do best when out of the moist, heavy clay and in a well-drained, sandy soil. Foliage of the *x Amarcrinum* is compact compared to most true crinums, and the bulbs are therefore easier to integrate into other plantings, taking less room in beds and borders than their traditional kin.

Close cousin of the crinum is the enchanting genus of spider lilies (*Hymenocallis*) with their fragrant, fragile, ghostly blooms and robust straplike leaves. Although different species abound, few find their way into commercial cultivation. Most commonly seen in the South is the evergreen *Hymenocallis spp.* 'Tropical Giant', whose dark green, shiny, amaryllislike leaves thrive in moist shade with river fern (*Thelypteris kunthii*). Midsummer is graced with spicy, sweet flowers on tall, naked stalks; the gaunt alabaster flowers are but thin strips of petals and protruding stamens embraced by a small white skirt at the bottom. The South American group of spider lilies (*Ismene*) contains mostly deciduous bulbs with shorter petals and larger cups. Of the several hybrids available in the trade, the best is 'Sulfur Queen', with compact, soft yellow flowers on short, sturdy stems. 'Sulfur Queen' is reliable in the most difficult weather conditions and is sweetly scented.

SURPRISE BLOOMS

Two late-summer-flowering bulbs that grace southern gardens in the hopeless days of heat also grow in winter, adding hardy green foliage to the cool-season palette. Both the oxblood lilies (*Rhodophiala bifida*) and red spider lilies (*Lycoris radiata*) bloom at about the same time of the year—September, where I live—and both have ruby-red flowers. Moreover, both of these bulbs have particularly hardy garden strains that differ from those that may be purchased commercially, so if at all possible dig some from a friend or neighbor's colony (with their permission, of course).

The fall emergence of red spider lily foliage means that the cool growing season is upon us, and the dark green straps with silver streak down the center make a valuable addition to beds and borders. The dense clumps of foliage thrive in the sunshine that penetrates bare branches overhead all winter, and the bulbs bloom in summer shade, successfully mingling with other shade-loving plants. The fanciful red flowers crown thick, naked stalks, with long, wispy, gold-tipped stamens protruding from two-inch blooms of recurved wavy petals.

The long, narrow, jade leaves of the oxblood lily are not as picturesque as the red spider lily, but they are a welcome green when so much else is dormant. They, too, can grow in open sun or under the branches of a deciduous tree, which sheds its leaves during fall to let in the sun. Their bulbs, the size of golf balls and with long necks, have the ability to pull themselves incredibly deep into the soil, making these challenging to dig from an established clump. In bloom, small groupings of three-inch, blood-red flowers top the short, naked stems, resembling little amaryllis. Happy in any soil, oxblood lilies last longer when their flowers are shaded and would make quite a splash popping through a golden carpet of *Ipomoea batatas* 'Margarita'.

The hardy surprise lily (*Lycoris squamigera*) thrives in the Upper South, where it flushes with leaves alongside other spring bulbs but doesn't share a flower. If grown

Towering Formosa lilies impress everyone who chances to see them.

among midsized garden perennials, the wide, bluish foliage can be tastefully eclipsed by other plants as it later yellows and fades. Those same perennial associates receive the welcome company of large, lavender-pink trumpets adorning tall, naked stems in midsummer, when the "naked ladies" come to enchant suitors. The blue foil of little bluestem grass makes a subtle background, as does the Indian grass cultivar 'Sioux Blue'.

TRUE LILIES

Although many bulbous flowers are given the common name "lily," that honor truly belongs to members of the genus *Lilium*. Most true lilies grow and bloom from spring to early summer, but some endure the heat later in the season. The tiger lily (*Lilium lancifolium,* syn. *tigrinum*) seems to be everyone's favorite despite the fact that it has orange flowers. The pendant blooms, shaped like Turkish caps, actually are a soft apricot suffused with black spots, more like a leopard than a tiger. This lily enjoys good garden conditions but blooms best with some shade. Blue flowers of bog sage or anise sage (*Salvia uliginosa* or *S. guaranitica*) make dashing companions for the graceful tiger lilies in bloom, as does white *Phlox paniculata*. *Lilium henryi* is another species with pendant Turk's-cap flowers, though they are unspotted and rather a gay mango color with bright green centers. It enjoys similar conditions and blooms a bit earlier.

At first glance the Formosa lily (*Lilium formosanum*) looks like an Easter lily with a thyroid problem, except that it blooms months after the spring holiday, during the hottest days of summer. The huge, white, flaring trumpets are impressive enough on their own, but when perched atop five-foot-tall stems, the sight is nothing if not astounding. Dark green, narrow leaves in whorls up the stem also add to the beauty of this hardy and heat-tolerant bulb. Formosa lily enjoys good garden conditions and tolerates some shade but does quite well in full sun as long as it has some moisture.

Despite its formidable height, the Formosa lily is such a narrow plant that it can be worked into smaller gardens, and the glistening white flowers find little conflict with other color schemes.

OTHER EXOTIC LILIES

The exotic climbing lily (*Gloriosa rothschildiana*) is not a true lily but a tropical look-alike. Solitary narrow stems grow to three or four feet, with each simple elliptical leaf bearing a grasping tendril at the tip. In the wild, these plants climb by grabbing onto twigs, often growing up shrubs; the domesticated boxwood hedge makes a suitable substitute in the tamed environs of the garden. The elaborate flowers consist of six undulating, red and yellow, windswept petals with pistil and stamens radiating out of the center where the petals are joined—it kind of looks like a tiger lily on acid, in a hurricane. Climbing lilies grow from finger-sized, fleshy rootstocks, which creep underground horizontally in moist, well-drained soil. In late spring a solitary tender shoot (susceptible to snail, slug, and pillbug damage) emerges from the tip of the tuberous root and begins its ascent into warm sunshine, grasping for a hold when about a foot tall. Plants bloom in midsummer and can be left in the ground if winters are not too wet. Otherwise, store the tubers in a cool, dry place until spring.

All pineapple lily species require good sun and rich soil with ample moisture and drainage.

The gold-flecked, red and green flowers of parrot lily (*Alstroemeria psittacina*, syn. *pulchella*) would be well suited for the winter holiday season, but these Brazilian natives love the summertime. Arising from clusters of peanut-sized tubers, pencil-thick stalks with whorls of spoon-shaped leaves at the top give the impression of small, two-foot-tall trees. The flowering stems, produced separately, are taller, sparsely leafed, and crowned with a circle of narrow, tunnel-like blooms (larger separate petals are collapsed together) that attract hummingbirds. In partial shade with adequate moisture, parrot lilies expand to form large colonies through spreading, stoloniferous roots, but the modest-sized plants cannot compete with woody plants, ornamental grasses, or perennials that rise above the tops of the leafy stalks. Red-leaf caladiums planted in the foreground contrast with the parrot lily foliage beautifully and harmonize with the flowers.

The odd-looking pineapple lily (*Eucomis bicolor*) prefers hot, humid summers, where it can revel in sun and moist soil. It is one of many summer-growing bulbs from South Africa that is less common than crinums. The whorl of long, broad leaves forming a basal rosette of foliage makes a perfect foil for the up to two-foot-tall erect flower stems. Hundreds of two-toned, greenish, pendant lilylike blooms crowd the upper half of the stalk, which is topped by another, smaller whorl of leaves—the result being similar to a pineapple. The flowers last a long time, then transition into

Abyssinian gladiolus is suprisingly heat- and moisture-loving, but watch out for thrips on the flowers.

showy green seedpods without any loss of visual effect, so that pineapple lilies look great for months. Green flowers are not most people's first choice for garden color, but these also have indispensable architectural form. Pineapple lilies are spectacular with orange cigar flowers and purple heart. The wine eucomis (*E. punctata*) has showier white, pink, or purple flowers, but the plants are not as robust in the face of adversity.

Rarer still, but no less valuable, is the simply beautiful *Anthericum saundersae*, which I would call grass lily because the dense clumps of long, narrow, creased leaves do look like any bunch of grass. The plant's nonstop supply of flowers, however, indicates otherwise. Many tall, wiry stems arc from the center of the clump, bearing small, white, starlike flowers densely arrayed at the tips of each stalk, which becomes pendulous with their floral weight. From spring to fall these industrious little plants bloom in sun or shade, whether they are in very wet or dry conditions. Ethereal *Anthericum* mingles pleasantly with a host of other flowers and foliage—its own white flowers and grassy texture are elegantly harmonious. As with garlic chives, I have yet to plant too much of this dainty beauty.

GLADS AND THEIR KIN

Gladiolus can be seen throughout the Southeast, as the corms are inexpensive and easy to grow—as long as they are planted early in the season, so that the plants produce their grand floral spikes before the weather gets hot and thrips take their toll. However, one species of glad grows and blooms well during the heat of summer and even perennializes where frost does not penetrate the ground: Abyssinian gladiolus (*Gladiolus callianthus,* formerly *Acidanthera bicolor*) thrives in rich, moist soil in a sunny exposure where its tall, ribbed, sword-shaped leaves thrust skyward in an imposing manner. The seminodding floral spikes later become erect as three-inch-wide, long-tubed, ivory flowers with dark eyes begin to open one at a time up the stalk. Due to the long floral tubes supporting each blossom, flowers gently bow their heads, encouraging closer inspection, which rewards the viewer with sweet perfume. Abyssinian glads thrive in moist, rich ground and would make a daring contrast with black-leafed elephant ears, with perhaps a group of white caladium 'Candidum' and orange cigar plants in the foreground.

Related to the gladiolus is a subtropical genus from South Africa known as *Crocosmia*. In the American South and on the West Coast there are thriving colonies of what I and many others still refer to as montbretias. These old hybrid corms are stoloniferous and spread in rich, moist soil to form dense colonies of flat, swordlike, grassy foliage producing narrow, semibranched spikes of small, brick-orange, nodding flowers with yellow throats. The dainty one-inch flowers look like six-pointed stars and are borne in graceful profusion at blooming time in summer, after which the foliage begins to fade as the corms ripen into dormancy. Variety 'Citronella' has a similar growth habit, with clear, peachy yellow blossoms, whereas 'Solfaterre' is similarly colored but has bronzed foliage. Montbretias are great for time-sharing bed space with daffodils and paperwhites, as they, too, enjoy similar conditions, but one sleeps while the other flowers.

The members of the genus *Crocosmia* with pleated, spear-shaped leaves and backward-arching floral spikes bearing upward-facing blooms are different enough in appearance to warrant separate identification, and I refer to these as crocosmias. The persimmon-orange, starlike flowers of *Crocosmia masoniorum* are larger than regular montbretias, and the two-inch flowers with protruding stamens face up for better viewing. This is one of the parents of the more commonly found *Crocosmia x 'Lucifer'*, which has similar foliage and form, but with vibrant, fiery red flowers. Flamboyant 'Lucifer' always garners attention and is best planted in groups of at least five or seven bulbs since they do not multiply as quickly as montbretias. *Crocosmia* bulbs survive cold winters and perform better in the Upper South than along the torrid Gulf Coast.

TUBEROSES

Intensely fragrant, waxy, ivory tuberose flowers (*Polianthes tuberosa*) are more frequently seen as cut flowers than in gardens, but this Mexican native (favorite of the Aztecs) adapts to life in southeast gardens. Tuberose is related to the century plants of the Southwest and Mexico, and the plant's fleshy leaves grow in grassy rosettes, forming dense clumps with smaller offshoots, until individual "bulbs" gain enough steam to produce a flowering stem (fortunately this doesn't take a century, but maybe a year). Like century plants, tuberose "bulbs" fade after they flower, but they surround themselves with a dozen smaller offshoots or pips so that the plant continues to grow.

Unmanaged clumps of tuberose quickly become too thick for many individual plants to develop into blooming-sized "bulbs," yielding only foliage instead. To have flowers, one must first grow the individual tuberose plant large enough to bloom, which means annual or biannual digging, thinning, and replanting of the largest of the unflowered "bulbs." These tuberlike roots have pointed tips and not a hole from a faded stalk in the center. Full sun, adequate moisture, and fertilizer will produce astounding results as the unassuming mound of leaves sends up three-foot-tall stalks of perfumed, starlike trumpets. Though a shorter-stemmed,

The sweet fragrance of tuberoses doubles after sunset. These 'Mexican Single' plants perfume an entire terrace at dusk.

double-flowered form exists ('Pearl'), the timeless cultivar called 'Mexican Single' does best in hot weather and is richly perfumed.

RAIN LILIES

Rain lilies are as many and varied as stars in the heavens; the genera *Zephyranthes* and *Habranthus* have countless New World species and resulting hybrids. Yet these are demure plants with petite but charming flowers—they must be planted en masse to rock your world when they bloom. Rain lilies erupt into colorful flowers as if by magic when the rains finally bless the sunbaked landscape. Even though the weather is still hot, they signal the coming end of summer, providing an epiphany that stirs the soul. Although some American species of rain lilies are native along the Gulf Coast, most of those in commerce hail from Mexico and South America.

The small white rain lily (*Zephyranthes candida*) grows as tight clusters of bulbs, creating large, dense, evergreen mounds of ten-inch, dark green, rushlike leaves capable of withstanding temperatures in the teens without flinching. Hot weather presents no challenge to these tough-as-nails bulbs as long as some moisture is available, but even bog conditions are acceptable. As early as August in the Upper South, clumps of this Argentine native are smothered in one-inch, white, crocuslike flowers with yellow anthers in their centers. In warmer regions of the Deep South the white rain lilies burst into bloom following the rains of September and October. The perky foliage is complemented by low-growing purple heart (*Setcreasia pallida*) or thrifty, dwarf Mexican petunia (*Ruellia* 'Katy').

Also from Argentina comes the large-flowered, pink rain lily (*Habranthus robustus*). Commonly listed as *Zephyranthes robustus* in catalogs, this subtropical evergreen bulb slowly increases to form relaxed clumps of flat, wide, grassy leaves. The semitender foliage needs protection from temperatures lower than 20° F, but the plants bounce back from losing their leaves. In summer, three-inch-wide amaryllislike flowers rise from the foliage sporadically, sometimes making quite a show. More frequently seen established in gardens of the South is Zephyranthes grandiflora, which is also a subtropical rain lily with large, pink flowers that tend to open facing up rather than out. Both rain lilies look great when planted with the compact, pink and creamy foliage of *Ipomoea* 'Pink Frost' and rosy-leafed caladiums.

The enchantment of summer bulbs is further extended by their ease of culture and long lives. Once planted in the proper site, bulbs reward the gardener with years of fanciful foliage and exotic blooms.

OPPOSITE: The delicate beauty of grass lily (*Anthericum saundersae*) belies a durable nature.

ABOVE: Each year I plant more sturdy white rain lilies in my garden; even the hardy jade foliage is a pleasure in winter.

171

CHAPTER 12

SUMMER ANNUALS

The Southeast's hot yet wet summer growing seasons are perfect for a myriad of annuals and tender perennials, which make the most of a long summer and then perish in winter. True annuals complete their life cycles without the intention of anything other than leaving behind seed for next year's crop. Tender perennials could live indefinitely if only the weather stayed mild

(or inside a greenhouse during winter's cold). Some of our favorite annuals for the South—impatiens, begonias, and geraniums—are actually tender perennials. During mild winter years some of these plants will even return for a second season of growth after narrowly escaping frozen doom in my Zone 8 garden. At the same time, some of our sunbelt's hardy perennials, like certain *Salvia* and *Verbena* species, are common annuals in the North. Nevertheless, I will lump the tender perennials together with annuals, since the entire Southeast covers the broad spectrum of mild to cold winters. The real focus is how well these plants perform in hot summers and the vital role that they play in our gardens.

Few plants can provide such a long season of colorful flowers or interesting foliage in the face of relentless heat and humidity as annuals. Annuals are such workhorses in the garden that it is easy to forgive the fact that they might need replacing next spring (some will readily reseed with abandon). Beyond the traditional bedding schemes most often seen, annuals are easily mixed into the garden to highlight permanent plantings. I am hardly a purist when it comes to garden motifs and do not see the point of having the perennial border ethnically cleansed of all nonperennials. I prefer the concept of the holistic garden with mixed plantings, including everything beautiful that works in a particular climate. Certainly shrubs, vines, grasses, bulbs, and, of course, annuals mingle with perennials in the garden, and the end result is most rewarding. Integrating hot shot annuals into the mixed border is a surefire way to add valuable color to southeastern gardens in summer.

SUCCULENTS

Some heat-loving annuals are drought-tolerant succulents that can bake in full sun with little additional watering. Moss rose (*Portulaca grandiflora*) sprouts large, brightly colored, crepe-papery flowers from low-growing, insignificant plants. The two-inch blooms can be double or single with a golden boss of stamens in the center, and they come in a range of white, cream, yellow, orange, red, pink, and magenta. The 'Sundial' hybrids offer separate colors from which to choose, making it possible to create impressive drifts of color in the summer garden or in pots. The six-inch-tall plants carpet the ground or skirt around other perennials and grasses, embellishing individual plants and combinations. Pastel orange

OVERLEAF: The sky is the limit when growing heat-loving summer annuals.

ABOVE: Colorful moss rose sprawls on stones by a pond's edge along with blue creeping morning glory.

Portulaca 'Sundial Mango' at the base of olive-green bear grass is a refreshing sight in my garden, and planting white moss rose at the feet of butterfly weed and gayfeather makes the most of a dry, sunny site.

Hybrid succulent purslane (*Portulaca oleracea*) takes even more neglect than moss rose and is therefore best for the forgetful gardener. Small, single flowers in sunset colors pepper the dense mats of tiny spoon-shaped leaves all summer long. The blossoms aren't as showy as those of moss rose, but what this plant lacks in flash it makes up for in fervor. The half-inch, bowl-shaped flowers are the perfect panache for subtle, blue-foliaged sotol or little bluestem grass, which both thrive in full sun and good drainage.

Baby sun rose (*Aptinia cordifolia*) is a foolproof succulent with heart-shaped leaves forming a low, dense ground cover sprinkled with tiny magenta flowers resembling daisies. While less than exciting, this tender perennial's cast-iron constitution makes it a sure thing even in the worst heat and drought, and the lush jade-green carpet can be a refreshing addition to otherwise parched plantings. A variegated form of baby sun rose sports wide, creamy white margins on succulent leaves that are densely arranged to create an exquisite brocade of cool color. This cultivar also has tiny magenta blooms like the original, but it appears to be less vigorous in brutal heat. Still, the variegated *Aptinia* is fabulous in containers, where it thrives despite drought, spilling over the edge like a waterfall.

Another succulent tender perennial that has made itself familiar in southeast gardens is jewels of opar (*Talinum paniculatum*). One of several species also called flame flowers, jewels of opar is a simple, branched herb about a foot tall and wide, with oval green leaves. The eighteen-inch-tall, open panicle of blooms yields a steady supply of tiny pink flowers on wiry stems followed by round orange seedpods. Minute black seeds spill about as the plant reseeds with abandon for the following season. An old variegated clone of the jewels of opar offers soft green leaves edged in ivory. This plant is a great accent in sun or shade even without the airy cloud of flowers overhead. Another clone, 'Kingwood Gold', is a lovely chartreuse form with the same habit and flowers, widening the range of application of this delightful plant. 'Kingwood Gold' reseeds true to color and is indispensable in sunny niches, where the foliage is particularly brilliant. It is great with magenta *Verbena* 'Batesville Rose' and compact, blue-flowered *Salvia glechomifolia*.

THE DAISY CHAIN

The charm of daisies is in short supply during the dog days of summer, especially in the Deep South. Fortunately, several annual daisies are available for inclusion in any garden. These are mostly small enough to tuck into the smallest niche or use in combinations where the round, familiar faces cheer up associate plants in beds and borders.

Low-growing creeping zinnia (*Sanvitalia procumbens*) looks very diminutive, yet the sturdy, mounding plants prove to be remarkably tough in relentless heat. This tidy, six-inch-tall, spreading sun-lover continuously covers itself in small yellow daisies with dark centers, looking like tiny black-eyed Susan flowers. Small oval leaves and uniform growth give this annual a neat appearance that balances the informal habit of other plants. A cultivar with orange petals, 'Mandarin', is highly touted, but it's not my favorite. Creeping zinnia makes a splendid summerlong contrast with red verbena and the orange tubular flowers of cigar plant.

The diminutive dahlberg daisy (*Dyssodia tenuiloba,* syn. *Thymophylla tenuiloba*) excels in dry, gritty soil. Cold hardy, too, this delicate-looking plant with ferny foliage and petite yellow flowers crosses the boundary between seasons, blooming in spring as well as in summer. In very wet conditions the eight-inch plants may play out, but they usually drop seed for the future. Inasmuch as dahlberg daisies enjoy sun and well-drained soil, they make wonderful companions for cacti, agaves, and yuccas in my garden, which might otherwise be lonely during summer.

Treasure flowers (*Gazania rigens* hybrids) also enjoy sunny, well-drained sites. The tufted rosettes of dark green, lobed leaves form a tidy backdrop for dozens of three- to four-inch daisies on short stems, borne in succession over a long period of time. Flowers range from white to yellow, shades of orange and dark red, and even pink (sometimes striped) with varying degrees of dark, zonal bands around the central disk. When in deep, well-drained conditions the plants may even persist for a couple of years. Due to their compact growth habit and compatible color range, treasure flowers are delightful accents for the desert denizens of my garden, and they complement the frothy dahlberg daisies.

Annual blackfoot daisy (*Melampodium paludosum*) bears nonstop, small, solid, sunny yellow daisies all through the hot weather on

In full sun, variegated jewels of opar blooms like fireworks amid the contrasting foliage of beefsteak plant and golden sweet potato.

rounded, twelve-inch-tall plants. Despite somewhat coarse foliage, the stalwart annuals are drought tolerant as well as able to take the heat in the worst of climates. Several new selections of *Melampodium*, such as 'Million Gold' and 'Derby', are a bit more compact (eight to ten inches), making them more suitable for containers than the species. Few plants can beat the annual blackfoot daisy where fail-safe, season-long color is needed, making it great company for other easy-care plants, like purple heart and variegated liriope.

Several species and named selections of tick seed (*Bidens*) offer gardeners an easily grown, sprawling summer annual with loose growth, lacy foliage, and an endless supply of one-inch, golden-yellow daisies. Both *Bidens ferulifolia* and *B. humilis* are robust enough to play with the big boys, blending well with larger garden perennials or in the front of borders. Their thin stems and wandering ways make it easy to wind *Bidens* in and out of perennials, grasses, and summer bulbs, and the trailing habit is perfect for large containers. The informal masses of golden daisies are great at the base of white or yellow variegated maiden grass, romping amid healthy plantings of orange montbretia, and mingling with vigorous purple verbena. And these plants always self-sow without fail

The big, frilly pom-pom marigolds that one sees everywhere are an enigma to me. They look like the oversized buttons on a clown's costume and hardly seem appropriate in a garden among refined and genteel blossoms. Call me old-fashioned, but I like flowers to have a natural appeal, as with the simplicity of daisies, not some blob of meaningless color. The dwarf French marigolds (*Tagetes patula*) are a bit of an improvement if one can secure the simple-flowered forms without such a confusion of petals.

Best of all are the miniature or signet marigolds (*Tagetes tenuifolia*), with ferny foliage studded with hundreds of tiny beguiling daisies. These twelve-inch-tall, dense, globose "shrublets" grow and bloom with gusto yet blend easily with other garden members, as the petite blooms are naturally proportioned. An orange cultivar, 'Tangerine Gem', and a yellow form, 'Lulu' or 'Lemon Gem', are readily available to grace the summer garden. Mixed with purple, red, or white verbena, these sweet summer annuals brighten up, but don't overpower, the garden.

Along with marigolds, zinnias are an age-old garden favorite, especially grown for cutting. The larger-than-life flowers of the bedding zinnia (*Z. elegans*) occur in a rainbow range of colors (white, yellow, orange, red, rose, and pink), and hybrids can be short-stemmed or tall. In the long, hot summers of the Southeast, zinnias can grow, bloom, reseed, and grow a second crop of luxuriant blossoms before frost. If grown for cutting or fun, and not for a sense of permanence in the garden, these annuals are quite rewarding despite a propensity for powdery mildew (well-fed zinnias are less prone to

'Lemon Gem' miniature marigolds always look fresh despite the heat, and heavy rains won't beat them into the ground.

disease). In wretched heat and humidity, the small, classic zinnia (*Z. angustifolia,* syn. *linearis)* is a superlative annual. These foot-tall, heavily branched plants have long narrow leaves that resist powdery mildew and always look neat. A steady stream of one-inch daisies in white, golden yellow, or orange keeps classic zinnias looking fresh without the need to remove spent blooms. With a yellow center contrasting most readily against alabaster petals, the white-flowered form is as close to hot-weather daisy perfection as can be found anywhere. Sun-loving classic zinnias are beautiful consorts for hybrid roses, softening their stems' rugged appearance and creating a cloud of white, yellow, or orange on which the larger regal blossoms can rest.

Golden cosmos (*C. sulphureus)* relishes torrid weather compared to its purplish-pink cousin, *C. bipinnatus,* which often folds halfway through southern summers. The narrow, three-foot-tall, branched annuals are scantily clad in dark green, ferny leaves that are resistant to powdery mildew. Semidouble, two-inch daisies in jewel-tone yellow, orange, and even red are carried aloft on thin stems, giving them an unusual presence in the garden that is nevertheless effective with tall perennials and ornamental grasses. Hybridization has resulted in compressed entities only a third or fourth of their original height that are good for planting at the front of the border, but one can

Creeping zinnia keeps a neat clean profile, hardly ever showing a faded bloom.

Spider flowers are pretty enough on their own, but they really add spice to the perennial border.

RIGHT: Colorful, tall bedding zinnias desire full sun, rich soil, and consistent water.

get better impact from classic zinnias if foot-tall annuals are needed.

Mexican sunflower (*Tithonia rotundifolia*) is a garden giant that easily grows to six feet tall with large, dark green, velvety leaves and three-inch flowers of pumpkin-orange, fat daisylike petals surrounding rich golden centers. Flowers are freely produced over a long period of time, but they never make a thick mass of color like smaller annuals, so it's a good thing that the foliage is quite handsome. Butterflies love Mexican sunflower, and its large size makes it a stylish companion for white or purple butterfly bush and yellow-striped zebra grass. Compact cultivars of *Tithonia* maturing at two or three feet are unfortunately all that most seed companies sell these days, but it is the grandiose size of the wild species that intrigues me. A promising new golden-yellow form with narrower petals called 'Aztec Sun' grows to four feet.

A GALAXY OF STARS

Tall-growing spider flower (*Cleome hassleriana*) is a stately annual that tolerates heat and drought with aplomb. Lightly branched, stout, spiny stems clad with five-finger, maplelike leaves are crowned with glorious floral explosions. Individual blossoms are unbalanced concoctions of four straplike petals framing long, wispy stamens that protrude dramatically outward, but collectively the many flowers blooming together at any one time are divinely inspired. A limited color selection of white, pink, or violet is as much a blessing as a curse since many people can't decide which one to choose and often plant mixed-color stands in their gardens. The three- to five-foot-tall annuals brighten up the perennial border throughout summer and are immensely popular nectar sources for butterflies, moths, and hummingbirds. The white *Cleome* is a particularly nice addition to the aforementioned combination with *Tithonia, Buddleia,* and *Miscanthus.*

Similar to the flowers of *Cleome*, with its whimsically protruding stamens, cat whiskers (*Orthosiphon stamineus*) offers the effect on smaller plants capable of tolerating light shade. Well-branched, two-foot-tall, tropical perennials bearing simple, elliptical,

Egyptian star flower imparts an elegant look wherever it is planted in the hot sun.

toothed leaves are indestructible in the most torrid conditions. Their long floral spikes consist of one-inch, white or lilac, slipperlike blooms with clusters of extensive wiry stamens flowing from each. Without frost the plants persist in cozy beds and borders, but in areas where freezing weather visits, it is easy to take a few cuttings to winter over.

Egyptian star flower (*Pentas lanceolata*) makes itself so at home in the South during summer it is a shame that this tropical perennial cannot bear any frost. The one- to two-foot-tall, compact, free-flowering shrublets bear a steady supply of short-tubed, five-point, star-shaped flowers in dense three-inch clusters. High heat, humidity, and even drought present no problem for the deep-rooting pentas, whose large, deep green, oval leaves have no apparent pest or disease problems. Butterflies are drawn like magnets to the red, pink, rose, white, or lavender blooms. Egyptian star flowers are unsurpassed in the long subtropical season of the Gulf Coast, where they yield nonstop bloom without becoming overwhelmingly large plants (ideal for courtyards and pots). The floriferous plants are a good color accent to balance the excess of tropical foliage from gingers, cannas, palms, and bamboos.

Wild types of annual vinca (*Catharanthus roseus*) have found a permanent home in southern Florida, where it is just another misplaced roadside weed. Further north, where winter's cold weather frequents, these everblooming, sun- and heat-loving, drought-tolerant plants are endearing and enduring. Dark green, glossy, two-inch, oval leaves clad the loosely branched, 12- to 18-inch-tall plants, making them handsome additions to the garden or landscape. A never-ending parade of one- to two-inch, phloxlike flowers in shades of pink, rose, lavender, and white with contrasting eyes continuously dot the plants in warm weather. Vinca doesn't make a carpet of color like some other annuals, but that makes the natural-looking plants a sensible addition to mixed gardens, where they easily integrate with other perennials, grasses, and bulbs. Pastel blue cape plumbago and white variegated dwarf bamboo meld with any of the vinca colors to create a refreshingly cool summer scene. Good drainage is essential for vinca, and these annuals prefer to be grown without too much supplemental water.

Although the hybrid petunias often make better winter annuals than summer ones in sunbelt climates, some petunias show particular tolerance to heat. The less hybridized or "old-fashioned" petunias (*P. violacea* or *purpurea*) tolerate both frost and heat. Lots of gardeners have self-sowing patches of these petunias with smaller, two-inch flowers in a simple mix of colors, usually lavenders, purples, and white. The sprawling plants can reach three or four feet in height, bearing little resemblance to the compact, modern bedding hybrids. The species *Petunia intergifolia* has won its way into many hearts and gardens and has been used in new hybridization programs, resulting in ever-blooming, spreading plants smothered in small flowers. In nature *P. integifolia* is a perennial that retreats back to tidy rosettes during winter, before sprawling stems creep through the foliage of neighboring plants again the following summer. It produces one-and-a-half-inch-wide, vibrant purplish-pink, cone-shaped flowers in a constant procession.

Tender, tropical scarlet sage (*Salvia splendens*) is much loved across the United States, and no less so in the South. In high heat and humidity these plants thrive and grow to a three-foot height that is proportionately balanced with their large, spade-shaped leaves and huge bloom spikes, making them less grotesque than the stunted bedding plants used further north. Scarlet sage produces thick, six- to eight-inch-tall floral spikes with both calyx and two-inch-long tubular bloom drenched in rich scarlet red. The robust, self-cleaning annual tolerates shade and revels in rich, moist soil, making it ideal for growing under the ubiquitous clumps of banana. Mixed with purple-leafed Persian shield, luxuriant scarlet sage brightens up the overwhelming green of canna and ginger lily foliage and is impressive with large ornamental grasses. The broadened color range of new hybrids is unfortunately only found on dwarf varieties, which also require the constant vigilance of deadheading to keep them clean.

A less common tropical perennial that is an excellent hot-summer annual is Ganges primrose (*Assystasia gangetica*). Even in weather so steamy it makes your eyeballs sweat, this perky little sprawling tropical loves life, and blooms continuously with short spikes of open-faced, funnel-shaped flowers. Butter-yellow and pastel purple clones are available, though the yellow clone is more compact, at about a foot high. The simple diamond-shaped leaves offer a subtle, disease-free background for the flowers. In the Deep South, plant the yellow form of *Assystasia* to complement similar-colored *Justicia* 'Fruit Salad' and purple heart (*Setcresia pallida*). Caladiums make zesty companions for the purple clone, along with yellow variegated dwarf sweet flag.

Pepper plants (*Capsicum annuum* hybrids) also revel in torrid weather so long as they are given moist, rich soil and sunshine. A multitude of midsized and dwarf ornamental peppers are available, with pea-size fruits or larger, in rainbow colors (yellow, orange, red, or purple). My personal favorites are the smaller plants with variegated foliage and those with black leaves. These plants add a refreshing foliage color and texture on multibranched, compact shrublets that also bear ornate, colorful fruits. I like the black-leaf pepper planted with red *Pentas* and orange *Lantana*, but next season I will plant some with *Caladium* 'Candidum', *Colocasia* 'Black Magic', and *Miscanthus* 'Variegatus'.

Black-leafed pepper revels in the same conditions as the variegated sweet potato: hot sun, rich soil, and moisture.

Where it is too hot for *Penstemon* to grow, a close relation can satisfy the urge for tall spires, packed with colorful bell-shaped flowers. *Angelonia salicariifolia* needs a common name to make it more widely accepted, but the genus name flows easily from anyone's tongue. *Angelonia* is a two-foot-tall tropical perennial frequently grown as an annual in climates that see a freeze come winter. It really doesn't look tropical, though, and blends effortlessly into mixed plantings of garden perennials and annuals with delightful results. The tall spikes of fragrant, lavender-blue, bell-shaped flowers amid simple willowlike foliage give plantings a much-needed alternative floral texture. Also found in pure white and bicolored forms, *Angelonia* thrives in full sun with average moisture, and it blooms consistently when given supplemental feeding.

Few annuals can bake in the hot sun of a western exposure framed with asphalt or rocks in 100° F heat without flinching. But that is exactly how I've seen *Turnera ulmifolia* getting along in the worst of a Texas summer. One would think this plant is used for flower boxes in the lowest level of hell, it is so tough. The common name, buttercup, is botanically misleading but does describe the two-inch yellow bowls formed by five satiny petals. The one- to two-foot-tall, shrubby plants are densely clad in two-inch elliptical leaves with toothed margins, looking very much like those of an elm tree (hence the name ulmifolia). Despite the size of flower and leaf, *Turnera* is deep rooting and therefore very drought tolerant, and the flowers open from late morning till afternoon so as to minimize water loss. A form with lovely creamy white flowers and black centers can also be found, making *Turnera* even more versatile in gardens.

Another heat-lover known for its ability to thrive in brutal conditions is blue daze (*Evolvulus nuttallianus,* syn. *pilosus*), with its low, creeping habit and simple, gray-green foliage. Small, light blue, circular flowers (with white centers like morning glory) punctuate the plant continuously, but never heavily, through the hot weather. Blue daze, though not a color knockout, is a lovely accent when grown at the base of other drought-tolerant plants. It makes a lovely consort for yellow or white *Turnera* and looks elegant at the foot of blue-leafed agave or yucca.

Like *Evolvulus,* some summer annuals have pretty enough foliage to compensate for meager bloom, and blue star (*Laurentia axillaris,* syn. *Isotoma axillaris*) is definitely in that category. Sharply cut, lacy foliage on clumping, branched plants under a foot in height make blue star a tidy accent piece to mix into low-growing beds. The one-inch, fine, five-point, bluish-lavender flowers dancing on the tips are an embellishment no more lovely than the foliage that frames them, and together result in a darling little annual. Blue star looks splendid against the bold backdrop of rock or stone, and it makes merry with vinca and moss rose.

Although the ebony leaves of this basil are edible, they are far more valuable in the garden for flavoring the petunias.

FOLIAGE ANNUALS

Not all summer annuals are grown for their floral contributions; instead, some plants are grown for the impact of foliage alone. The self-sowing perilla, or beefsteak plant (*Perilla frutescens*), is a perennial favorite in the Southeast, and once you have this annual in the garden it will be there every year. One does find the need to perform several thinnings in a season as the sun-loving plants get to two or three feet in height and can become overwhelming (drought limits their growth, however). Yet the large chocolate-brown leaves with metallic sheen are a valuable contrast to the sea of green that summer brings. Perfect with a multitude of other annuals and perennials, perilla makes a dramatic foil for yellow, orange, and red flowers such as Mexican milkweed (*Asclepias curassavica*) and is intriguing with blues like cape plumbago (*P. auriculata*) or lobelia (*L. syphalitica*). By late summer the plants bloom in a lackluster finale; the spikes of the insignificant flowers mature into next year's seed crop.

The many forms of basil (*Ocimum basilicum*) thrive in subtropical summers, and the dark-leafed cultivars particularly add a touch of class to floral compositions. Shiny, purplish-ebony, oval leaves, sometimes ruffled, on compact, mounding, one- to two-foot-tall plants give the garden an enchanting depth. Flowering spikes of small pink blossoms, each set like a jewel in a dark calyx, whorled in tiers up long thin stems, embellish the elegant basil plants and need not be removed. The purplish-hued foliage harmonizes well with the purple flowers of verbena, petunias, *Salvia greggii* 'Dark Dancer', and perennial *Lobelia* hybrids. For those who prefer high contrast, try dark-leafed basil with white pentas, white classic zinnia, and variegated liriope. Thai basil 'Siam Queen' is a uniquely ornamental plant even with green leaves. The one- to two-foot-tall herbs are crowned for months with a tight, dark, domed inflorescence (rather than spikes) punctuated by good-sized, pale pink flowers.

The South African genus *Plectranthus* has of late revealed an abundance of tender perennial herbs with colorful foliage that all prosper in hot weather. This plethora of *Plectranthus* seems formidable to the uninitiated until one realizes that we already know at least one species: Swedish ivy (*Plectranthus australis*). Some of these varied species prefer sun whereas others like shade, and some add delightful flowers to the bounty of beautiful leaves. *Plectranthus* is a member of the mint family, and as such most of the individual species have distinctly aromatic foliage and are quite easy to propagate from cuttings (so they need not perish in winter).

Cuban oregano (*P. amboinicus*) is perhaps the best known *Plectranthus* in most of the South, and the short, creeping plant with large, deltoid, succulent variegated leaves of green and ivory does smell like its name suggests. Tough as nails, Cuban oregano excels in full, hot sun where its slowly trailing habit complements lavender-flowered Mexican heather, rain lilies, and dwarf Mexican petunia 'Katy'. The versatile variegated plant can be used as easily to contrast with orange Lantana 'tangerine' plant and rich-foliaged purple heart.

The silver plectranthus (*P. argentatus*) alas has no common name associated with a foreign country, but it is a valuable addition to hot, humid gardens where so many other silver-leafed plants melt out. This two-foot-tall, branched herb sports large, velvety, oval leaves, which develop the best silvery cast in full sun. Silver plectranthus makes a smart partner for so many other perennials, annuals, bulbs, and grasses. One can hardly fail when using its silvery foliage to mix with any of the color forms of annual vinca, or adding it to pastel or moonlight borders. Late summer brings on long, wispy spikes of tiny pale blossoms, making the plant glamorous well into fall.

An exceptional, robust *Plectranthus* species without a well-known name, perhaps due to some horticultural witness protection program, is nevertheless a wonderful addition to hot-weather gardens. Though frequently seen in nurseries and gardens from coast to coast, this anonymous tropical perennial could be named *P. mysteryensis* since few people know its name. The thick-stemmed, lightly branched plants grow to two feet tall and bear large, succulent, felted leaves with ivory scalloped margins. This sun-

lover takes the heat and happily makes a commanding presence in the garden. When mixed with summer phlox, fountain grass, and lilies (Turk's cap or Formosa), this plant demands attention. It also blends well with all colors of large cutting zinnias, giving their rainbow flowers a refreshing foreground. Other *Plectranthus* species and clones with cream, chartreuse, or golden variegated leaves are popping up, unidentified and shamelessly nameless, at nurseries all the time, and deserve a chance in our gardens.

In shaded venues other *Plectranthus* species also thrive despite heat, drought, or excessive moisture. My new favorite, *P. ciliatus*, is so in need of a common name that I will hereby call it "maiden d'shade"—corny, but it works for me. This plant is a gangbuster in impossible conditions. A single individual will spread out to cover a three-foot-diameter area in heavy clay soil and dark shade. The stems rise a bit over a foot in height with durable, pest-free, deltoid leaves that are dark green above and purple below. Not bothered by floods, drought, or hundred-degree heat, maiden d'shade blooms luxuriantly for two months in late summer into fall with six-inch spikes

Beefsteak plant, or perilla, offers a sophisticated foliage that complements almost any color flower in the garden.

185 ॐ

Brilliant use of the more subdued clones of coleus are displayed here in a simple context.

of not-too-small lilac flowers. This plectranthus is great company for ferns and spider lilies in darkened niches with limited options.

Also good in beds with only a little sun and lacking a common name is the variegated *Plectranthus coleoides*. This multistemmed herb has two-inch, ivory-mottled, spade-shaped leaves that smell like cedar when crushed. Even with plenty of moisture and in good soil, *P. coleoides* is well behaved, staying about a foot wide and two feet tall (several years in a frost-free environment will produce a larger plant). The light-colored foliage is a delightful change of pace for dark corners, where it can highlight the white blooms of orchid pansies or impatiens, and oakleaf hydrangea.

Coleus (*Solenostemon scutellarioides*, a.k.a. *Coleus x hybridus*) needs no more introduction to southerners than does high humidity. The only problem seems to be that, like the latter, gardeners have become tired of the commonly seen, multicolored, tropical perennials. Flashy bicolored and tricolored leaves of cream, yellow, green, orange, red, and pink have been around for over a hundred years and yet have left many a gardener oddly unfulfilled of late. Fortunately, as with cannas, a renaissance of these antique foliage plants is under way, and gardeners can now obtain exciting new choices of leaf shape and color. The latest trend is toward monochromatic leaves in rich, sophisticated colors that blend with other plantings or make dramatic statements on their own. I find it easier to integrate a single-colored coleus with other annuals and perennials than to plant an ungainly kaleidoscope that is reminiscent of an LSD flashback, but for gardeners who like the color selection, chartreuse, orange, bronze, scarlet, russet, mahogany, and even black planting permutations in the garden are possible. As long as coleus has rich, well-drained soil in light shade or part sun, these tropicals will be happy and rewarding.

Another iconoclastic annual of the South is copper plant (*Acalypha wilkesiana*), whose broad, undulate leaves mottled with bronze, dark green, and pinkish-copper are a common sight where summers are hot and humid. This tropical shrub unfortunately seems to be permanently cast out of the garden, like Adam and Eve, and has to survive in shabby, unimaginative bed plantings with little or no company. The powder-blue foliage of some palms and perennial grasses, like Lindheimer's muhly, little bluestem, and 'Sioux Blue' Indian grass, provide the perfect patina for sun-loving copper plant. Sky-blue cape plumbago would also be enchanting with the coppery foil of this three- to five-foot-tall plant, as could peach or apricot roses. Many cultivars of copper plant exist, including some dwarf specimens good for small gardens that bear narrow, two-inch leaves and giants with broad foliage eight inches across.

A tropical shrub in the same family as the copper plant, but with less public exposure, is the bronze spurge (*Euphorbia cotinifolia*). Although a dandy permanent bush for mild winter climates, bronze spurge makes a fabulous annual accent for any hot-weather climate. When grown in full sun, the rounded leaves take on a rich purplish-red color that is hard to beat, and with ample moisture bronze spurge can quickly grow to three or even five feet in height. This tender shrub is a superlative foil for zesty tropical colors; reds, yellows, and oranges all look outstanding against the rich, glowing foliage. Even among hardy perennials the foliage of bronze spurge is a plus. White garden phlox, blue bog sage, and golden black-eyed Susan are a knockout together with this tropical addition.

Castor bean (*Ricinus communis*) is yet another member of the diverse Euphorbia family. The treelike tropical goes by the name palm of Christ and in warm climates will easily reach 15 to 20 feet in height. As a summer annual, one can expect castor bean to grow from seed to eight or ten feet tall by frost, all the while imparting a lush, dramatic exuberance to the garden. Both green and ruby-bronze forms of the enormous, maple-shaped leaves are easily available from seed catalogs. Tight clusters of ruby-colored flowers and later burrlike seedpods are held along branches of the sturdy stems. When a quick and easy taste of the tropics is called for, nothing beats castor beans.

THE AMARANTH FAMILY

The Amaranth plant family holds many heat-loving species, including some grown solely for their beautiful foliage. Joy weed (*Alternanthera ficoidea* 'Versicolor') is often found in tropical gardens as a colorful ground cover, but the low, mounding herb has uses in gardens throughout the Southeast. Tiny yellow or red, marbled leaves arrayed densely on heavily branched, thin stems create compact foils of color. This tropical perennial thrives in full sun with moist soil, even taking to bog conditions, but well-rooted plants tolerate drought as well. Used sparingly in the front of borders, by ponds, or in containers, joy weed adds a delightful splash of color, but one would want to avoid planting too much, creating a messy spill.

Dwarf forms of the ubiquitous copper plant are perfect for integrating into small gardens and even containers.

Rare yet simply invaluable are *Alternanthera* 'Ruby' and the variegated mystery *Plectranthus*.

Larger yet more sedately colored is sophisticated *Alternanthera dentata* 'Ruby'. The tropical perennial grows to two feet tall, bearing colorful, two-inch, oval leaves loosely on upright, slightly sprawling stems. The leaves themselves seem a jewel-toned, blackish-red mix of onyx and ruby with a glossy sheen to match. Happiest in full sun with ample moisture and rich soil, 'Ruby' is intriguing in any garden motif, tropical or temperate. It's fun to add the scintillating foliage to plantings of ginger lilies and the yellow-striped foliage of *Canna* 'Pretoria', but one could as easily juxtapose it with daylilies, hybrid cardinal flower, and tall verbena. Planting *Alternanthera* 'Ruby' at the base of white variegated maiden grass or yellow-striped zebra grass would be simply stunning for months.

Globe amaranth, or, in my neighborhood, bachelor's buttons (*Gomphrena globosa*), is a true friend in tough times. The reseeding annual makes itself quite at home in any open patch of soil, facing summer's floods and drought with equal equanimity. The two-foot-tall plants produce a myriad of stems, each loosely clad with elliptical foliage and terminating in one-inch, violet, spherical "flowers" composed of densely whorled bracts. Hybrids now expand the color range to soft pinkish-lavender and white, with dwarf varieties called 'Gnome' in white and rose-violet. The old-fashioned color, bright as it is, is my favorite. It easily mixes in with perennials and grasses and can even spark life into a barren bed of red, yellow, and white hybrid tea roses. The species *G. haageana* is a thinner plant with several named varieties of orange-red or red flowers.

Cockscomb, especially the plumed varieties (*Celosia argentea* 'Plumosa'), makes itself at home in the hot, steamy Southeast and readily reseeds for years. Direct seeding is, in fact, the preferred method of starting this jewel-toned amaranth since nursery-grown plants often are sold in bloom and don't develop into their true selves in the garden. Green- and reddish-bronze foliaged cultivars are readily available on one- to two-foot-tall, narrow plants with floral colors running the fiery range of yellow, orange, scarlet, red, and pink. The unique—maybe even bizarre—plumes of flowers are not easy to meld into an ordinary perennial border, so try tempering celosias with the foliage palms, grasses, dwarf bamboo, or bear grass.

Spike-flowered celosia (*C. argentea* 'Spicata') is so happy during hot summers that plants assume massive proportions, four to five feet tall, when given adequate moisture. Their overwhelming success in hot climates is balanced by the fact that they don't have a very large bloom or much of it, for that matter. However, the often purplish-tinted, three-inch, lanceolate foliage is lush and clean, embellished with a smattering of four- to eight-inch-long, dense, pink spires on top of the plant. 'Pink Candle' and 'Flamingo Purple' are the two most often found, with the former keeping to a modest three feet in height, bearing green, willowy leaves. These are best used in large gardens or as part of the bigger landscape with gigantic ornamental grasses, flowering shrubs, or lusty bamboos.

Several annual species of the genus *Amaranthus* make grand, stunning accents for the garden. Summer poinsettia, or Joseph's coat (*Amaranthus tricolor*), produces lush, pendant leaves up heavy stalks reaching four feet in height, with the upper third of the plant crowned in magenta, gold, and green banded leaves. Love-lies-bleeding (*A. caudatus*) is a branched annual growing equally as tall with surprisingly luxuriant, large green leaves for such a drought-tolerant plant. In summer it produces many long, weeping tresses of dense, red bloom spikes, which sometimes even drape on the ground. The imposing ornamental amaranth (*A. paniculatus*) grows from three to five feet tall, depending on site conditions. Branched stems clad in large, sometimes russet-colored leaves terminate in a pyramidal series of long, thick, erect red spikes, creating an organic candelabra effect. As with the gaudy celosias, these amaranths should be situated in the garden carefully with simple, sedate grassy foils.

ANNUALS FOR SHADE

Annuals for the shade are far more limited than the options that exist for sunny sites. Fortunately, some summer bulbs also thrive with little sun, and a multitude of

Familiar, reliable impatiens grown in a shallow pot are an exquisite way to brighten a shady corner.

ferns and even variegated English ivy (*Hedera helix*) broaden the palette. Using shade-loving annuals as an embellishment for foliage combinations is perhaps the best way to parlay the restricted palette into elegant, colorful plantings in sunless areas.

The original wild form of *Impatiens walleriana* is a robust, tropical perennial bedecked with a lush array of large, three-inch-long, broad, elliptical leaves suffused with a metallic sheen and garnished with hot-pink, one-inch blooms. After a century of focused selective breeding, the plants are much more compact, with leaves one third smaller, and the blossoms are now twice the size of the original and come in assorted shades of pink, coral, red, purple, lilac, salmon, orange, and white. Variations on the floral theme include double blooms, picotee, darker eyes, and brush marks. Some cultivars sport bronze foliage, although the enchanting silvery sheen of the wild plants was lost in the pursuit of bigger, better flowers.

Hybrid impatiens are hands down the number-one flowering annual for shade. Plants can take the heat as long as there is enough moisture and good soil. Their low-growing habit seduces many gardeners who want carpets of color to fill dark, dull areas. However, the biggest impact can be achieved in gardens when the fail-safe summer blooms are used in combination with lacy ferns, bold hostas or cast-iron plant (*Aspidistra elatior*), and linear sedges or liriope. Colorful leaves of caladiums, coleus, plectranthus, or sweet potato vines make remarkable foils off of which the colorful blooms of impatiens are reflected, synergized, and magnified. The endearing five-petaled blossoms of impatiens are best used sprinkled through sophisticated arrangements of foliage with endless permutations of texture and color, like jewelry adorning the well dressed.

New Guinea impatiens (*I. hawkeri* hybrids) are also tropical perennials grown as annuals. The succulent-stemmed plants bear deeply veined, narrowly elliptic leaves that are deep green and often colored with yellow bands or purplish cast. Flowers of the New Guinea impatiens are slightly larger than their cousins and are generally more richly colored, too, with each petal slightly cleft. The vivid hues of these hybrids will electrify sedate shaded plantings and as such should be used sparingly. The higher cost of these mostly cutting-propagated plants also lends them to be planted such. The cultivar 'Tango' is a well-known, frequently purveyed New Guinea with large, brilliant orange flowers and dark green leaves suffused with purple on two-foot plants. Enjoying moist, rich soil and even tolerant of some sun, 'Tango' makes an exciting dance partner with *Alternanthera* 'Ruby' or *Caladium* 'Candidum'.

The genus *Begonia* is dazzling in the number of diverse species that flourish around the world. Most of these tropical perennials impart luxuriant foliage texture and color with only a modicum of floral interest, but one species in particular has launched a thousand hybrids of flowering annuals. The wild-type *Begonia semperflorens* is a one- to two-foot-tall, succulent-stemmed tropical perennial bearing lightly bronzed, semiswirled, rounded leaves, and a nonstop output of loose, pendant clusters of white, monoecious (separate male and female flowers on the same plant), one-inch flowers. It is a commonly planted perennial in the Deep South, where the sturdy clumps return faithfully from even a hard freeze (it is a garden persona non gratus in south Florida, where it seems to be just another weed to pull).

The many hybrids of *Begonia semperflorens*, also called fibrous-rooted begonias to

Small scarlet blooms and green oval begonia leaves balance the flashy coleus in this exuberant planting.

distinguish them from their tuberous cousins, still only cover an expansion of color that now includes pink, rose, and scarlet red. The many cultivars include some with bronze-toned foliage as well as the ever-present green. Most notable, unfortunately, is the reduction of a dignified, graceful plant into a squat, compressed, albeit floriferous, bedding annual. Why the glories of the garden must become two-dimensional for mass consumption, I'll never understand. Nevertheless, today's hybrid begonias display an ironclad constitution and tolerance of heat, drought, and even full sun that make the six- to ten-inch-tall plants delightfully indestructible. The tight-mounded forms are desperate for companions with exuberant textural contrast; in shady venues bold caladium leaves, grassy spider plant foliage, and lacy ferns all conspire to liberate begonias from the restrictions of their breeding.

The many foliage types of begonias also should not be overlooked when it comes to adding some pizzazz to dark and difficult places. The small- and large-leafed angelwing begonias, creeping rhizomatous begonias, and flashy-leafed Rex begonias cover an incredible scope of species and hybrids. Some of the rhizomatous species even grow quite well as perennials in my Zone 8 garden. These tropicals are frequently kept over the winter in a pot on the windowsill and planted back into the garden for summer, or they can be kept solely as container specimens, where they will continue to become more impressive with each succeeding year. In either venue, these begonias mingle elegantly with ferns, ivy, and even bromeliads.

Polka dot plant (*Hypoestes phyllostachya*) is another tropical perennial that has become a weed in southern Florida, but that shouldn't dissuade anyone from using the perky little numbers as annuals further north, where cold weather renders the winter-bloomers harmless. Compact, branched plants sport many two-inch, oval, marbled green leaves, which are presumably heavily spattered with white, pink, rose, or red paint. The effect is mottled two-tone foliage with just enough green evident to make it seem alive. Polka dot plants impart a fun and carefree ambiance to shady areas or pots, but they will probably be shunned by the too serious gardener. Mixing the variegated foliage with that of caladiums might be a dizzying experience; instead, plant them amid hybrid begonias or impatiens in an informal setting that includes subdued greenery.

Wishbone flower (*Torenia fournieri*) is a compact, mounding tropical annual bearing small spade-shaped leaves. It prefers light shade, warmth, and moisture. More interesting than showy, the intricate flowers are two-toned and thimblelike, with flared petals resembling open-mouthed faces. Their quaint appearance has endeared them to many, and hybrids now include white-throated bicolor flowers of blues, pink, rose, violet, burgundy, and plum. Like any proper annual, however, wishbone flower steadfastly makes seed for the next generation, resulting in fewer blooms and more empty calyces over time, thus rendering the plant ineffective for long-term interest. The tropical perennial species *T. flava* forms dense, low mats of creeping foliage studded with golden-yellow flowers framing dark throats, and it blooms continuously through the season. Perhaps most promising is the recent hybrid between the two species, which yields a continuous supply of darling, solid blue flowers (and no seed heads) on compact creeping plants. This plant will get a thorough trial in my garden this coming summer, when I mix it with orange impatiens and white polka dot plants.

White polka dot plant and yellow coleus create colorful foliage fanfare.

TROPICALS

Absolutely tropical, yet indispensable as part of summer's annual shade-garden composition, are bromeliads. These resilient members of a dozen different genera offer structure, texture, and color for the darkest, most difficult corners of the garden. As tree-dwelling epiphytes, bromeliads are quite at home in small pots with very little soil. This not only makes them easily mobile to thrust, pot and all, into the ground for accenting shady plantings, but also

allows them to be retrieved lock, stock, and barrel at the end of the season to overwinter indoors. A cast-iron disposition gives them the ability to survive extended drought, deep shade, and endless heat, which makes them perfect for neglected portions of beds that would otherwise be vacant. Of the many species and hybrids of *Billbergia, Vriesea, Neoregelia, Guzmania, Aechmea,* and *Tillandsia* that grace my garden in summer, the only problem is their tendency to multiply, becoming larger clumps by the end of each summer.

Bromeliads, here nestled for summer in wood sorrel at the base of a pecan tree, endure the dry shade later on when the perennial goes dormant.

Another tropical epiphyte at home in the shady summer gardens of the Southeast is the ubiquitous Boston fern (*Nephrolepis exaltata* and other species). Readily available for cheap at almost any home-and-garden or grocery store, Boston ferns make dandy additions to shady beds, patios, or pots. The fresh, spring-green foliage belies a sturdy disposition—these ferns take heat and even drought in stride, and their elegant texture is a vital addition to many other foliage and flower combinations for shady plantings. These ferns perennialize in the Deep South (they can survive light frosts), but further north they make great annuals that can be easily obtained fresh each year and used with abandon in otherwise difficult spots.

Some perennial enthusiasts disdain the inclusion of annuals in the garden, as if it were somehow cheating to indulge in "temporary" horticulture. But nothing lasts forever, and I've seen plenty of perennials perish after only one year of service, so the distinction can be mute. I hate to pass up the possibility of adding six or seven months of unadulterated excitement and nonstop color just because I will have to plant again next year. I relish the extra punch of foliar and floral color and enjoy the fact that in following years I can create different garden combinations with new and different plants.

PART III
Southwestern
SUMMER
GARDENING

SUMMERS ARE HOT IN THE DESERT SOUTHWEST, but it's a dry heat, or so the joke goes. Dry, however, is the operative word for this area of scant rainfall and low humidity. Less available moisture and low humidity mean few clouds and lots of sunshine. Furthermore, lacking abundant rain, the landscape is devoid of the tall, dense forests that dominate the Southeast. The desert landscape is different, but it is not desolate.

Some trees do grow naturally in the Southwest. The mesquites, acacias, and palo verdes are comparatively small, of low stature, and occur somewhat sparsely, but they still create microhabitats in the realm of their thin, vital shade. The harsh environment is also conducive to a surprising host of other plants in a myriad of forms. Visually, the effect of the natural landscape is one of austere but diverse natural beauty that is for half the year bathed in intense, hot sunshine.

Not only is the dry air noticeable to our human skin, but it particularly affects the leaves and flowers of plants. Thick, succulent, or tough, leathery leaves and petals, sometimes with waxy coatings, are adaptations to an arid climate. Mostly, though, it is the size of the leaf that is markedly different in hot, dry climates: Leaves tend to be much smaller on plants adapted for desert survival. This is not the land of big, billowy blossoms and huge tropical leaves. Foliage is often dissected into tiny, feathery components (called compound leaves), or it can even become deciduous in a pinch, therefore avoiding greater water loss in times of drought.

Southwestern soils are distinctively different from those in the rest of the country, and indeed many gardeners would suggest that these are not soils at all. Generally clay in structure, sometimes with gravel mixed into it, southwest soils are difficult to wet and slow to drain. Many situations also include an impenetrable hardpan layer below the surface that limits the depth of the soil. Almost

OVERLEAF: A lush, waterwise desert planting.

ABOVE: A rich, dynamic composition of cacti, agaves, and friends.

always low in organic matter (scant vegetation growth adds very little over time) with a relatively high pH, these thin, poor soils are not amenable to plants foreign to such frugal living.

Obviously, plants with drought tolerance and heat endurance are going to be true survivors, even great performers, in the desert garden. Native or not, many plants are well adapted to withstand the dry soil and drier air during the long, hot desert summers; these become the mainstay of the garden in arid climates. Small areas are given extra irrigation to support a more diverse assortment of thirstier, but still heat-tolerant, flora. In this way, one can achieve a sensible, water-wise garden and still include some luxury plants and frivolous eccentricities on a reasonable scale.

In nature, desert trees and large shrubs create a special environment under their canopy, which many other plants find to their liking. Additional organic matter from fallen leaves accumulated through time enriches the impoverished soil and improves its water-holding capacity. The gentle, albeit thin, shade of the branches above gives an all-important respite to many other plants that would fare poorly without its help. Oddly enough, few home gardens and landscapes take advantage of the rich horticultural possibilities of these sites. My friends speculate that it is the result of designing on paper, since when a tree is drawn in on a plan, there is no room on paper to fill in any additional plantings. In the real world of the garden, however, many annual and perennial flowers as well as agaves, aloes, and yuccas prosper under a tree's canopy.

Soil improvement markedly changes the success rate of anything planted in the hot, dry garden. That and the final addition of a gravel mulch to inhibit water loss, as well as encourage infiltration (instead of surface runoff) of natural rainfall, yield the best horticultural payoff in a hostile environment. I would note here that "decorative gravel" is an oxymoron. Creating a deeper, more moisture-retentive garden soil in the first place allows greater root growth and overall success of most landscape and garden plantings without pouring on the extra water. Within the smaller microniche that receives additional irrigation, soil improvement creates a veritable oasis in which almost everything will thrive.

If the soil is restricted by a subsurface layer of caliche or hardpan, it is important to find out how thick of a barrier there is and if it is possible to break through. Alternatively, one can build up the soil so as to create a deeper, more stable root run. This can be accomplished by bringing in topsoil (which may be a contradiction of terms in desert areas) or adding other mineral components, such as coarse sand or gravel. In clay soil conditions, the incorporation of gravel is far superior to fine sand, which only tends to make a good brick once it bakes dry in the sun. Small aggregate gravel (like decomposed granite) when mixed with existing soil creates the type of rocky conditions that many desert plants favor in the wild.

After adding more mineral components to the soil, the addition of organic matter is a must. Using a compost (many urban areas now recycle yard waste into this precious resource) instead of manure, the incorporation of a good amount of organic matter well into the soil will yield amazing results. Thin, barren clay becomes a delightful clay loam, which is the ideal base for a great garden. The resultant earth will have a superior water-holding capacity as well as enabling good aeration. Also, the naturally high soil pH will become buffered, allowing for better availability of essential nutrients—especially iron. As in gardening anywhere else, a little soil preparation goes a long way toward ensuring success of everything planted.

When creating a garden microniche such as a mini-oasis, it is helpful to seriously improve the soil (an ongoing process in hot climates even after initial preparation). This area of greatly improved soil will allow for the expansion of the plant palette from which we choose. Alternatively, outlying areas can be left alone with little improvement, as long as only those plants that can be grown "lean and mean" are chosen for the site. Plants that can succeed in such difficult places are a special breed, but the selection is not as broad as those that prefer better soil. ☼

CHAPTER 13

THE MINI-OASIS:

DESERT FLOWER POWER ON A WATER BUDGET

Everyone who spends any time in a hot, dry environment yearns for the quintessential desert oasis replete with a cool-water spring, exotic flowers, delicious fruits, and lush foliage. Our American ideal is for everyone to have such a chance at making the desert bloom, but the reality is that

there is just not enough water available for that to happen. However, we need not let go of that dream, just the massive scale of it. It is still quite possible to have in our gardens an intimate, lush portion that invites the soul thirsting for a respite from oppressive heat. It is called the mini-oasis.

The mini-oasis is an integral part of a sensible garden or landscape in hot, dry regions. It sometimes includes small portions of irrigated turf lawn (since the larger version of the American dream takes excessive watering), and ponds, pools, and fountains are also possible. It is, however, primarily a habitat conducive for growing a wide variety of flowers, which in turn attract butterflies, hummingbirds, and other jewels of nature.

Usually the mini-oasis is situated close to the house in the outdoor area most frequently used. Ideally, a door and even a few windows should open out onto the oasis for easy physical and visual access. This is a place you will want to frequent and live in; consider it an additional room of the house. It is therefore best designed with some protection from sun and wind (comfortable conditions that many plants will appreciate as much as human visitors).

A courtyard setting is most often seen as the site for the mini-oasis, with walls enclosing, defining, and protecting the space from some of the hot sun and dry winds. Arbors, pergolas, trellises, and screens are different approaches to the same end and can be dressed with an assortment of flowering vines as well. Of course, the delightful shade of a choice tree or two can't be beat and is perhaps the easier means to an end if one has the same construction skills as I.

Water features are always welcome within the space of the oasis. Be sure to create any type of fountain or waterfall with a large enough reservoir to handle the daily water loss through evaporation without running dry (moving water evaporates quickly). Water in an arid climate also attracts a variety of birds and other wildlife—an added bonus. The enriched, improved soil and protected site of the oasis allow gardeners the indulgence of many flowers, which generally need sustained moisture to perform admirably. This includes hot-season annuals that would otherwise be difficult to grow (see Chapter 12).

Nevertheless, even if the space is mostly paved, it is an ideal situation for growing in containers. The

additional depth, structure, and dimension that containers lend intimate settings like the mini-oasis are immeasurable. All manner of succulents, cacti, aloes, agaves, yuccas, grasses, and even herbs can be easily grown in pots. A quick study of the space on a sunny day will let you discover the best places to situate your containers (putting the most resilient, tough-as-nails prospects up against hot, west walls). Shaded sites can safely harbor pots of asparagus fern, purple heart, and fibrous-root begonia, or even tropicals like bromeliads.

In the cooler months of winter, the mini-oasis undergoes a change. The rich, improved soil on the inside successfully supports all manner of cool-season annuals, vegetables, and bulbs as the space undergoes a horticultural renaissance. Gardeners can broaden their horizons and enjoy the floral delicacies that heat and drought prohibit the rest of the year, and do so in the one part of the garden that they visit the most. Containers in the mini-oasis also add splashes of winter/spring color as they are planted with assorted bulbs and annuals and moved into the best sunshine afforded for outstanding growth (see Chapters 2 and 3).

The mini-oasis is the jewel of the desert garden. It is not the result of climactic denial but rather the embellishment of one of nature's best ideas. Gardening in such a site expands the range of horticultural possibilities enough to leave no one frustrated about the limitations of the American Southwest. In fact, it quickly becomes apparent that there are more wonderful things to grow there than ever imagined. ✳

OVERLEAF: Even thirsty cannas can be grown in the mini-oasis.

LEFT: With a little extra water, effusive plantings are easy to achieve (the desert rose needs to be potted, though).

ABOVE: Winter annuals pack into a mini-oasis during the cool season.

CHAPTER 14

PERENNIALS FOR SUMMER BLOOM

Herbaceous perennials are as rare in southwest gardens as they are scarce in the wild desert ecosystems. The reason for this is somewhat simple, in that a sustained source of water—sorely lacking in most of the Southwest—is needed to grow the entire plant structure anew each year (remember, growth equals water for cell expansion). Also, in a climate that experiences little killing cold during winter, it is not a crucial survival tactic to retreat back to ground level to maintain life's hold.

Many flowering plants of the desert region tend to have permanent, woody stems, even though they are not really shrubs (by our definition). Woody stems sporting small leaves in a variety of shapes and sizes give flowering plants the opportunity to grow flowers with meager water resources when the time is right for reproduction. Because many of these woody-stemmed perennials are less than three feet in height and return quickly if cut to the ground by cold or hand, I have separated this group of plants from the more robust woody shrubs. (See Chapter 15 for a discussion of flowering shrubs for the Southwest.)

Some of the nonwoody perennials tend to live life in the fast lane. We enjoy their long season of bloom but are disappointed by their early demise, as these plants seem to bloom themselves to death after only a few years. Many times I am faced by sad, confused faces and questions such as "What went wrong—weren't these supposed to be perennials?" Of course, these plants are perennials—but they are not immortal. Nothing is permanent in the garden; even trees come and go. We should enjoy the performance as certain perennials bloom their heads off for a couple of years and then give up the ghost. Such plants are still worth their weight in gold, and openings in the garden can always be filled with more of the same or something new.

The perennial garden is an enigma in the desert Southwest. This mainstay of the English simply does not stand on its own in hot, dry climates. Instead, perennials must be combined with grasses, succulents, bulbs, shrubs and sub-shrubs, and the woody lilies. The result is the mixed border, which reflects all the extraordinary diversity of plant forms in nature's dryland garden.

Perennials are best used to accent the dramatic architectural form and bold structural elements of desert plants like agaves, yuccas, sotols, aloes, bear grasses, and cacti. In contrast to the common sight of austere plantings of these unappreciated elements, with unseemingly wide berths given between each specimen (surrounded by lifeless dirt and gravel), the accompaniment of choice flowering perennials lends a beautiful depth and dimension unrivaled in the greatest gardens of the world. Their zesty splashes of color add a contrasting or harmonizing element and sometimes lend subtle sophistication by creating color echoes with their complementary plantings. Following are my suggestions for some of the best perennial plants and design combinations for southwest gardens.

COMPACT PERENNIALS

Foliage is often the last thing on a gardener's mind when he or she thinks of adding color from perennials. However, the rich purple, succulent leaves of purple heart (*Setcreasea pallida*) are outstanding in their ability to lend a splash of royal color to gardens in the hottest, driest climates. Purple heart is able to grow in a wide range of soils, sun, and moisture; indeed, it is cultivated across the sunbelt, from coast to coast. The stems rarely exceed a foot in height as the clumping perennial grows, making it an ideal consort for many other flowers in a variety of sites. Purple heart does bloom, but the small, three-petaled, pinkish-lavender flowers appearing at the tips of stems are merely the frosting on the cake.

In the neighborhood of my south-central Texas garden, people tend to look down their noses at purple heart. I love it (I've got a thing for the color purple) and use it in many settings. It is always a good idea to include some tough-as-nails plants in the garden when you are experimenting with so many other uncertain flowers. The deep purple foliage of *Setcreasia* sets off the shiny, dark green, grassy leaves of white rain lily (*Zephyranthes candida*) in one part of my garden and complements the delightful, compact *Ruellia* 'Katy' in another. It works great in containers when mixed with an assortment of other annuals or perennials. Purple heart is a dynamic contrast to the lime-green, frilly leaves of foxtail fern (*Asparagus densiflorus* 'Myers') in the hot sun, as long as all receive irrigation in desert situations.

There are several cultivars of the Mexican petunia (*Ruellia brittoniana*) in the world of gardening, but one in particular is undaunted by the arid heat of the Southwest. Dwarf *Ruellia* 'Katy' is remarkable for its ability to thrive and bloom in the sun or shade and in moist soil or drought. The compact, six-inch-high plants bearing large, narrow, dark green, simple leaves make an impact even without being constantly studded with the purple-blue blossoms. 'Katy' is also a stable clone that reproduces itself by seeding about if conditions are right (especially in a mini-oasis). It can be used singly to punctuate other low ground covers, or massed for an effect all its own. I am fond of the contrast of ornamental grasses against a foreground of this delightful perennial.

A species of evening primrose good for spring through fall bloom in the Southwest is *Oenothera stubbei*. Also known as the Baja primrose,

OVERLEAF: Purple heart intermingles with variegated St. Augustine grass.

BELOW: Dwarf Ruellia 'Katy' and white rain lilies both thrive in desert gardens as long as they are watered.

this plant sprouts from a clump of coarse green leaves with a parade of large, butter-yellow, silky blooms. It also sends out long runners that colonize an area as large as four feet in diameter. Like its pink cousin (*O. berlandieri*), this perennial offers a commanding presence in the garden and has an iron constitution. The foliage and form of Baja primrose complement small-flowered perennials like cherry sage (*Salvia greggii*), Texas betony (*Stachys coccinea*), and rock verbena (*Verbena pulchella*).

More demure is the tufted evening primrose (*Oenothera caespitosa*). The foliage is somewhat silky with a blue-green cast, forming large, tight rosettes (about a foot across) with flowers in the center. Pinkish buds precede the large, glistening white flowers that seem to be composed of four white hearts connected at their points (immortalized by Georgia O'Keeffe). These flowers turn a soft pink again as they age. Tufted evening primrose makes a delightful punctuation in a sea of tiny white daisies when grown with *Erigeron karvinskianus* 'Profusion'. It combines well with pink fountain grass, variegated narrowleaf agave (*A. angustifolia*), and white cenizo (*Leucophyllum candidum*). As with the Baja primrose, good drainage is a must.

A well-drained sunny site is all the tufted evening primrose needs for months of bloom.

Closely related to the evening primrose, with similar but smaller flowers, are the sundrops (*Calylophus spp.*). Low-growing, prostrate herbs with small, simple leaves, the plants reach 12 to 18 inches across. Sundrops are very floriferous, with a two-toned effect being created by sulfur-yellow, new flowers juxtaposed against faded blooms, which turn apricot. Several species of *Calylophus* prosper in the Southwest, but *C. hartwegii* seems to be the most common in the nursery trade. Different, seemingly in name only, are several other species found throughout the southwestern states and into Texas. The delicate ambiance of the plants makes them wonderful for contrasting at the base of meaty cacti, aloes, and agaves.

A trademark wildflower of the desert in spring, *Baileya multiradiata*, or desert marigold, lives life in the fast lane. Desert marigolds bloom early in the season but persist into the summer and fall with brilliant sulfur-yellow daisies held high above compact mounds of gray-green filigree foliage. These flowers seem to literally bloom themselves to death, and the more rich living they enjoy, the bigger the display they make on the way to an early grave. A lean and mean approach to cultivation of the

Plant the thin sprawling sundrops along with aloes, cacti, or agaves for a lively color and textural contrast.

desert marigold seems to yield fewer blossoms at any one time but prolongs the life of these free-blooming "perannuals." At any rate, it is best to allow the plants to seed about the nonirrigated landscape so as to keep a population going well into the future. Their bright yellow flowers sharply contrast with red fairy duster (*Calliandra californica*), purple cenizos (*Leucophyllum spp.*), and *daleas*.

A perennial with a more permanent lifestyle is the angelita daisy (also unfortunately known as Perky Sue). Both *Hymenoxys acaulis* and *H. scaposa* are common in the nursery trade, and the difference between them is minute. Plants form low, dense, tufted mats of dark green, linear foliage from which arise a chorus of golden-yellow daisies on eight- to ten-inch stems. If ever there was such a thing as a rock garden plant for the desert, this is it. Neat and compact, the only maintenance required is a bit of cleaning up during the long bloom season, as the spent flower stems tend to collect over time. The dainty yellow flowers create a delightful color echo with the gold trimming found on the blue leaves of *Yucca rostrata* and *Y. pallida* and are marvelous surrounding the glowing globes of golden barrel cactus (*Echinocactus grusonii*).

Golden yellow blooms of angelita daisy sprout nonstop from thrifty mats of evergreen foliage.

Perennial Indian blanket (*Gaillardia aristata* and hybrids) tends to have a short but glorious life even in northern gardens. Nevertheless its hot-colored flowers, with banded concentric rings of orange, red, and yellow, are always welcome in southwestern settings. Indian blankets don't hold back their enthusiastic blooms, which is obviously what sends them to an early grave. However, the foot-tall perennials will usually last a couple of seasons and seed about when not deadheaded religiously, therefore persisting in the garden. The spicy colors work well with sobering greens of bear grass (*Nolina spp.*), prickly pear cactus (*Opuntia spp.*), and ornamental grasses (*Muhlenbergia spp.*). Pure, dark red ('Burgundy') and solid yellow ('Aurea' and 'Yellow Queen') cultivars are also available but may not reseed true to color.

Chocolate flower (*Berlandiera lyrata*) has a beguiling charm that encourages further interest piqued by its common name. Yes, blooms do smell of chocolate—the bitter-sweet kind used in baking—and on warm days the fragrance is quite strong. The flower is less glorious once you pull your nose out of it and give it a good look. The seminodding, yellow daisies with reddish-brown centers are borne in profusion by sprawling plants with lax stems. When petals drop from the flowers (daily, as with many desert species), they leave behind a pronounced green cup surrounding the central disk, which persists until the seed ripens. They benefit from a strong structural counterpoint of yuccas, aloes, grasses, cacti, or agaves.

Like the wild species, this red hybrid Indian blanket is a short-lived but glorious perennial.

Although most people are familiar with annual garden varieties of zinnias, the Southwest is also home to some perennial species. Not as flamboyant as their ephemeral cousins, these are still wonderful additions to landscapes and gardens. Prairie zinnia (*Z. grandiflora*) is a wisp of a plant with wiry stems mounding to only four or five inches, and bearing threadlike leaves. Its delicate appearance belies an ironclad constitution, however, and when covered in golden, one-inch, papery blooms, prairie zinnia is quite showy. Nestled at the base of hummingbird trumpets (*Zauschneria spp.*), red yucca (*Hesperaloe parviflora*), or golden barrel cactus (*Echinocactus grusonii*), prairie zinnia makes a lovely consort.

Desert zinnia (*Z. acerosa*) is more of a shrublet than an herbaceous perennial, and it is even more tolerant of drought than its aforementioned cousin. One finds this gray-leafed species growing in hostile, rocky soil with little available water, and yet it still puts on a parade of little white, papery flowers (turning cream colored as they dry) persisting throughout the summer and into winter. A little extra water makes it a wonderful perennial, but too much water will kill it, so desert zinnia is best used where there will be a minimum of irrigation. Its white flowers reflect the creamy, central bands in the bold leaves of *Agave americana* var. *marginata* 'Medio-picta', and the two enjoy the same dry, sunny setting.

Damianita (*Chrysactinia mexicana*) is very much a woody plant, but this shrublet keeps such a low profile (only a foot tall) and is so floriferous that it performs more like a garden-variety perennial. Tiny, narrow, dark green leaves densely cover the branches, creating a jade-green mound that is deliciously aromatic (I plant it more for foliage scent than the blooms). From late spring through fall, however, one can hardly see the foliage for the thick cover of tiny yellow daisies produced generously by damianita. As a guaranteed consort for the hard-to-predict summer blooms of *Leucophyllum candidum, L. pruinulosum,* and *L. zygophyllum,* damianita is a shoe-in ground cover. Its need for good drainage and full sun also makes it perfect combined with the red-spined barrel cactus (*Ferocactus pringlei*).

SALVIAS

The world of salvias is large and daunting even to the experienced gardener or botanist. New species, special selections, and hybrids are constantly showing up at progressive nurseries everywhere, and most are worth trying. Though decidedly few of these prosper in a hot, dry climate, many are worth trying in the microniche of the mini-oasis, where they will receive the extra moisture needed.

Cherry sage (*Salvia greggii*) is quite woody compared to most perennials already discussed; it could be classed as a shrub except the wood is very brittle. Stems are

cloaked in small, simple, aromatic foliage and crowned by many loose spikes of one-inch flowers with a pronounced lower lobe. Vermilion red is the most common form, but hot pink, white, coral orange, and soft yellow are also easily found (orange and yellow are more temperamental in the hottest climates). Although plants grow two to three feet tall and wide, winter shearing maintains a more compact, shapely form, and plants can even be cut to the ground for renewal.

Cherry sage enjoys full sun and tolerates some shade in my south-central Texas garden, but it really needs some shade when grown in places like Phoenix, Arizona. Eastern exposure with afternoon shade seems to give it enough protection to keep this sage happy in the hottest climates. This is a great impetus for expanding our desert gardens and landscapes into the shady areas under trees, which often go ignored and unplanted. Since many yuccas, aloes, bear grass, and agaves, along with other perennials, also flourish in dappled venues, there is no shortage of complementary foliage or flowers to create interesting combinations. The vermilion flowers consort well with green, linear textures produced by bear grass (*Nolina* spp.) and

Cherry sage grows well with minimal water or in the irrigated mini-oasis, as seen here with variegated maiden grass.

twin-flowered agave (*A. gemniflora*). The soft blue foliage of *Dasylirion wheeleri* or *Yucca rigida* makes an ideal foil for pink or coral-orange cultivars. The white form of cherry sage mixes well with blue cape plumbago (*P. auriculata*) and lavender trailing lantana (*L. montevidensis*) for a cool-looking respite from the summer's heat.

Tropical sage (*Salvia coccinea*) also prefers some shade protection from the blistering desert sun, but this is hardly a limitation on its use in the garden. This herbaceous perennial was relatively unknown in many circles despite the fact that it is a widespread native. The scarlet-red blooms in loose spikes top the two- to three-foot-tall plants, which are quite narrow by comparison (there is also a salmon and white bicolored form). The floriferous, compact hybrid 'Lady in Red' put this species in the forefront of mainstream gardening and moved this plant to the front of the border. Other new cultivars include pastel 'Coral Nymph' and its white relation 'Snow Nymph', which both have a shorter posture than the wild species. Wild tropical sage sows itself about in the shaded beds of my garden, where it looks splendid with the metallic purple leaves of Persian shield (*Strobilanthes dyerianus*) and adds color once the spring display of perennials has ended.

Another salvia known to most gardeners at any latitude are the bedding hybrids of mealy blue sage (*Salvia farinacea*), which are usually sold as annuals. As nice as those hybrids are, they don't seem to have the same hot-weather vigor and persistence as wild-type plants (collectors are finding populations in the western part of their range that show greater adaptation to drought and heat). Plants form a dense mat of two-inch-long, simple leaves, and stems begin to lengthen early in spring. Finally, tight blue spikes powdered with white (the mealy part) appear at the end of two-foot-tall stems from which purple-blue flowers erupt over a long period (all-white and bicolored cultivars are also available). Plants bloom from spring though frost and can be cut back at most any time if they start to flop. Vigorous wild clumps slowly increase in size to form large colonies, but the plant is in no way invasive. Mealy blue sage also appreciates protection from the hottest sun in Phoenix gardens. It is hard to find other plants with which this flower doesn't look good—it combines well with everything.

Thanks to the gentlemen of Yucca Du Nursery in Hempstead, Texas, who discovered and introduced this plant, we can enjoy *Salvia darcyi* in our summer gardens. Recently christened lipstick red sage, this herbaceous salvia's leaves are rather large (two inches long and wide) with a strong aromatic smell and sticky undersides. Still, they weather well (needing some shade in Phoenix) and make a beautiful green foil for the plant's long terminal spikes of two-inch, fire-engine-red blooms. A real workhorse, *Salvia darcyi* blooms tirelessly (it helps to feed and water it) all summer and fall, yet it is reliably perennial. The two-foot-tall plants simply need to be cut back to the ground in winter, as this sage retreats to the ground during winter weather.

LEFT: In full sun the scarlet-red blooms of tropical sage enliven pastel green pads of Texas native prickly pear, yet it flowers equally well in the shade.

211 ~

Plants are a bit stoloniferous and send up new shoots in an ever-widening clump. Excess moisture has never hurt this sage in my garden, so I often pair it with the equally vivacious, royal-purple *Verbena* 'Homestead' for the sheer joy of it. In drier sites, it would look great with fiery Indian blanket and golden damianita.

At home in conditions good enough to grow zinnias, native mealy blue sage makes a worthy partner.

MORE COMPACT HERBACEOUS PERENNIALS

Texas betony (*Stachys coccinea*) looks like it could be another sage at first glance, but the coral-red flowers radiating from foot-tall spikes, amid mounding, aromatic foliage, are more balanced (without the big lower lip like *Salvia*). This herbaceous perennial also enjoys desert shade with only moderate moisture necessary to keep a steady stream of flowers for you and your hummingbird friends. Although the odd coral color is hard to work with, it does harmonize well with the coral-orange *Salvia greggii* and always looks good contrasting with blue-flowered desert ageratum (*Eupatorium greggii*) or the olive-green leaves of tree bear grass (*Nolina matapensis*).

Most of the succulent "ice plants" that grow in the Southwest bloom heavily in the springtime but fail to carry on during summer's heat. Not so with the Rocky Point ice plant (*Malephora lutea*), which produces a steady supply of small, yellow, daisylike blooms throughout summer. Although the flowers are not large or incredibly showy like many of its kin, it is a pardonable sin because the plant is so reliable. Given good sun and drainage, Rocky Point ice plant forms a bright green mat that is perfect for cloaking the ground about boulders, cacti, or other sculptural elements within the garden. It looks great married with the low-growing, sun-loving blackfoot daisy, which is equally reliable for summer bloom.

Blackfoot daisy (*Melampodium leucanthum*) needs a name change to launch it into well-deserved greater fame. It is a widespread

Southwest native that blooms from spring till frost but usually dies from overwatering when planted in normal garden conditions. When given the heat and drought that it deserves, the 10- to 12-inch-high, mounding perennial grows to two feet across and blooms brilliantly, smothering itself with a myriad of tiny white daisies with lemon-yellow centers. As long as it gets full sun and good drainage (thin, unimproved soil is actually preferred), blackfoot daisy blooms long and lives long. This plant is a knockout combined with the architectural Queen Victoria agave (*A. victoriae-reginae*), where the tiny white flowers play off the intriguing white lines edging each succulent, sculpted leaf.

Peruvian verbena hybrids combined with even the simplest companions make a refreshing change.

The small white daisies with fringed petals of creeping fleabane (*Erigeron karvinskianus* 'Profusion') are indeed produced in such a profusion that there is a constant sea of frothy blooms. New buds tend to have a ruddy cast, which gives the mass of blossoms a slightly two-toned appearance. No taller than six or eight inches, the thin, branched stems bearing tiny leaves spread out to form a mat up to two feet across. *Erigeron* 'Profusion' is the perfect mate for a number of small to midsized plants, whether they are other perennial flowers, ornamental grasses, or desert denizens like aloes and agaves. Its color and stature are perfect for setting off the bold fishhook barrel cactus (*Ferocactus emoryi*) and pinkish-gray ghost plant (*Graptopetalum paraguayense*).

Though most people are familiar with the common bedding gazanias, the altogether different creeping gazania (*G. rigens*) is a superb creeping perennial for southwest gardens. Small, felty gray leaves densely cover the ground, forming a mat that spreads up to four feet across. The two- to three-inch, golden-yellow daisies dot the silver carpet for most of the warm season, giving the plant a unique look. Creeping gazania makes a wonderful ground cover beneath various Aloe species since its golden blooms mix well with the yellows, oranges, and reds of the succulent's flowers, and the silver leaves form a foliage contrast.

VERBENAS

Few people who see verbenas in bloom will have any but good things to say about the plants; verbenas are everything expected from a traditional garden flower. The low-growing, tidy plants keep clean, healthy foliage, and they bloom with large clusters of otherwise small flowers so that they put on quite a show.

Rock verbena (*V. pulchella,* a.k.a. *V. tenuisecta*) sports finely dissected leaves and a very prostrate habit, slowly spreading in the garden when blessed with good soil. Rounded heads of tiny, light purple flowers are displayed against a background of dark green foliage. Although rock verbena makes a splendidly simple ground cover on its

213

Rough-leaf verbena, a weed in my garden, is easily tamed when grown lean and mean in the arid Southwest.

own, I like to jazz it up by punctuating the sedate carpet with a few clumps of golden prairie zinnia and scarlet hummingbird trumpet (*Zauschneria spp.*). The carpeting growth habit of rock verbena seems to have an ebb and flow to it—spotty dieback in one place, and new growth in others.

Anyone who has visited nurseries in warm climates has already come to know the Peruvian verbena (*V. peruviana* hybrids; the actual species is small with red flowers and not as common), as this old standby has long dazzled customers every season when the quest for color begins. If the indestructible blooming ground cover suffers from anything, it is familiarity (which, as the saying goes, breeds contempt). However, as with many overused flowers, the "plant-combination makeover" breathes new life into otherwise tired gardens. Try using the bright pink flowers of this familiar old friend with silver foliage from trailing indigo bush (*Dalea greggii*), *Artemisia* 'Powis Castle', bush morning glory (*Convolvulus cneorum*), or blue-foliaged *Encelia farinosa* (the equally common brittle bush). Add the pinkish-white flowers of whimsical, long-blooming appleblossom grass (*Gaura lindheimeri*) and you can enjoy Peruvian verbena in a new light. The bright red clone can be outrageously shocking grown with purple heart (*Setcreasia pallida*) and angelita daisy (*Hymenoxys acaulis*).

The foot-tall *Verbena rigida* (sometimes called rough-leaf verbena) is not a creeping ground cover like the preceding two species, but it does get around. Vigorous underground runners invade surrounding soil one to two feet (furthest in light soil) from current stems as the *V. rigida* makes its way through the landscape. In heavy, calcareous soils of the Southwest, this process is forgivably slow (but watch this verbena in the sandy soils of the Southeast, where it runs rampant and winter's cold isn't severe enough to stop it). When it blooms, *V. rigida* produces a parade of dense, bright purple heads prominently displayed on upright stems. Big, tough plants that can compete with this bold perennial are the way to go. Bold clumps of deer grass (*Muhlenbergia rigens*), bear grass (*Nolina* spp.), and red bird of paradise (*Caesalpinia pulcherrima*) enjoy the company of this erstwhile invasive verbena.

WOODY PERENNIALS

Lantanas are similar to verbenas in that they also have rounded floral heads consisting of smaller, colorful flowers, and they are equally common and familiar to most gardeners. The difference is that there is sometimes a range of colors within a single floral head of lantana. In addition, *Lantana* species are woody plants instead of herbaceous perennials. However, since lantanas can be cut to the ground annually (and likewise rebound from freezing temperatures), they can be used as a drought-tolerant perennial in garden settings. Some varieties can also be used as a permanent shrub where weather permits.

The large shrubby forms of *Lantana* are either *L. camara* or *L. horrida,* and more commonly the hybrids of these species. Flower colors of yellow, orange, and red together within a single head—or yellow, peach, and pink combined in one cluster— make this plant quite a sight. It excites the inner child in some people and turns the stomachs of others who find the multicolored plants rather unsophisticated. As with the overused verbenas, the best remedy for the lantana blahs is to break old patterns and recombine these sturdy flowers with new elements (preferably foliage elements, since we are trying to treat a floral imbalance here). The green tones and linear texture of deer grass (*Muhlenbergia rigens*) or bear grass (*Nolina* spp.) with the white flowers of blackfoot daisy (*Melampodium leucanthum*) help to calm the sassy, hot-colored forms. Burgundy fountain grass (*Pennisetum setaceum* 'Cupreum') or purple hop bush (*Dodonaea viscosa* 'Purpurea') along with the silver foliage of prairie sagebrush (*Artemisia ludoviciana*) breathes new life into the pinkish lantanas. A chance encounter in Phoenix between an Arizona cypress and pink hybrid of

Lantana horrida—carefree but needing a "plant combination makeover." Mix these vintage shrubs with new and different foliage elements.

L. camara resulted in the pastel yellow, peach, and pink flowers spilling out from the cool blue foliage up to 15 feet high as the lantana grew up into the branches of the tree; breathtaking!

A more demure woody perennial with a similarly indestructible nature is the trailing lantana (*L. montevidensis* and its hybrids). Bearing small, simple, green leaves, the plants usually stay about a foot high unless they find a more erect shrub to climb (a situation rich in design possibilities), but the species can spread up to six feet across when conditions suit them, with hybrids being less rambunctious. Trailing lantana looks best doing just that, if it's possible to grow it cascading over a wall where the trailing nature of the plant is displayed. The original species has small, dark lavender flowers with white centers, clustered into rounded heads, and blooms nonstop throughout summer, fall, and into winter. It can be planted with other shades of purple: at the base of cenizo (*Leucophyllum fructescens* 'Compacta'), with *Dalea* bicolor, and with *Salvia lyciodes*. Red yucca (*Hesperaloe parviflora*) makes a lovely color and texture contrast for trailing lantana, with an equally long bloom time. Yellow, soft yellow, and white forms of this lantana are easily found, expanding the use of the flower in gardens and landscapes.

Cape plumbago (*P. auriculata,* syn. *capensis*) is by nature a monstrously sprawling shrub with thin, arching branches vining their way toward ever higher reaches, the branch tips crowned with sky-blue, phloxlike flowers. Where winter's cold does not take this plant to the ground to start all over again the following spring, cape plumbago can be daunting. Unfortunately this woody perennial is often shamelessly sheared into blocks and balls of tortured twigs so that the graceful, arching beauty and delightful clusters of flowers are eliminated. When not treated like a hedge, but rather cut back hard once a year like a perennial, the blue flowers of plumbago can easily grace any garden. The sky-blue cape plumbago is great with white or pastel flowers, along with silver and bronze foliage. Dwarf oleander 'Petite Pink', lavender trailing lantana, and purple hop bush make wonderful consorts for the plumbago.

The cape plumbago is also found in a white-flowered cultivar, but there is in fact another white plumbago that is even better for gardens. The southwestern native *Plumbago scandens* first caught my eye during winter (both in the wild and at a nursery) when the foliage of this three-foot-tall perennial had turned a dark garnet red. Seeing it bloom, undaunted, through the summer with endless clusters of white flowers is also a sight, although the flowers are smaller than those of the cape plumbago. The profusion of bloom more than makes up for the smaller blossoms, and the added bonus of rich winter color puts *P. scandens* over the top. Shade to part shade suits this three-foot, rounded plant quite well and further expands the realm of gardening out of the sun. The white flowers mingle splendidly with anything, and the plant is stunning against the verdant green trunks of the palo verde tree or parkinsonia.

Quite out of left field, but interesting nonetheless, is wild Texas pepper, or chili pequin (*Capsicum annuum*). This two-foot-tall perennial loves hot weather and shade, where it smothers itself with tiny white blooms along with green and red, jellybean-sized fruits (they are very hot). In mild winters the plants keep their small green leaves year-round, but with freezing weather, they are cut to the ground. *Salvia coccinea* and *Plumbago scandens* are two shade-lovers that echo the red and white of the chili pequin in summer and enjoy similar moisture.

Hummingbird trumpets (*Zauschneria californica, Z. arizonica,* and *Z. cana*) seem to suffer more from an identity crisis than from the heat of summer. These native perennials of the Southwest are also called California fuchsia (even the Arizona one), and taxonomists bicker about the difference between *Z. arizonica* and *Z. californica* while someone else went and changed the genus name from *Zauschneria* to *Epilobium.* Yikes! Like the artist formerly known as Prince, perhaps it would be best if these snappy perennials were now given a symbol instead of a name. Nomenclatural madness

Late summer is peak time for hummingbird trumpets and their fine feathered friends.

217

notwithstanding, these are wonderful heat- and drought-tolerant perennials that give a long season of bloom and attract hummingbirds as well. The one- to three-foot-tall plants enjoy deep soil with only modest waterings and will put up new shoots from the ground as old, tired stems are removed. Midseason shearing keeps them smaller and reduces the incidence of stem breakage. The scarlet/orange trumpet-shaped flowers contrast well with golden prairie zinnia (*Z. grandiflora*) or angelita daisy (*Hymenoxys acaulis*) in the foreground.

Hot-weather perennials with spicy orange and red flowers, but with slightly less taxonomic confusion, belong to the genus *Justicia*. Mexican honeysuckle (*Justicia spicigera*) has somewhat large, felty, bright green leaves, which make for a handsome three-foot-tall shrub even without the crowning touch of terminal clusters of tangerine-orange, tubular flowers. Mexican honeysuckle is able to enjoy the good life in a mini-oasis where the bold and the daring might add the bright purple foliage of *Setcreasea pallida* at its base, punctuated with white spider lily (*Hymenocallis sonorensis*). Lovers of the color orange can plant sunset-hued lantana and red bird of paradise (*Caesalpinia pulcherrima*) with Mexican honeysuckle and let the chips fall where they may.

The red justicia (*J. candicans*) is a charming woody perennial with a narrow, erect shape (about three feet tall) that contrasts nicely with many other garden plants having more spreading habits. Small red flowers resembling gaping mouths are produced from spring through fall amid little heart-shaped leaves, and hummingbirds do love them. Red justicia looks best where it can tower above lower plantings (like purple or yellow trailing lantana) and its erect habit can be appreciated along with that of the statuesque Mexican grass tree (*Dasylirion longissimum*).

A relative unknown but dynamite hot-weather bloomer is *Justicia sonorae*. This sparsely foliaged perennial herb has green stems heavily cloaked with rosy-purple flowers. After a heavy spring show, blooming seems to come in waves, but even during slow periods the plants have a smattering of flowers as they prepare for the next big wave of blossoms. The color contrasts brilliantly with the acid-yellow desert marigold (*Baileya multiradiata*) or with the subdued pastel greens of prickly pear cactus or bamboo muhly (*Muhlenbergia dumosa*).

Desert ageratum (*Eupatorium greggii*) is a southwest native that has recently found mainstream approval. The one- to two-foot-tall perennial has beautifully cut leaves that make it a striking foliage plant even before the flowers begin. Clouds of cottony, lavender-blue blossoms resembling the common bedding plant ageratum are

Even in frost-free areas blue cape plumbago can be cut back hard in December to keep it manageable and make room for winter annuals.

produced from spring to fall, and butterflies love them. Since this perennial enjoys some shade, try it in the dappled realm of mesquite or acacia along with white-flowered desert plumbago for a cooling combination.

The southwestern deserts are also home to shrubby perennials with dark green leaves and yellow daisies known as goldeneye (*Viguiera deltoidea*, also *V. dentata* and *V. stenoloba*). These tough-as-nails plants bloom for a long season through the hottest months, but they suffer from being "yet another yellow composite." However, in areas where there is not much extra irrigation, goldeneye gives a lot and asks little in return. It makes a handsome partner for the many species of green-leafed yuccas that have thus far waited for a companion.

Bat-faced cuphea shows best spilling over the edge of a raised bed or container.

OTHER GARDEN-WORTHY PERENNIALS

Mexico is home to a host of interesting members of the genus *Cuphea*, and so far we've only scratched the surface of perennials with garden potential. One old standby found throughout the South is Mexican heather (*Cuphea hyssopifolia*). Commonly sold as a bedding annual, but perennial in my Zone 8 garden, Mexican heather tolerates the extremes of both dank and drought in a heavy clay soil and blooms nonstop through the heat. Tiny reddish-purple flowers are produced amid small green leaves that densely cover the little branches, giving this plant a tight, but graceful, formal look. White- and lavender-flowered forms, as well as a golden-leafed clone, are available, expanding the use of this perennial. In the mini-oasis, Mexican heather will thrive in the sometimes wet soil at the base of fountains, and it combines well with many other garden flowers.

Bat-faced cuphea (*C. llavea*) definitely has a name that gets your attention, and if it doesn't, the flowers will! Loosely spreading branches, thinly clad with simple leaves, terminate with a steady stream of odd-shaped, one-inch-long flowers. These blooms consist of red floral tubes with two big (relatively speaking) purple petals, resembling ears, perched at the end, creating a face. The flowers are modest, although interesting, but tend to droop a bit, making the plant display itself best from a raised planter or pot (where it also gets the good drainage it needs). In such a venue, bat-faced cuphea looks good with purple heart (*Setcreasia pallida*), foxtail fern (*Asparagus densiflorus* 'Myers'), and *Agave desmettiana* 'Variegata', with the container lightly shaded for best results.

The common and rather boring anise hyssop (*Agastache foeniculum*) has some relatives from the mountains of the Chihuahuan Desert that warrant an invitation to your garden. The sunset hyssop (*Agastache rupestris*) is an unpretentious multibranched perennial that looks almost like a small tumbleweed with its tiny gray-green leaves thinly cloaking the stems. Being a member of the aromatic mint family, though, this herb has a refreshing minty-licorice fragrance, with some plants even smelling like root beer. I plant it just to have a chance to keep in close contact with the heady aroma, but in summer the two-foot-tall plants reward you and hummingbirds with a bonus of peachy tubular flowers on six-inch-long spikes. Full sun and good drainage are essential for *A. rupestris*, which is also a perfect site for the complementary powder-blue foliage of *Schizachyrium scoparium* (little bluestem grass) and white blooms of *Gaura lindheimeri*.

The more obscure Pringle's hyssop (*Agastache pringlii*) has small spade-shaped leaves with an interesting ginger aroma. Also bearing many thin stems, this two-foot-tall, branched perennial becomes transformed into a willowy cloud of lavender spires. The almost foot-long spikes are covered with a multitude of minute flowers, keeping the plant shrouded in a pastel purple haze for weeks on end. It is a splendid accent for the subtle elegance of bear grass (*Nolina* spp.).

Appleblossom grass (*Gaura lindheimeri*) is a charming perennial that grows well throughout the southern latitudes but performs impressively in the arid Southwest so as to warrant inclusion here. Also known as whirling butterflies (a name that makes me dizzy), this perennial starts out as a simple rosette with three-inch elliptical leaves bearing red blotches. The first stems bolt and begin flowering in spring and continue through summer as the plant takes on an ethereal appearance with small pinkish-white flowers massing on long, graceful wands. Flowers don't stay open for more than a day but are replaced with freshly opened buds as old blooms fade. Quite tolerant of drought, appleblossom grass consorts with many desert elements, and the veil of blush-pink and white flowers is wonderful to gaze through at robust blue agaves in a moderately irrigated site.

Not surprisingly, many plants of the middle plains of America can go both ways—east or west, where they thrive in gardens from coast to coast. Purple coneflower (*Echinacea purpurea*) is such an adaptable perennial that it is a summer star in gardens across the United States. It

This hybrid hyssop 'Firebrand' was a chance seedling of sunset hyssop. It has larger darker flowers and extra vigor.

Purple coneflower is an industrial-strength perennial as long as it receives ample moisture.

thrives in clay soil and enjoys the type of moisture one would expect to find on the prairies rather than in the deserts, so include it in the mini-oasis of desert settings. The bright pink flowers (I don't know why they call it "purple") show splendidly against the silvery foliage of cenizo or Texas ranger (*Leucophyllum frutescens*), and since *Echinacea* is a prairie native, blue Lindheimer's muhly grass (*Muhlenbergia lindheimeri*) is the perfect consort. Either way, include the subtle beauty of long-blooming appleblossom grass (*Gaura lindheimeri*) and you have a knockout combination.

The inclusion of summer-blooming perennials in our southwest gardens and landscapes makes it possible to embellish the desert scene with floral color, depth, and panache. Though shrubs, cacti, and the woody lilies will always create the backbone of the garden, the addition of herbaceous and woody perennials gives each of those elements a new dimension as the subtle interplay of color and texture enlivens the scene. Flowering perennials can be used in such an endless variety of ways that no two gardeners will likely eschew the same combinations, yet everyone will enjoy the results.

CHAPTER 15

FLOWERING SHRUBS
FOR HOT, DRY GARDENS

A visit to the Sonoran or Chihuahuan Desert will quickly reveal the predominance of shrubs and scrubby trees in the landscape. Many woody plants thrive in hot, arid climates, and so it is logical that they form the backbone of gardens in the Southwest. Yes, grasses, cacti, yuccas, and agaves

are included in the desert's botanical palette, and their silhouettes, in turn, are reflected in our southwestern gardens. Nevertheless, the importance of shrubs should not be overlooked. If one is to create a colorful, beautifully diverse, and permanent garden or landscape in the desert Southwest, the incorporation of flowering shrubs is a must.

In order to stretch the realm of perennials, I included some woody plants in the previous chapter because they can resprout from the ground and quickly bloom on new growth. These can also play larger roles as shrubs in the garden, although in some areas winter's cold takes them to the ground annually. In the same vein, I will include here some summer-blooming woody plants that are large bushes, even growing to the size of small trees. The use of these is definitely limited for the person with a small garden (as I well know from my home experience).

LEUCOPHYLLUMS

If there is one genus of heat- and drought-tolerant shrubs that no southwest gardener should be without, it is the *Leucophyllum*, or Texas rangers (in Texas we call them cenizos, oddly enough). Though I don't always

embrace Latin plant names with great enthusiasm, I like how the word *Leucophyllum* just rolls off the tongue, and it is delightfully descriptive (unlike some meaningless plant names that are just people's names). "Leuco," meaning white, and "phyllum," meaning leaf, aptly describe the look of these nondeciduous bushes bearing small silver or gray leaves. Even without flowering, the species of *Leucophyllum* are gorgeous additions to the garden. Most of these sun-loving shrubs bloom on a whim during hot weather when humidity is high, with purple, lavender, or violet flowers, although white and pink selections are also available. The five-petaled, funnelform flowers pop out from the leaves, along the stems en masse, with a striking similarity to penstemons and other members of that family.

The first Texas ranger to find its way into gardens and landscapes was *Leucophyllum frutescens*, a large, loosely rounded shrub with silver-gray leaves and light purple flowers. Its thin, informal shape confounds many gardeners who demand a tight, controlled appearance from this otherwise six- to eight-foot-tall shrub. Please don't shear them, as doing so ruins the lush, graceful appearance of this desert shrub, resulting in an

unpleasant, butchered skeleton of twigs and few leaves (note that all leucophyllums tend to lose some of their leaves during winter). It is better to control the bush's size by cutting it back hard in late winter and letting it remake itself as it regrows. Better yet, try one of the more compact selections. This species has seen the most selection and breeding of all the leucophyllums, and its application in the garden and landscape has fortunately been expanded.

'White Cloud' is a selection of *L. frutescens* that has the same silver leaves, loose habit, and rather large proportions as the regular species, but it blooms with white flowers. Perfect for the moonlight garden, and an unobtrusive foil for other flowers with soft colors, 'White Cloud' makes a quiet statement for the back of the border. The light shade of mature, eight-foot-tall specimens is the perfect venue for *Plumbago scandens* and white *Salvia greggii* for those hoping for snow in summer.

'Green Cloud' is also a selection of *L. frutescens*. Sporting light green foliage instead of the usual silver-gray, this selection is seen by the less adventurous crowd as a more "normal" bush for mainstream home use. However, this variety still gets quite large (to eight feet tall and wide), and one should plan on that inevitability. 'Green Cloud' has bright pink flowers that show well with light purple trailing lantana (*L. montevidensis*) clambering up into its sparsely clad lower branches.

For smaller gardens, there is *Leucophyllum frutescens* 'Compacta', which is a smaller version of the wild shrub, bearing silver-gray leaves and light purple-pink blooms. This plant can't be beat; it can be used as a medium-sized shrub instead of a small tree. Planted with Arizona yellow bells (*Tecoma stans* var. *angustata*) as a companion, compact cenizo puts on a dazzling display against the clusters of lemon-yellow flowers. To push the envelope, add the pink and yellow *Lantana camara* 'Confetti' for a flowering shrub combination that will give months of fabulous color.

Another cenizo suited for gardens with limited space is *L. frutescens* 'Convent'. This compact, silver-leafed selection has a more archaic branching habit that I find wonderfully informal, and bright magenta-purple blooms that make the inner child in me squeal with delight. Desert marigold (*Baileya multiradiata*) scattered about in the foreground, offers wonderful contrast with its acid-yellow flowers. Perhaps an equally brilliant, hot-pink bougainvillea included in the rear of this planting would be enough to shake up the whole neighborhood.

Also a rather large shrub, the species *Leucophyllum pruinosum* grows to about six feet in all directions, with a rather erratic, rangy habit. The foliage is a dark shade of steel gray, and the flowers are a deep, rich purple. Best of all, the blooms are incredibly fragrant (they smell like grape bubble gum). In an informal setting, *L. pruinosum* planted with Arizona yellow bells (*Tecoma stans* var. *angustata*) and red coral tree (Erythrina spp.) makes a rich summer display. Alternatively, the shrub can be the backdrop for a simple, low-key planting of deer grass with rough-leaf verbena (*V. rigida*).

Perhaps better suited for the small garden (as long as there is good sun and good drainage) is *Leucophyllum candidum*. The leaves on this three- to four-foot-tall shrub are almost white, and the flowers are a rich, deep violet. In the nursery trade there are two cultivars, 'Silver Cloud' and 'Thunder Cloud', with the latter growing to a more petite three-foot maximum. The key to success with these shrubs is full sun, good drainage, and minimal irrigation, so I'd recommend integrating them into the usually too-barren plantings of cacti, yuccas, and agaves, along with equally drought-needy desert zinnia (*Z. acerosa*) and damianita (*Chrysactinia mexicana*).

Leucophyllum zygophyllum is a small bush with gray leaves and light blue flowers, the source behind its common name, blue ranger. It is one of the best for small gardens receiving modest irrigation since the blue ranger tolerates the extra watering that kills *L. candidum*. Indian mallow (*Abutilon palmeri*), with its light, mango-colored flowers, makes a grand companion for *L. zygophyllum*. The pastel blue with cream-centered *Agave americana* var. 'Medio-picta' in the foreground of such a planting would complete the picture quite nicely.

YELLOW BELLS

Both the Sonoran and Chihuahuan Deserts are home to a beautiful, indomitable shrub called yellow bells (*Tecoma stans*). The common name aptly describes the large, bright, terminal clusters of flowers on this six- to eight-foot-tall shrub (more compact under xeric growing conditions), but I love the Spanish name for this plant—*esperanza*, meaning "hope." The name certainly indicates that *Tecoma* will produce refreshing showers of golden-yellow trumpets during the most bleak, hot summer months. Hummingbirds find the flowers irresistible.

Several varieties of yellow bells are available to the gardener. The hardiest is Arizona yellow bells (*Tecoma stans* var. *angustata*), which proudly displays clusters of bloom against a backdrop of bright green, narrow, compound leaves. In fall the shrubs carry decorative, pencil-thin seedpods that birds love. Even though the leaves may drop in winter, the seedpods remain, lending the shrub an interesting seasonal aspect. The large shrubs can be used with other bushes that have the same scale, like *Leucophyllum frutescens*, purple hop bush, and oleander hybrids, or even small trees like mescal bean (*Sophora secundiflora*) or Arizona rosewood

The blue linear foliage of Lindheimer's muhly grass perfectly compliments the clustered bells of Tecoma hybrid 'Orange Jubilee'.

(*Vauquelina californica*). Arizona yellow bells is the perfect large specimen plant for a small courtyard or mini-oasis, cavorting shamelessly with windmill palm (*Trachycarpus fortunei*). Its beautiful, clean foliage and long bloom time make esperanza indispensable.

A wonderful peach-colored hybrid between *Tecoma* and cape honeysuckle (*Tecomaria*) called 'Orange Jubilee' is also available to gardeners. The foliage is a bit broader, and the plant's habit is also somewhat larger than the yellow species. The clusters of pastel orange trumpets crowning the tips of branches are lovely against the powder-blue foliage of Mexican blue palm (*Brahea armata*) or pindo palm (*Butia capitata*). With the dwarf oleander hybrid 'Petite Pink' or pink and soft yellow lantana massed at its feet, the effect is enchanting. 'Orange Jubilee' is not as cold hardy as Arizona yellow bells, but though the specimen in my Zone 8 garden freezes to the ground most winters, it returns with gusto, enjoying a blistering southwestern exposure and becoming a seven-foot-tall flowering extravaganza by summer.

If one travels further south from the deserts to the tropics of Central America, one encounters the tropical version of yellow bells (*Tecoma stans* var. *stans*). This shrub is bigger all the way around: in overall habit (up to 20 feet tall!), in leaf (twice the size), and in flower (huge clusters of big yellow trumpets). However, it is tropical, and though a lovely, large evergreen specimen for frost-free environments, it can be damaged by even a light freeze. In a warm garden, sassy yellow bells, exotic red bird of paradise (*Caesalpinia pulcherrima*), and coconut-looking pindo palm (*Butea capitata*) generate a calypso rhythm all their own.

A member of the same exotic family as Tecoma, desert willow (*Chilopsis linearis*) bears extravagant, trumpetlike blooms followed by long, thin seedpods. Although it is a small tree (to 25 feet) and not as easy to place as any bush, it is a choice specimen for any hot, dry garden. The fine, narrow leaves are indeed reminiscent of a willow, giving the tree a delicate cast. But when desert willow blooms, the light pink bells with ruffled petals remind one of orchid flowers. A deep pinkish-purple clone expands the variety of this colorful small tree. Cool blue Arizona cypress (*Cupressus glabra*), the blue-foliage palms (*Butia* and *Brahea*), and silver-leafed leucophyllums make exceptional companions that highlight the gorgeous blooms.

CORAL TREES

The very name coral tree (*Erythrina* spp.) conjures visions of the tropics and hot climates. Certainly the ability to grow coral trees in the hot Southwest makes up for our inability to successfully cultivate cold-loving plants like lilacs and forsythias. The genus contains several species and hybrids that have the same lush, trifoliate leaves and perform well in hot, arid gardens and landscapes. The brilliant, exotic, vermilion flowers are quite stunning on their own, but they also show well with yellow bells, red

LEFT: The coral tree is one of my absolute favorite plants on the property. The fact that it's so easy to grow only endears it further.

bird of paradise, and other tropical-looking elements. These choice shrubs are sometimes difficult (but not impossible) to find.

Rocky, foothill sites in the desert are home to the Arizona coral bean (*Erythrina flabelliformis*), where the thick stems annually produce large, handsome spikes of long, scarlet flowers on top of lush green foliage. Blooms occur in late spring and again when the summer rains come. In fall and winter, the leaves depart, leaving sculpted, dangling pods, split open to reveal bright red seeds adhered to the insides. The three- to five-foot-long stems are fat and minimally branched, giving the desert coral bean an odd profile during winter months. In the wild, these stems persist for a few years, then die, as new, bigger stems rise from the slowly progressing rootstock. Desert coral beans are complemented by the equally compact goldeneye (*Viguiera*) and red bird of paradise (*Caesalpinia pulcherrima*).

Texas coral bean (*Erythrina herbacea*) is actually considered an herbaceous perennial in much of its home state, where cold weather trims it to the ground on an annual basis. It is a tree, however, in subtropical climates, where it may only lose its leaves for winter. In the dry heat of Phoenix this coral bean relishes afternoon shade. In my Zone 8 garden, Texas coral bean usually freezes to the ground in winter but enjoys life in the heavy, black clay enough to always return to its six-foot height and spread with a dazzling floral display. Although my Texas coral bean stands alone, gracing an understated boxwood hedge with its flamboyant blooms, it would look smashing with the robust orange and yellow lantana (*L. horrida*).

The ever-blooming coral tree (*Erythrina x bidwillii*) is a hybrid between *E. herbacea* and the arborescent, tropical *E. crista-galli*. Vigorous and large, the ever-blooming coral tree produces huge, two-foot-tall spikes of bright, cardinal-red flowers virtually nonstop as long as the weather is warm. It is a bit of a giant and will command any corner in which it is planted (also needing a canopy of shade in Phoenix). The sight of this would no doubt make the pastel-loving English swoon, but then so would the blistering heat in which the coral tree thrives.

INDIAN MALLOW AND FAIRY DUSTER

It was the olive-green, velvet-soft leaves of Indian mallow (*Abutilon palmeri*) that caught my eyes when I first saw this plant. The sprays of small, glowing tangerine, cup-shaped blooms reminded me of orange sherbet, and I was sold. Even out of bloom, Indian mallow is a beautiful, stately plant, although one that I can't keep from touching all the time (plant it near a path for easy access). With just a little extra water, the three- to five-foot-tall shrubs will flower themselves ragged, so late fall finds them in need of rejuvenation. Wait until winter is finished before pruning back the plants, however, so you can enjoy the golden, starlike seed heads. Indian mallow prospers with shade (as it

does in sun), and I recommend planting it with a skirt of white-blooming *Plumbago scandens* in such a protected site. Also try this *Abutilon* with sky-blue cape plumbago, white *Salvia greggii*, and bear grass.

The intriguing tropical powderpuffs (*Calliandra* spp.) include a couple of desert species. These two arid-land shrubs have smaller flowers and leaves than their Central and South American cousins (blooms still have the look of a shaving brush), and they are given the charming name of fairy duster. The Arizona fairy duster (*C. eriophylla*) is very compact, with tiny, pink, wispy flowers occurring in spring and fall. Although it is an indispensable flowering shrub for the water-wise garden, it sadly does not bloom during the heat of summer.

The Baja fairy duster (*Calliandra californica*), however, does offer its quaint, red, one-inch flowers all season. The five-foot-tall shrub is thinly clad with small, dissected leaves and has an open, informal appearance—all the better to appreciate the almost magical display of lipstick-red tufts. I easily imagine garden fairies grabbing hold of one of these to tidy up other flowers while I'm not looking. Baja fairy duster makes a marvelous asset to the garden even if it doesn't have the weight to be a strong focal point. I love its vivid red blooms hovering over golden barrel cactus (*Echinocactus*

The enchanting, tiny red tufts of bloom on the Baja fairy duster can cast a magical spell. (Photo by Charles Mann.)

The golden shower bush combines equally well with xeric desert companions or lush elements of the mini-oasis.

grusonii). Winter-, spring-, and fall-blooming daleas (*D. versicolor, D. pulchra,* and *D. bicolor*) make good companions with equally loose habits and small purple flowers. For summer floral companionship, try yellow damianita at its feet. Since the Baja fairy duster does not bounce back from freezing temperatures with gusto, I grow mine in a container where it joins other tender desert denizens on the pot patio (they are then moved in from the cold).

GOLDEN SHOWER AND MORNING GLORY

Golden shower bush (*Galphimia glauca*) is a compact shrub from Mexico with small, glossy, gray-green leaves. It is almost constantly in flower, and that includes the hottest time of the year. The plant produces terminal clusters of small, bright yellow flowers shaped like a five-point star with a reddish center. In my garden, golden shower bush withstands frost stoically but gets cut to the ground in a hard freeze. This is just as well since I need to keep it smaller than its ultimate five-foot size. In southwest gardens with milder winters, grow golden shower bush with the vermilion Baja fairy duster. At home I enjoy it blooming through the hottest months in concert with compact lantana 'Tangerine' and red floribunda rose 'Europeana'.

Shrub morning glory (*Ipomoea fistulosa*) is a resilient, heat-loving plant that acts like a huge perennial for those of us living where cold weather cuts it annually to the ground. Elsewhere the six- to eight-foot-tall woody bush keeps a year-round appearance of several to many thickened stalks. An array of large, heart-shaped, green leaves and flowers clothe a rather stark profile that can be used in the garden to advantage when paired with palms or ornamental grasses, which balance its naked demeanor. The large pink, funnel-shaped flowers with dark wine-colored throats are clustered at each leaf with buds of assorted sizes, promising blooms over a long period. Winter finds groups of decorative pods bearing large, furry, brown seeds. Pink-flowering, olive-foliaged *Leucophyllum* 'Green Cloud' makes a nice partner for bush morning glory, as does blue-leafed pindo plam (*Butea capitata*).

OLEANDERS

A common shrub originating far from the desert Southwest but enjoying life there nonetheless is oleander (*Nerium oleander*). The narrow four-inch leaves are simple, dark green, and look as if they should belong on a much thirstier plant, but oleanders are quite drought tolerant. Five-petaled flowers appear in terminal clusters and are quite showy (some cultivars are scented, others bear double blossoms), with red, hot pink, light pink, white, apricot, and yellow being the color range from which to choose. Specimens grow from seven to ten feet tall and wide, but old hedges twice that tall can be found. These robust, fast-growing evergreens are so foolproof that they have earned a certain measure of disdain from some gardeners (excessive roadside planting by city landscape crews has perhaps been part of the problem). As with any shrub that has seen overuse or misuse, there is hope in new combinations with other plant partners.

The dense, rounded form of oleander lends itself to formal uses in gardens and landscapes, yet this sometimes seems out of place with the eclectic, rugged appearance of many desert shrubs. The best way to avoid this culture clash is to couch oleander between distinctively contrasting textural elements like palms, bear grass, sotols, and ornamental grasses. Red and white cultivars look especially handsome with green foliage accompaniment, while apricot- and pink-flowered forms benefit from a soft blue foil. The white oleander cultivar 'Sister Agnes' is deliciously fragrant and worth growing in an intimate courtyard setting.

Two compact hybrids of the common oleander also expand the range of uses for this shrub. Unfortunately, though sweet and long blooming, 'Petite Pink' is not very cold hardy. I can't grow it in my Zone 8 garden, but most urban areas in the Southwest and all along the coast can enjoy the four-foot-tall bush sporting clusters of soft pink blooms with just a touch of peach in the center. A foreground of lavender or white trailing lantana (*L. montevidensis*) and the companionship of pastel blue Lindheimer's muhly grass (*Muhlenbergia lindheimeri*) or sotol (*Dasylirion wheeleri*) create a satisfying scene. 'Little Red' is a dwarf cultivar that is hardy in my zone. Its dark vermilion flowers are choice, but the plant does not bloom for as long as most oleanders.

BIRD OF PARADISE

Red bird of paradise shrub (*Caesalpinia pulcherrima*) also goes by the names Barbados

Red bird of paradise shrub thrives in blast furnace heat and is hardy enough to survive zero-degree cold.

The brilliant blooms of bougainvillea are best appreciated against a simple background.

pride and dwarf poinciana. The variety of names is indicative of this plant's wide exposure and almost universal cultivation in warm climates. Finely dissected, pale green, compound leaves adorn this plant, giving it a fernlike texture that contrasts wonderfully with other foliage in the garden. Stems terminate in bold spikes of large, frilly flowers of fiery orange and scarlet, with bright red stamens whimsically protruding from each bloom. The multiple stems of this six-foot-tall, flamboyant shrub are sometimes armed with thin spines, but that is little deterrent to including it in gardens. In cool weather, the foliage takes on a rich bronzed cast, crowned with a smattering of plump, plum-colored seedpods hovering above. Do enjoy this seasonal color of an exceptional plant if winter's cold doesn't take it down to the ground as it does in Zone 8. It faithfully and vigorously returns to bloom again from such cold.

The airy texture of red bird of paradise is as much a consideration when planting it as the flaming floral display. Since ferns don't do well in hot, dry climates, this shrub is a pleasant addition for contrasting with strong architectural elements and linear textures in the garden. The flowers stand alone in their exuberant brilliance, and I recommend planting red bird of paradise amid spring- and fall-bloomers to carry on the color parade in areas of the garden through hot weather. But if one wants to run with the whole glorious fiesta theme, include orange bougainvillea, yellow bells, red coral tree, Mexican honeysuckle, burgundy fountain grass, and a palm or two.

BOUGAINVILLEAS

Another flowering plant grown around the world in hot climates is the brilliant, rainbow-colored bougainvillea. Technically a shrubby vine capable of clambering up to 20 feet, the various species and hybrids of the genus *Bougainvillea* are more often than not used as shrubs in the landscape and in gardens. The true flowers are almost insignificant, enclosed by large papery bracts creating the color extravaganza in shades of purple, red, pink, orange, yellow, and white. Two-inch, simple leaves hide vicious thorns that occur along the stems. Plants enjoy well-drained soil and hot sun but may seem fickle in their ability to drop all their leaves in one moment (a botanical tantrum common to chilled or overwatered specimens) and burst into unpredictable, outrageous bloom the next.

Bougainvillea brasiliensis is a vigorous grower with violet blossoms that are refreshingly smaller than most other species and hybrids. The color echoes and complements the varied hues produced by leucophyllums in their sporadic bloom, and sharply contrasts with Arizona yellow bells. Shocking magenta-purple is the color of flowers shamelessly produced by *B. glabra* and some of its hybrids. Sophisticated gardeners are supposed to eschew such vulgar colors, like sensible home decorators should shun velvet paintings. However, if you like the color (and I confess that I do, but don't own any velvet paintings), try planting magenta bougainvillea on its own or juxtaposed with complementary-toned stucco walls. Hot pink *B. spectabilis* and its hybrids also present a similar color conundrum in the garden, easily solved by using it as a solo performer. The difficult-to-harmonize color forms of bougainvilleas are perfectly suited for growing in containers, where their brilliance can be thoughtfully positioned.

Whether it is a small courtyard or an entire landscape, any size of a Southwest garden can be designed around some or all of these wonderful woody plants. The flowering small trees and shrubs discussed here create the foundation of a great garden, should it be on the Pacific Coast, in the hot desert, or in Texas.

CHAPTER 16

PALMS, ORNAMENTAL GRASSES, AND BEAR GRASS

Whereas palms have long been planted in the Southwest as successful components of city landscapes and home gardens, drought-tolerant grasses are only recently appearing at the same venues. Both palms and ornamental grasses add structure and texture to gardens and landscapes.

The two are stunning planted together; their subtle color harmonies and textural contrasts add an exciting new depth to the garden while remaining essentially trouble-free. In addition to those plants in the palm family and the grass family, one should not forget the bear grasses. Although these agave relatives belong to yet a different family, bear grasses (*Nolina*) are similar to true grasses in their linear foliage effect. Plants in the genus *Nolina*, however, are evergreen and somewhat shade tolerant as well as extremely heat and drought tolerant, so their contribution to gardens is immense.

PALMS

Everyone's first impression upon arrival in the southern parts of California, Arizona, or Texas is of the towering palm trees growing along the streets and in front of homes. The feathery leaves of date palms topping sturdy trunks dominate the landscape, conjuring images of Cleopatra and Mark Anthony in Egypt, and of ancient Babylon (I save imagery of Moses and the pharaohs for association with papyrus whenever seen). The fan palms are also striking components of the landscape: the native California fan palm, with its bold, swarthy trunk; and the

Mexican fan palm, with its tall, spindly, sinuous trunk topped by a rounded ball of foliage (reminiscent of Dr. Seuss cartoon trees). These and other large palms should be placed in the home garden or landscape with the same deliberation as would be afforded any large shade tree. Also, do consider the overall suitability of a mature specimen with the architecture of the home, as these large specimens will dominate the landscape. Some house styles look smashing with a well-placed palm to accent them, but others look awkward juxtaposed with visions of Cleopatra and Babylon.

Fortunately for the gardener in the dry southern environs, small to midsized palms that fit into many intimate settings are available. One of the most delightful comes from the south of Spain: the Mediterranean fan palm (*Chamaerops humilis*). This very tough, clumping plant sports dark green leathery leaves that range from one to two feet across, crowning stems that can attain 12 feet in height but usually are seen at half that. Older specimens will have several distinct trunks, with the overall effect being quite stunning. Underneath such established clumps of Mediterranean fan palm is a site perfect for the cultivation of shade-loving and shade-tolerant plants such as desert plumbago (*P. scandens*), cherry sage (*Salvia greggii*), and twin-flowered agave (*A. geminiflora*).

The windmill palm (*Trachycarpus fortunei*) looks similar to the Mediterranean fan palm with the exception that it has only a single, not multiple, trunk (which is covered by a hairy fiber). This feature lends the windmill palm to use in restricted spaces and tight corners where larger plants might not fit. Both palms share the same needs and tolerance of frost (down to single-digit temperatures without damage), and both are widely available. In my south-central Texas garden, a windmill palm punctuates the sunny terrace that I call the pot patio, consorting with container specimens of ponytail palm, agaves, and cactus while also shading amaryllis, plumbago, and yellow columbine planted at its feet. A large clump of golden bamboo, a pomegranate, and the palm define this space as a sunbelt garden.

Harder to come by, but well worth the effort, is the Mexican blue palm (*Brahea armata*). This delightful bold-trunked beauty has large, rigid, fan-shaped leaves softly colored powder blue. It is a bit slow to develop but can be coerced into faster growth

OVERLEAF: Devil's shoestring prepares to bloom in spring with cherry sage and bluebonnets.

Large mature clump of Mediterranean fan palm— a lifetime's achievement.

with liberal watering and feedings during hot weather. At any rate, the Mexican blue palm will reward any patient soul who invests in it. A favorite combination composed around the powder-blue palm echoes the soft blue with the foliage of *Agave parryii*, Santa Rita prickly pear (*Opuntia violacea*), and Lindheimer's muhly grass (*Muhlenbergia lindheimeri*). Adding just a touch of peach from the blooms of Indian mallow (*Abutilon palmeri*) and copper mallow (*Spheralcea ambigua*), with the support of *Tecoma* 'Orange Jubilee' or dwarf oleander 'Petite Pink', creates one of the coolest spectacles ever seen under the hot sun. In my more moisture-rich garden, the blue palm is planted on a small, broad berm to allow for extra drainage, while in the lower positions front and back (with extra water available) reside the delectable flowering maple (*Abutilon* 'Linda Vista Peach') and large, peach angel's trumpet (*Brugmansia* 'Charles Grimaldi').

Incredible as it may seem, another blue palm is even harder to find and is also slower growing than the Mexican blue palm. It is the Afghan mazari palm (*Nannorrhops ritchiana*). Although this palm takes years to develop, it does have a reputation for being the cold-hardiest palm around. This could potentially extend palm mania into gardens much further north. I have yet to acquire my own mazari palm, but when I do I will be certain to get several so that I can plant one in northern Arizona and even in southern Colorado, as well as in my own Texas garden.

While on the subject of frost-hardy, blue-colored palms, we must include the delightful pindo palm (*Butia capitata*). This is the only feather palm with blue pigmentation, and it is incredibly resistant to heat and drought. Coming from southern Brazil and Uruguay, the pindo palm enjoys a long hot summer and will readily tolerate cold weather in winter. This resilience enables Butia to be quite happy in pot culture as long as the pot is relatively large. The pindo palm will outgrow the Mexican fan palm in less than half the time, but a five-gallon nursery specimen will still be delightfully small for its first decade of residence, all the while playing center stage to a host of horticultural accompaniment. The feathery leaf fronds are best echoed by soft blue grasses like little bluestem (*Schizachyrium scoparium*) or blue sotol (*Dasylirion wheeleri*), and the silver leaves of trailing indigo bush (*Dalea greggii*), as well as the sky-blue blossoms of cape plumbago (*P. auriculata*).

For those gardeners with very small spaces, or those who want the Polynesian village look for dollhouses, the only palm to plant is the pygmy date palm (*Phoenix roebelenii*). Its full, dark green crown, slender trunk, and dwarf stature make this miniature coconut look-alike an ideal plant for patio, pot, or small garden. Being tropical, the pygmy date palm is happy anywhere similar to its home in Laos, but it performs admirably in frost-free parts of the arid West when given ample water. For those gardeners living in hot climates sometimes visited by freezing weather, the pygmy date palm makes an ideal pot specimen that is at home in a container, needing only to

Mexican blue palms can endure drought but grow faster when given the good life during hot weather.

be whisked in from the cold of winter. In a pot on the patio, this palm makes quite a statement standing alone or as a dramatic focal point for other container plantings.

Though it is not a large tree, the queen palm (*Arecastrum romanzoffianum*) is the largest of the garden-sized palms appropriate for the Southwest. Its strong, clean trunk and long, graceful fronds of shiny green leaves lend an air of tropical beauty to any garden that can accommodate a queen palm. Whenever I see queen palms growing, I must resist the overwhelming temptation to declare a holiday and order refreshing, fruity rum drinks with umbrellas in them while I relax in the shade. You can, however, have too much of a good thing, I decided when viewing a newly built mansion with nothing but 15 queen palms and lawn as the landscape. They are an excellent addition to the garden or landscape, used as one would a small flowering tree, but I would not invest solely in queen palms.

In southern Brazil and Argentina, where they originate, the queen palm does survive the occasional freeze. Having heard of specimens surviving temperatures in the teens, I decided to try a queen palm in my Zone 8 Texas garden, although they are usually categorized as Zone 9 plants. In Texas, gardening around the random visits of a killing freeze is like playing Russian roulette, and I figure there might be a chance for the palm to get established before the next "big one." I purchased my specimen at the local discount mart for a steal, and even if it fails I will have enjoyed it for several years before its untimely end. Besides, I needed a holiday.

ORNAMENTAL GRASSES

Most people are ready to discuss grass for the landscape or garden as long as it is a green, manicured turf. We know how grass fits into the scheme of things when we mow it, control it, and walk on it, but what about when it is a larger component of our garden landscape, integrated with other plants, flowers, and shrubs? What about ornamental grasses? Most of us envision only the monstrous pampas grass (*Cortaderia selloana*), which has been overused and misused in the past. Pampas grass is everyone's first—and usually last—ornamental grass. Fortunately, great varieties of tried-and-true grasses from our own wilds and from other countries are now available, and they are revolutionizing garden design. There are selections and hybrids of our native grasses that are every bit as beautiful and valuable as the shrubs and flowers we now plant in our gardens. Grasses offer us a whole new texture and look for our gardens, and they are easy to care for, too. Believe it or not, plant breeders have even created new and improved forms of the pampas grass. Many of these ornamental grasses deserve greater use in southwestern landscapes and gardens, where they add carefree elegance.

Pink fountain grass (*Pennisetum setaceum*) grows so well in the American Southwest that it was transplanted from its home in the highlands of Ethiopia for use in erosion control and revegetation of road cuts in Arizona and southern California. Decades later, pink fountain grass has become naturalized in desert ecosystems and along the coast of the Pacific Southwest. The showy pink plumes of this fountain grass are a delight to see anywhere, but this comes at a cost since the *Pennisetum* tends to replace native *Stipa*, *Muhlenbergia,* and *Sporabolus*. Although the ecological disturbance is unfortunate and permanent, it demonstrates the resilience and adaptability of pink fountain grass in hot, dry climates. Further north, pink fountain grass is widely planted and enjoyed as an annual that can take the heat and perform well in difficult sites.

For those who do not want an ornamental grass that grows up to three feet in height and width, there are dwarf selections of *P. alopecuroides* called 'Hamlen' and 'Little Bunny' that are only half-sized or smaller. Fountain grass is easy to integrate into most plantings receiving good sun. The subtle, almost neutral hues blend into nearly every color scheme, and the fine-textured foliage creates an effortless contrast with most perennials, shrubs, and cacti. In autumn, plants are crowned by myriad two- to three-inch-long plumes that are great for cutting.

Another fountain grass for southern gardens, but requiring a little extra water in the arid Southwest, is burgundy fountain grass (*Pennisetum setaceum* 'Cupreum'). The rich burgundy leaves are twice the width of the pink fountain grass foliage on a plant that attains the same stature. The foliage alone of the purple fountain grass adds stunning contrast of color and texture to plantings in beds or containers. The added bonus of coppery pink summer and autumn blooms makes this plant a sure winner in any site.

Combinations with other foliage and flowers are really what makes purple fountain grass special. Silver- or blue-foliage plants like the "sages" (*Artemisia* spp., *Salvia* spp., and *Leucophyllum* spp.), Arizona cypress (*Cupressus glabra* 'Blue Ice'), and brittle bush (*Encelia farinosa*) take on a new dimension when planted with this *Pennisetum*. Green

hues are given lively depth when mixed with the burgundy fountain grass. Whether it is with the dark jade foliage of rosemary, the pastel olive-green of desert cactus, or the vivid chartreuse leaves of *Helichrysum petiolare* 'Limelight', the addition of linear-textured burgundy tones creates dynamic duos for the garden.

Overused garden favorites can be viewed with a new eye when planted together with the versatile burgundy fountain grass. The common lavender trailing lantana (*Lantana montevidensis*) looks great as a companion plant, as do pink ivy geraniums (*Pelargonium peltatum cv.*) or blue cape plumbago (*P. auriculata*). I enjoy the lively interplay between white-flowered cherry sage (*Salvia greggii*) and burgundy grass foliage. Include the pink, antique China rose 'Old Blush' in the rear and *Artemisia* 'Powis Castle' as a foreground for a combo that won't quit. The garden potential of this plant is unlimited, but purple fountain grass does need a yearly cutting back, followed by a good feeding, to keep it at its best. Subtropical by nature, this grass is only frost tolerant and must be replanted as a short-lived perennial or annual in my Zone 8 garden, depending on the whims of the north wind.

California, Arizona, New Mexico, and Texas are home to many grasses now finding their way into our gardens and landscapes. These plants enjoy a hot summer, will tolerate drought, and add a variety of colors, textures, and forms to any site. They are all cold hardy at least to 0° F, which expands their range of use in our gardens considerably.

One of the largest groups of ornamental grasses is the genus *Muhlenbergia*, or muhly grass. Lindheimer's muhly (*M. lindheimeri*) is a midsized bunch grass with steel-blue foliage and beautiful golden blooms. Its soft blue hue echoes the similarly colored *Yucca rigida, Y. rostrata,* and *Y. pallida,* as well as sotol or desert spoon (*Dasylirion wheeleri*) and the blue palms (*Brahea* and *Butia* genera). In Texas, three-foot-tall specimens are the norm, but in southern California along the coast, I encountered well-fed, well-watered giants over twice that size. Lindheimer's muhly is the perfect evergreen grass for gardens and landscapes where the steel-blue foliage can complement the pink blooms of *Penstemons, Salvias,* and *Echinacea.*

Deer grass (*Muhlenbergia rigens*) is a clump-former with thin, rigid green leaves and somewhat inconspicuous, tight, narrow flower spikes. A three-foot-tall, mature clump dancing in the breeze looks almost like a moving sculpture. Deer grass makes a versatile, neutral-colored element that is easy to add to gardens, providing depth and dimension. It is very drought tolerant and enjoys full sun, so this muhly is finding its way into more southwestern landscapes these days. It appears, however, that maintenance personnel have not quite figured out how to handle the *Muhlenbergia's* minor cosmetic requirements. They need only a little cleanup in late winter—not severe pruning or shearing down to a stump after summer. Some plants really are low maintenance.

LEFT: Rich color, linear texture, and fluid form combine to make burgundy fountain grass versatile in the garden or landscape.

Needing a bit more moisture than the others, the gulf muhly (*M. capilaris*) is simple in appearance most of the year. It is a modest-sized but tidy clump, dressed casually in relaxed, fine green leaves. It is simply breathtaking in the fall when the grass is crowned by numerous branched inflorescences forming a vivid ruby-pink cloud. Backlighting is a must for this grass, so plant it where it can be viewed with the autumn sun behind it. The pink blooms are a delightful contrast to blue-leafed brittle bush (*Encelia farinosa*), and swarthy blue agaves such as *A. americana* and *A. colorata* are exceptional when viewed through gulf muhly's misty veil.

My favorite muhly (not to be confused with my favorite Martian) is the bamboo muhly (*Muhlenbergia dumosa*). As the common name suggests, this grass looks like a neat, clumping, fine-textured bamboo. Growing anywhere from three to six feet in height with the top spreading as wide, the bamboo muhly is a small, safe alternative to regular bamboos, which can become five to ten times bigger. The plant sends up sturdy stalks or canes that branch out and become loose, light green plumes. The leaves turn a tawny brown in winter but green up again in spring, after flowering with small,

Gulf muhly grass softens the appearance of this Parry's agave. (Photo by Charles Mann.)

insignificant spikes. In my Zone 8 garden, a hard freeze will sometimes cut the plant to the ground, but it sprouts new growth in spring, and the dead stems make a wonderful dried arrangement inside the house.

I use bamboo muhly mixed with shrubs in delightful contrast to their rigid form. Wind makes the difference even more pronounced as it whips the graceful six-foot-tall canes to and fro against a backdrop of stolid resistance. Oddly enough, this Arizona native is not widely embraced in its home state, no doubt because some landscapers have not figured out how to use a plant that cannot be sheared into a gum ball or pillbox shape.

Wire grass *(Stipa tenuissima)* grows a thrifty mop of bright green, fine, wiry foliage topped in summer by buff-colored spikes. Whereas some grasses add a dramatic touch to gardens, the effect of wire grass is more subtle. Its fine texture and diminutive stature (only a foot tall) allow multiple use in even small gardens. Both orange and purple shine when juxtaposed with this verdant green grass. In my garden, I plant wire grass as contrast to stiff, starfish-shaped aloes that bloom orange in the spring. I add orange Iceland poppies and purple sweet alyssum as winter annuals to further complement the lime-green tufts. There are many more species of Stipa to choose from in nature, and we need only be willing to try them.

Little bluestem's ascendant foliage punctuates these rather pedestrian mums.

Similar in stature to wire grass is the purple three awn *(Aristida purpurea)*. This versatile bunch grass has thin, light green leaves that are crowned with gently arching, rust-hued wands. Purple three awn is quite drought tolerant and blends well with small-statured perennials, cacti, aloes, and agaves. Clumps of this resilient, compact grass add a new dimension to a planting of white-flowered blackfoot daisy *(Melampodium leucanthum)*, prairie zinnia *(Z. grandiflora)*, red-needle barrel cactus *(Ferocactus pringlei)*, and Queen Victoria agave *(A. victoriae-reginae)*.

Starting in the Sonoran Desert of Arizona and sweeping northeast into the Great Plains is a group of warm-season grasses called the bluestems (genera *Andropogon* and *Schizachyrium)*. Foliage on the bluestems is, surprisingly enough, not always blue, but selections are being made to bring us more consistent steely-blue cultivars. More noteworthy, perhaps, is the fall and winter color of most bluestems, embracing all tones from reddish-orange to cinnamon brown. These grasses really turn the corner on the season's shift toward cooler weather, as they are more valuable in fall and winter than they are in spring and summer.

The largest, blooming up to six feet, is the big bluestem *(Andropogon gerardii)*, and it requires the most water by comparison. Blue foliage selections do exist, but I would suggest basing one's color choice on the reds and oranges that develop when the leaves

ripen in autumn. Big bluestem is very drought tolerant, but it is a component of the tallgrass prairie, so it prefers deep soil and regular water for best performance. When in bloom, big bluestem lends a strong vertical element to the landscape; pair it with tall, late-blooming perennials like pitcher sage (*Salvia azurea*) and Maximillion sunflower (*Helianthus maximillianus*).

Little bluestem is, in contrast, smaller and much more drought tolerant. It used to be included in the genus *Andropogon* as well, but little bluestem had a name change and now has the tongue twister *Schizachyrium scoparium* (this happens on a regular basis to at least some of the thousands of plants in horticulture, just to keep us on our toes). Little bluestem is a sun-loving bunch grass forming a soft mound of pastel blue leaves, two feet tall and wide. In autumn, when the clump forms thin, vertical bloom stalks, the leaves and stems begin to include red and purple hues. This transformation continues with the fall season until the stalks rise 18 inches above the foliage, and the grass is bathed in autumn's colors. By winter, little bluestem is a rich cinnamon brown, with tops of the lightly branched seed heads expanding into soft white tufts. In the summer, use little bluestem in combinations where the gentle pastel foliage and drought tolerance complement plantings (echoing the color and texture of the pindo palm, *Butia capitata*, against the bold, blue *Agave parryi*). Later, enjoy the contrast offered by the winter foliage of the grass against the still-blue companions, with a cool-season foreground planting of white sweet alyssum.

Only rarely found in nurseries, but well worth the search, is the sugary bluestem (*Andropogon saccharoides*). This native gem keeps a low profile during the summer season with its rather wide green blades arching to only 12 or 15 inches. The clump of grass begins to put on a show in late summer, when flower spikes begin to form. These consist of many naked stems radiating out of the base at all angles (rather than ascending in parallel unison like the little bluestem) and topped by tight, cottony inflorescences. During this time, the leaves begin to mature into rich shades of orange-red, and the combination of white flower spikes waving above the ripening foliage is indeed a beautiful sight. The colors are muted as the leaves continue their procession into winter, finally becoming a peachy rust. Silver fringed sage and large, olive-colored prickly pear cactus found growing in the wild with the tawny bluestem have etched the visual memory of a divine foliage combination with subtle contrast.

BEAR GRASS

I am not so fond of the common name bear grass as I am of its Latin alias, *Nolina*. The name *Nolina* just rolls off the tongue with little effort; indeed it is even fun to say (like "salsa"), and it precludes confusion with the northern native also called bear grass. Also, these are not in the grass family but are members of the *Agave* genus, and plants

LEFT: Normally perky wire grass adopts a languid habit when grown in the shade.

245

My young specimen of tree bear grass is a pleasure to design and plant around. This cool-season combination includes cardoon, Iceland poppy, and desert fleabane.

produce stalks of many small, cream-colored blooms. Everyone knows at least one *Nolina* (*N. tuberculata*, labeled by some taxonomists with the Latin name *Beaucarnea recurvata*). It is the ponytail palm. Only a few nolinas form trunks as does the ponytail palm, but all have the same olive-green linear foliage with leathery texture, similar to their more familiar cousin. In the Southwest, from California to Texas and into Mexico, there are quite a few species to choose from. All are evergreen and tough as nails, with at least Zone 8 cold hardiness.

Three southwestern native species of *Nolina* similar in form and available in the nursery trade are *N. texana*, *N. lindheimeriana*, and *N. microcarpa*. These plants slowly develop into grasslike clumps of sturdy, leathery foliage, which are occasionally punctuated with tiny cream-colored blooms clustered atop woody stalks. Basket grass (*N. texana*) has thin, shiny, bright green, supple leaves that develop a low, relaxed, moplike mound. Devil's shoestring (*N. lindheimeriana*) forms somewhat flattened rosettes of narrow, gently curving foliage and is perfect for small spaces. Arizona bear grass (*N. microcarpa*) forms a larger, more upright clump of tough, rigid, linear foliage, with each narrow leaf tapering to a brown coach-whip wisp on the end.

In all three species the mounding foliage is more rigid than the willowy blades of grasses, but the form is still graceful, and the overall effect of nolinas in the garden is enchanting. Best of all, the foliage is evergreen, so the plant is a constant feature of the garden or landscape, and they are winter hardy to Zone 7. In the wild, nolinas can be found growing in the dry shade of live oaks as readily as sprawling on sunbaked hillsides.

Such adaptability makes these plants the perfect substitute for shrubs in mixed plantings, and ideal for growing at the base of small palms. I am especially fond of the simple contrast between the tough but graceful nolinas and large boulders or giant pads of prickly pear cactus (*Opuntia* spp.). They make great companions for coral- and orange-flowering aloes, too.

Several *Nolina* species from the mountains of northern Mexico form trunks and make imposing specimens for the garden. *Nolina nelsoni* is an architectural delight even when young. From a sturdy stem, three-foot-long, silvery green leaves radiate in all directions. It becomes a six-foot-tall, trunked tower of rigid, but not dangerous, foliage when mature, and the overall effect is almost hypnotic when hundreds of inch-wide leaves vibrate in the breeze. I grow my specimen in a slightly raised bed to ensure good drainage, accompanied by hardy gloxinia (*Rehmannia elata*), prairie penstemon (*P. digitalis* 'Husker Red'), and purple coneflower (*Echinacea purpurea*).

Two other trunk-forming species from Mexico, *Nolina matapensis* and *N. longifolia,* grow long, relaxed, weeping leaves emanating from the crown of the plant. A mature specimen of *N. matapensis* (tree bear grass) standing seven feet tall and four feet wide with perfect leaves in a lush mop is truly a magnificent sight. The small specimen in my garden will take some time to reach those proportions, but I enjoy planting around it with different winter annuals and summer perennials as I play off the delightfully long, olive-green leaves. *N. longifolia* closely resembles a ponytail palm with wider, shiny, flattened leaves, but it is hardy to Zone 8. These plants lend an elegant, luxuriant look to the hot, dry garden that is difficult to find. Although my garden has no large rocks or rock walls, it would be a great venue for these weeping nolinas to grow with their foliage cascading over stone. For the time being, a large pot will have to do.

Let us not exclude the lowly ponytail palm (*Nolina tuberculata*, a.k.a. *Beaucarnea Recurvata)* from our gardens either. Once as popular as macramé, these plants have become as passé to many people as the art of knotting string. They are, however, very tough container plants for hot regions that experience freezing weather and thrive in the ground in frost-free climes. Very large plants are happy in small pots, and they are forgiving of the forgetful waterer even in 100° F heat. All they ask is to be brought indoors during freezing weather, and they will reward you for decades with their exotic, sculptural beauty. My 20-year-old specimen is five feet tall with weeping foliage flowing down to the pot, and it looks for all the world like "Cousin It" from the *Addams Family.*

Cherished member of the family, our ponytail palm along with windmill palm back a cluster of containered plants.

Although palms do not produce colorful blooms like flowering shrubs and perennials, they add dramatic texture and atmosphere to the hot, arid garden and landscape. These sturdy plants can be the structure around which the rest of the garden is built, and they easily complement a host of flowering shrubs, vines, and perennials. The wonderfully contrasting linear foliage and subtle colors of ornamental grasses and nolinas lend a graceful respite to the otherwise too-rigid plantings in the Southwest. They are a foolproof addition to the garden, and their effect is simple and harmonizing. Most of all, these plants' ease of cultivation and iron constitutions make them a pleasure to grow.

CHAPTER 17

VINES FOR SOUTHWESTERN GARDENS

Summer-flowering vines do more than simply add color to the garden. They expand the garden into new dimensions, bridging the gap between earth and sky. Architecturally, vines can transform blank spaces and naked outdoor structures, soften harsh corners or excessive expanses of walls or fences, and, of course, hide unsightly views. Flowering vines impart a lush green cloak upon the

garden wherever they prosper, but the icing on the cake is their glorious bloom. What I find most endearing about vines is the way that they stitch together the garden as meandering stems gently intermingle with other elements of the garden, interjecting a flower here and there. Yet vines are underrated and underused in gardens, and this is no doubt due to a dearth of appropriate structures upon which they can be grown. Most ready-made trellises and the like are woefully inadequate in size and strength for lending real support for these plants. Although not very glamorous, nothing beats a chain-link fence for growing vines.

Somehow, flowering vines suggest both genteel sophistication and primal wildness in their conquest of the impediments keeping them from their inevitable embrace of the sky. Their ability to shroud whatever structure they may climb—and celebrate the victory of their day in the sun with profuse bloom—is profoundly inspirational to me. This is, admittedly, downright scary to most Texans, who suspect vines of tearing down trees, destroying houses, and creeping in through windows to steal babies.

The confines of a courtyard or mini-oasis are perfect for including summer-flowering vines. Walls that delineate these private spaces and shade structures built to make them more liveable both benefit from the softening effects of greenery and colorful blooms. In my eyes, such landscape is naked without the gracious mantel of green.

The best approach is to plan for vines from the start by building the right supporting structures for them. I have had great success designing trellises made from iron bars, which local craftsmen can weld easily and affordably. Pergolas, fences, and latticework are perfect for growing vines, and any construction of such should be solid enough to support the additional weight of the plant. Additionally, a few long, sturdy, vertical wires discretely anchored on stout nails firmly pounded onto any sunny wall can successfully hold a clambering vine as it ascends toward the sun (see Chapter 10 for further discussion of vines). A number of heat-loving vines also capable of enduring the arid conditions of the Southwest make the world of vertical gardening explode with possibilities. Most are early bloomers (late winter to early spring), but some endure the dog days stoically blooming during hot weather.

Native to the Baja peninsula, the heat-loving coral vine (*Antigonon leptopus*, a.k.a. coral vine) doesn't break

249 ॐ

dormancy in spring until the weather is very warm and settled. Then, frail-looking shoots with triangular leaves and tiny tendrils emerge from a large underground tuber, and begin their climb toward the light. Coral vine needs to get a head of steam before it begins to bloom, but by midsummer the dark green foliage is joined by lacy clusters of delicate, heart-shaped, pink flowers. This display continues through fall where weather allows, and the vines continue to grow out as long as there is something upon which they can cling. A darker-flowered cultivar, 'Baja Red', is available, as well as a pure white selection. This is a vine that needs well-drained soil and loves to climb far and wide; give it room so it can ramble up to 20 feet. It is ideal on a terrace arbor, where it creates some much-needed shade in the heat of summer, and one can enjoy sitting beneath its airy canopy and viewing the dainty floral clusters above.

A drought-tolerant relative of the morning glory and wood rose, the yellow morning glory vine (*Merremia aurea*) is in a genus of its own. The clean, trouble-free foliage is deeply lobed like a rounded maple leaf and imparts a good foliage contrast with most

OVERLEAF: No wall or fence is too hot to grow yellow morning glory vine. (Photo by Greg Starr.)

Coral vine transforms an ordinary fence into a splendid garden wall.

other garden elements. Leaves of the yellow morning glory tend to be evergreen in mild winter areas but can get damaged by frost, so place it in a protected location. If the vine does get frozen, it returns from an underground tuber, but do situate it in the hottest spot possible since it responds best to blast-furnace conditions (it, too, is from Baja, California). The scattered summer bloom of canary-yellow, two-inch disks looks like a host of glowing suns peaking out from the leaves. The vine twines around its support rather than using tendrils, so plan on using something narrow enough to accommodate this behavior. Yellow

Lavender trumpet vine is quite elegant even before the onset of its beautiful flowers. (Photo by Greg Starr.)

morning glory vine covering a latticework wall would be the perfect way to define an intimate space in the mini-oasis of a hot, dry garden.

The yellow butterfly vine (*Mascagnia macroptera*) is, like the preceding vines, also from Mexico and enjoys heat and drought. Thin, twining stems spiral up as the sturdy evergreen vine climbs to keep its handsome, dark, glossy, simple leaves in the sun. In the hottest weather, the plant produces hundreds of small, five-petaled yellow flowers resembling tiny orchids, in umbrellalike clusters, but that is not what inspires the name butterfly vine. It is the winged seedpods following the flowers that give the vine its common name. At first lime green and unpronounced, the interesting fruits continue to grow until they mature, becoming chestnut brown and quite noticeable. Freezing weather will cut *Mascagnia* to the ground, but it quickly recovers in the spring. If one needs to cover something like an ugly chain-link fence (God forbid), there is no better candidate than this beautiful, vigorous vine.

Lavender trumpet vine (*Clytostoma callistegioides*) is an evergreen vine with neat, clean foliage consisting of simple, elliptical leaves that look good even in light shade. From spring through midsummer the plant is absolutely cloaked in large (three- to four-inch), trumpet-shaped, lavender flowers with white throats. Although it is a robust grower that tolerates frost, this vine does not bounce back vigorously from a hard freeze, so it is best grown in regions where winters are not severe. In such mild winter climates lavender trumpet vine makes a high-class escort for otherwise lonely walls, fences, or pergolas in a courtyard setting. As the *Clytostoma*'s foliage and habit are similar to that of the yellow butterfly vine (*Mascagnia macroptera*), the two create a lovely marriage when grown together; contrasting floral shapes and colors seem to magically appear on one plant in early summer.

Pink trumpet vine (*Podranea ricasoleana*) also goes by the name Zimbabwe creeper, which alludes to its African origins. The foliage and habit of this rampant, creeping vine are quite similar to its American trumpet-creeper cousin, *Campsis radicans*; glossy, compound leaves with serrated leaflets occur in opposite fashion on long, sprawling stems that adhere by suckering roots. This is not a vine for the timid, as a well-watered

RIGHT: Red passionflower prospers from consistent water and rich soil—perfect for the mini-oasis or courtyard wall.

specimen can easily spread 20 feet on the appropriate structure (strength is key). Yet, in such a venue pink trumpet vine is absolutely stunning. Uncommonly luxuriant foliage is dominated by masses of large, pastel pink trumpets with yellow throats. While I can't resist having one in my garden, its performance is no doubt altered by an almost annual freezing to the ground. It much prefers to grow in areas that do not receive hard freezes like Phoenix, Arizona. In climates free from such troubles, the free-flowering *Podranea* continues to bloom well into winter.

Snapdragon vine (*Maurandia antirrhinifolia,* a.k.a. *Asarina*) is a southwestern native that is charmingly small compared to most other vines. Tiny spade-shaped leaves cover the almost thread-thin stems as this delicate species climbs by grasping petioles. Accordingly, the vine needs particularly fine support wires attached to whatever it climbs to ensure a good grip. Spring through fall the snapdragon vine sprouts two-inch-long, tubular, lavender flowers with five-petaled faces that protrude cleanly out from the dense foliage on two-inch-long stems.

I thought my snapdragon vine would be cute growing up a dead ocotillo as the thorn-clad stalks made the perfect trellis with a southwest ambiance. However, the end of summer found the diminutive monster quite unsatisfied with such meager trappings as it had swarmed the six-foot skeleton, laying it over, and proceeded into the nearby holly bush. Autumn found its continued profusion of lavender trumpets intermingled with red berries of the holly. Snapdragon vine apparently enjoys rich soil and ample water, and always returns from a cold snap as well as seeding in a few new plants. Pink and white hybrids are also on the scene.

Recently large nurseries out West have produced and shipped quantities of red passion flower (*Passiflora vitifolia*), which has given many people a chance to experiment with this exciting creeper in hot climates. So far the results are encouraging, as the vine appears to enjoy hot, dry weather as long as its roots receive some extra water. The rough, dark green leaves are three-lobed and rather large (three to four inches) but are unfazed by an arid environment. The stunning, intricate, scarlet flowers are a good three inches across and last for a day but are constantly replaced as successive blooms open along the creeping, tendril-laced stems. The evergreen plant shows an obvious distaste for freezing weather but would make a splash on a protected, sunny courtyard wall that also showcases weeping bottle-brush (*Callistemon viminalis*) and coral tree (*Erythrina* sp.).

CHAPTER 18

Agaves, Cacti, Yuccas, and Sotols

No journey to the Southwest is complete without seeing at least a few of the most resilient inhabitants of the desert region, either in the wild or planted by humans. The bold, dangerous-looking agaves and cacti, as well as the woody lilies—yuccas and sotols—have the most potential for hot, dry gardens and landscapes, yet these are the most misused of all the desert plants.

They are most often seen in situations that are desperately barren and frightfully uninspiring: desolate, sparse "plantings" including only one or two of these desert gems cheapened by a setting that is a vast gravel wasteland. This post-apocalyptic vision is surely an aesthetic fate worse than death that unfortunately only leads to others copying a bad idea. Moreover, the misguided use of these beautiful plants in gardens and landscapes is seen throughout the Southwest from Texas to the California coast and has thus become the norm. Yet a quick trip to the wilds will reveal these plants living in complex, intimate relationship with other trees, shrubs, grasses, and flowers, creating a very lush appearance.

Fortunately, a few talented, plant-loving garden designers have enthusiastically embraced these tough but classy plants with artistic finesse and are using them in diverse, colorful settings that celebrate their unique beauty. In these exceptional designs, the desert denizens are not separated by huge, empty expanses but are interplanted with contrasting or harmonizing flowers, ground covers, and grasses as they would grow in nature. The right use of any sort of plants in the garden and landscape is to *create and define* space, and not necessarily the more common, woefully inadequate attempt to *fill* space. The usual motif of tired desert wannabes, the "zeroscape," is aesthetically unfulfilling, lacks exuberance, and indeed makes it look hot. Creative plant design illustrates this need not be the case.

Agaves, cacti, yuccas, and sotols are like living sculptures with dramatic architectural beauty that is easily enhanced with the appropriate companion plants. The structural quality of a choice specimen is embellished by additional foreground and background plantings. Furthermore, the muscular texture of an agave is perfectly complemented by the grand symmetry of yucca, star-burst sotol, and bold forms of cactus so that all work together with additional synergy. This is preferably done without so much dead space between the plants, with any number of drought-tolerant perennials and grasses for summer panache, and drifts of winter-growing wildflowers for an explosion of color in spring. This approach to planting can turn a vast wasteland to a veritable florgasm, and still use very little water.

HESPERALOE

OVERLEAF: Agaves and cacti
offer innumerable textures,
forms, and colors.

BELOW: Red yucca stays in
bloom for months.
(Photo by Charles Mann.)

Most of these aforementioned plants sometimes have showy spring blooms, but it is really the foliage texture and color, as well as plant structure, that contribute to gardens in summer.

One widely adapted desert plant, however, blooms famously through the hot season. This garden dynamo is distractingly called red yucca (*Hesperaloe parviflora*), but it is not a true yucca at all. Red yucca isn't even red; rather, the waxy, semitranslucent flowers are a rich, pastel coral with creamy interiors. The one-inch blooms are densely clustered along tall (three to five feet), arching stalks. The narrow, leathery foliage with white threads along the edge is only somewhat reminiscent of a yucca, and the two- to three-foot-tall, dark green, unarmed leaves erupt from tight clumps that slowly increase the individual blooming crowns. In cool weather the foliage takes on a bronzed hue that adds to the winter interest of this graceful plant. Red yucca tolerates a wide range of conditions, including the cold winter temperatures of Santa Fe and even Denver. It is moderately shade tolerant and thrives in drought as well as in my heavy clay soil during a wet year (50 inches of rain was not too much for it).

The design potential of red yucca is unlimited as it easily combines with many other perennials, shrubs, cacti, and other desert plants. The relaxed, slightly curved leaves impart an informal feel to its associates, and the glowing coral flowers held aloft on long wands cavort with flowers in most hues (yellows, white, lavender, blues, and pinks). While quite stunning on its own, give this garden gem the company of blooming shrubs, ground covers, and perennials for extra pizzazz. A nice, butter-yellow-flowered selection of *Hesperaloe parviflora* is also on the scene, so there is no reason for this splendid plant to be left out of any hot-weather garden.

AGAVES

The genus *Agave* is huge and diverse enough to include many shapes and sizes of plants growing from arid deserts to steamy jungle regions. The quick tour that follows looks at just a few of the many garden-worthy species and cultivars that perform well in gardens of the Southwest.

Perhaps one of the most recognized, if not most planted, of the agaves is the classic century plant (*Agave americana*). It is also one of the biggest agaves (six by

six feet) used in the landscape and the large garden, and its size does limit its use. A six-foot-wide mature specimen nevertheless makes a stunning, sculptural focal point. The pastel blue century plant is complemented by mango-colored California poppy (*Eschscholzia californica*) or African daisy (*Dimorphotheca aurantiaca*), both of which can be easily sown about the agave in fall to create a shimmering pool of orange. Watching a breeze toss the gay flowers about in contrast to the rigid century plant is quite a sight.

The variegated century plant (*A. americana* var. *marginata*) is a slightly smaller creature with pale blue leaves edged in creamy yellow, including a few faint streaks of color running through the centers. The leaves also tend to be a bit less stiff, with randomly curving features giving specimens a more fluid look. The creamy margins echo the similar color found in the yellow-flowered selection of *Hesperaloe parviflora* (indeed, it makes an ideal companion). An underplanting of the rather invasive pink evening primrose (*Oenothera berlandieri*) is perfect since the foot-tall wildflower cannot outcompete the larger agave. The sight of variegated century plant growing in a sea of soft pink, poppylike blooms is breathtaking and easy to create.

The smallest variegated form of the century plant (*A. americana* var. *marginata* 'Medio-picta') displays a wide ivory band down the center of each bluish leaf, with the whole plant assuming a more truncate posture than its relatives. This midsized cultivar may also be less tolerant of freezing temperatures than the basic species, so I have mine in a white clay pot in the company of other desert dwellers on my pot patio. In a more benign winter climate, 'Medio-picta' could be planted in the dry garden with tufted evening primrose (*Oenothera caespitosa*), *Erigeron* 'Profusion', and desert zinnia

Variegated century plants develop character over the years, improving their sculptural quality.

Saguaro cactus and tree bear grass contrast the twin dancing forms of octopus agave.

(*Z. acerosa*). The white and cream flowers with subtle pink hues and the bluish-gray foliage all work together to paint a long-blooming picture that is sublime.

Agave scabra is also a large, blue-colored species, but its slightly undulating leaves have a more ascendant posture, so the plant appears to have thrown its hands up to embrace the sun. You may not want to embrace this century plant, which bears large, black, marginal teeth and spines on the tips, but its less wide-reaching habit actually makes gardening under the giant easy. Planting clusters of equally blue *Yucca pallida* and sotol (*Dasylirion wheeleri*) repeats the cool color with a variety of textures. Adding a carpet of bright pink, hybrid Peruvian verbena or silver-leafed *Dalea greggii* heightens or tones down the planting, depending on which you choose.

Octopus agave (*A. vilmoriniana*) is just as big as the preceding two species (five feet in height and width) but has a decidedly disarming appearance. The huge, green, untoothed leaves look like sinuous arms of its namesake, due to their gentle, random undulations. The fluid movement implied by the plant has led one ingenious garden designer to plant it as the focal point of a raised planter, where it plays the role of a dry fountain. In the landscape, this large species needs the willowy, graceful companionship of ornamental grass like *Muhlenbergia rigens* or *M. dumosa*, and shrubs such as feathery cassia (*C. artemisioides*) or yellow bells (*Tecoma stans*). You might also try planting lavender-flowered trailing lantana at the base and let it weave through the lower limbs of this captivating agave (hardy in Zone 9).

Agave bracteosa, fondly called squid agave, is somewhat similar in form to the aforementioned species, except the avocado-green leaves all gently coil away from the center, symmetrically, on this smaller clumping plant. The distinctive habit is pronounced even on young individuals, so it is easy to interject squid agave's whimsical form into the garden, where it looks great with the coral hues of Texas betony (*Stachys coccinea*) or cherry sage (*Salvia greggii* cultivar). It also looks splendid with the two-toned orange blooms of *Bulbine frutescens* 'Hallmark' dancing about on long, slender stems. Fortunately this agave is classic in containers where the pot and plant together become fine art, even though it can survive our coldest Zone 8 winter temperatures. And without any spines or teeth, squid agave can be planted close to high-traffic areas without worry.

Cow horn agave (*A. bovicornuta*) is one of the more dangerous looking of the group with prominent, mahogany-red teeth along the leaves and thick spined tips on a compact, two- to three-foot-tall plant. It is quite decorative, however, because of such colorful armament and has the air of a serious, toothed tulip. Cow horn agave makes quite the punctuation point in the garden and landscape, and its inclusion breaks the monotony of excessive, ambiguous texture from too many small-leafed perennials and shrubs (it needs shade in the Phoenix area). Hummingbird trumpet (*Zauschneria californica*) makes a splendid companion for this bold, beautiful agave in summer, and red Drummond's phlox echoes the color of the teeth in spring. It cannot survive hard freezes, so cow horn agave is best used in Zone 9 gardens.

The mescal ceniza (*Agave colorata*) is similar in size and armament to its bovine cousin, but the blue-gray leaves are wide, with horizontal bands of silver dusted around both sides. Like most agaves, each leaf bears the ghostlike imprint of the toothed margins from other leaves, making every one a unique work of art. The foliage is also arranged in a loose manner that allows individual inspection of each beautiful leaf. *Agave colorata* shows off best in containers when the perfect pot can be chosen and the botanical sculpture is displayed upon a pedestal (pot culture is a necessity in my Zone 8 winters). In the garden, the compact mat of silver foliage from *Gazania rigens* creates a brilliant stage for the mescal ceniza. A backdrop of red yucca is also nice.

Of all the century plants in the Southwest, Parry's agave (*A. parryi*) is the hardiest; some selections are capable of surviving Zone 5 winters. In hot climates with milder winters, this plant is still a wonderful addition to the garden or landscape. The blue-

Agave geminiflora (top) and variegated *Agave desmettiana* (bottom) both make exemplary user-friendly container plants for shade.

green leaves are tightly whorled, resulting in spiny, artichokelike rosettes. Plants offset readily, forming clumps over time, and when individuals come of age (no, it doesn't take a hundred years) they bolt and bloom on a spectacular, branched flower stalk. *Agave parryi* is quite variable in the wild, and many forms of this choice plant can be found (from one to two feet in mature size), so don't be surprised if two different Parry's agaves eventually show up in your garden. The shade tolerance of this agave allows the gardener a broader application in its use, but it always looks great with bear grass, prickly pear cactus, and a smattering of winter ephemerals, or summer perennials.

The Queen Victoria agave (*A. victoriae-reginae*) doesn't even look like a plant, but rather an artifact carved from wood. Thick, stubby green leaves with odd angular edges marked in white cluster in a tight rosette, usually a foot across. The leaves are further etched in their centers so that the random-looking pattern of green and white creates an unsurpassable objet d'art. This unearthly agave is cold hardy in my zone and stays happy as long as I can keep it from getting too wet, so it's planted on the edge of the gravel pot patio, flanked by snowy alyssum in winter and spring. In summer, equally drought-needy blackfoot daisy (*Melampodium leucanthum*) echoes the ivory plant petroglyphs with an endless display of white daisies.

The tropical *Agave desmettiana* produces wide, dark green, succulent leaves that gently sweep up and away from a central core. Tender, pliant leaves are tipped with minor spines, but these are not imposing. The flowing form of the two- to three-foot rosettes is quite lush and picturesque, and plants quickly offset pups, making larger colonies. Because *A. desmettiana* prospers in shade, it is perfect for highlighting the oft-barren areas under trees. Desert plumbago (*P. scandens*) is an ideal companion in such a setting, as is tropical sage (*Salvia coccinea*). The variegated form of this plant (a favorite of mine) sports a simple, thin band of gold along the leaf margins, but it is only hardy to about 29° F, so I keep it in a pot where it mingles with foxtail fern and ivy geraniums.

Twin-flowered agave (*A. geminiflora*) is another tender, shade-loving dynamo. Looking nothing like a century plant, it is a ball of pencil-thin, dark green, straight but supple leaves with white threads fraying from the margins—it looks like a sea creature. Tiny spines on the leaf tips do not deter me from stroking this pet since the foliage flexes away from the touch and causes no pain. As with the preceding agave, this choice plant is easy and fast growing but freezes readily, so I keep mine in a pot where it can be protected from damaging cold. Where it can be used in the ground, *Agave geminiflora* contrasts well with starfishlike *Aloe saponaria* and white *Salvia greggii* in dry shade.

CACTI

In Arizona, cactus is an inevitable part of the garden as it is in the wild landscape. But in other parts of the Southwest it is embraced less enthusiastically as an important structural element, perhaps because it's thought that cactus is the last resort for the gardening impaired. Ideas are changing, however, as the appreciation of these desert denizens begins to spread to gardeners far and wide who enjoy the form and substance that cacti lend to the garden. Western gardeners now are less afraid of the stigma attached to the cultivation of these spiny plants as we celebrate our western heritage and regional style in the garden. Without exception, these cacti enjoy full sun and well-drained soil and yearn for the company of other flowers and plants needing similar conditions.

Beaver tail cactus (*Opuntia basilaris*) is loved by many for its luxuriant magenta-pink blooms in spring. It is one of the few prickly pear cacti that stays low, and the slowly spreading clumps are perfect for very small spaces. The flat, gray-green pads are spineless but *not* unarmed, as they are dotted with small, cinnamon-brown clusters of minuscule spinlettes (technically called glochids, and worth avoiding). The plant is nonetheless charming, but it needs to be kept dry in summer as it is from the Mojave Desert and resents summer moisture. In a small, dry garden beaver tail cactus looks good with agaves, yuccas, and barrel cactus liberally punctuated with winter-growing wildflowers like desert bluebell (*Phacelia campanularia*) and California poppy.

The hardy, spineless prickly pear (*Opuntia ellisiana*) really is user-friendly—virtually no little glochids. Its plump, naked, olive-green pads form a bold structural counterpoint amid the flowers and shrubs in a raised gravel bed in my garden. The neutral color blends well with most flowers and is lighter than the surrounding greenery, so it stands out. The yellow flowers of this prickly pear are the icing on the cake, but they are not the reason that I grow it. Winter-growing bulbs and linear, evergreen nolina play off the base note of the opuntia, creating a delightful foliage melody.

Two of my favorite cacti are considered by some taxonomists to be the same species, but since they exhibit different profiles and common names, I'll be among the dissenters who give them separate botanical names, too. The Santa Rita prickly pear (*Opuntia violacea*) is a large, branching plant with spineless, pastel blue pads that are still definitively armed with lots of glochids. The medium-sized plants (four by four feet) fill the role of shrubs in the very dry landscape but lend a swarthy texture and a wonderful blue foil off of which other flowers play. The tall, elegant, pink *Penstemon parryi* shows very well against the blue pads. Cheerful yellow flowers grace the plants in midspring, but the real color show is in winter, when cold temperatures turn the cactus a brilliant violet-purple (lean and mean conditions improve the color). Mixed with

This hybrid between the beaver tail cactus and Santa Rita prickly pear needs container culture in my garden in order to avoid rot.

Golden barrel cactus, gem of the desert garden, glows in any setting.

green yuccas, bear grass, or agaves, and with golden barrel cactus in the foreground, the colors and textures are beyond compare. Adding a splash of cool-season annual flowers makes a showstopper.

Opuntia macrocentra, the long-spined alternative to Santa Rita, has slightly smaller pads of the same hue, but with long, black spines like a porcupine. Most are clad with the ferocious, three-inch-long needles on the top crest of each pad, but one very compact clone is cloaked in unusually pliant, long spines. With the chill of winter comes the transformation into the purple prickly pear. They contrast splendidly with other textural elements in the garden, and the plants make colorful foils for wildflowers. Lavender-blue Tahoka daisy (*Macheranthera tanacetifolia*) and rosy purple horsemint (*Monarda citriodora*) enjoy a long season of floral fun, both thriving in the same well-drained soil as the cactus.

Golden barrel (*Echinocactus grusonii*) must be one of the most recognized and widely planted cacti in areas that never see a hard freeze. The robust, globose cactus covered head to toe with rows of translucent, yellow spines definitely catches the eye. Though six- to ten-inch-tall individuals are available and fun to use in the garden, a mature, two-foot specimen unfortunately takes years to grow. As a result, unscrupulous (and impatient) people have taken to stealing large golden barrels from the landscapes of others. A friend suggests laying chicken wire in the soil around the base when these cacti are planted to thwart the shovels of any midnight marauders. Golden barrel cactus makes an ideal focal point around which many perennials and flowering shrubs can radiate. I love the violet heads of *Dalea versicolor* and vermilion puffs of Baja fairy duster (*Calliandra californica*) hovering over the rotund gold jewels. A young specimen beautifully highlights a drift of petite pink owl's clover (*Orthocarpus purpurescens*) and is a great counterpoint for the gilded blue leaves of *Yucca rostrata*.

There are, of course, other barrel cactus, and they play a base note in the botanical desert music. The genus *Ferocactus* includes several swarthy species that add structure and color to the garden. Compass barrel (*F. acanthodes*) is the biggest and most common of the group. The plant grows to four feet tall, in a columnar shape, with large and small, rose-hued spines clustered densely about it. The subtle colors of the spines are captivating when coral flowers of red yucca float overhead, and the massive silhouette contrasts with any of the muhly grasses.

Red-spined barrel (*Ferocactus pringlei*) has a nice, spherical shape, but the green succulent tissue is deeply pleated (like an accordion) with sparse clusters of thick, ruby spines arranged along the crest of each rib. The translucent spines glow in the sunlight and are splendid when backlit. For company, the tidy, purple three awn grass (*Aristida purpurea*) is just the right size with feathery, red seed heads and a willowy habit. Annual purple net toadflax (*Linaria reticulata*) and perennial angelita daisy (*Hymenoxys acaulis*) easily join in for a sweet, jewel-toned planting.

Grappling hooks come to mind whenever I see the huge, daunting spines on *Ferocactus emoryi*. The gray-green flesh with blush-lavender overtones is unearthly because of its overall shape: many moundlike protuberances, each sprouting a starry cluster of bold, hooked, dusty rose spines. The cactus is enchanting on its own but is magical when planted with tufted evening primrose (*Oenothera caespitosa*) and *Erigeron* 'Profusion'. The soft velvety leaves of the *Oenothera* and frothy masses of daisies contrast the formidable cactus in texture, while the white flowers with subtle pink blushes create a color harmony with its showy spines.

There are many species of hedgehog cactus (*Echinocereus* spp.) from which to choose in any part of the Southwest, although the greatest availability is for Zone 8 and 9 gardens. All have gorgeous spring blooms and are modestly to heavily armed with spines. These clumping plants stay low and slowly spread out as they form ever-increasing

Potted Santa Rita prickly pear surrounded by containers of ponytail palm, blue sotol, and agave.

A mature specimen of Joshua tree lends characteristic structure to the driest garden or landscape.

colonies, which makes them ideal as living boulders, adding depth and substance to ground covers in the garden. Hedgehog cacti are also perfect for container culture, where their tight, mounding crowns of assorted heights remind one of a distant mountain range.

YUCCAS

Although it is always wonderful when a plant's scientific name is learned and used commonly, this seems to work against popular culture's embrace of yuccas in the garden. For most people, "yuck" is learned in life long before *Yucca*, but in the psyche the two become inseparable, and most folks end up making faces at the mention of these plants in the garden. Nevertheless, this sturdy group of evergreen woody lilies is a dynamic source of color, texture, and drama in the garden that horticulturists the world over appreciate. They are indispensable for hot, dry gardens and landscapes, even though some species originate in the more humid Southeast.

Some yuccas are quite large and take the place of trees in the desert landscape. The arborescent Joshua tree (*Yucca brevifolia*) is one such plant. It is the icon of the Mojave Desert, where its brave silhouettes dot the landscape. In sites where there is no irrigation to start even a desert tree like mesquite or acacia, one can still grow a Joshua tree with its stiff, short, densely arrayed leaves. It does take some time, and unfortunately, shortsighted people will plant large specimens dug from the wild for instant gratification, but this should by all means be discouraged. Seed-grown individuals are being produced by talented nurseryfolk, and these should be planted where one wants to enjoy its classic form. Even when young, *Yucca brevifolia* is a distinctive plant that contrasts splendidly with agaves and cacti.

The soaptree yucca (*Y. elata*) is another arborescent species that commonly grows into a multibranched tree of 15 feet. The gray-green leaves of soaptree are long, thin, and relaxed with wispy white threads laced along the margins to give it a softened look. The old leaves tend to persist after turning brown, putting a shaggy semblance on this weeping character that melds with desert willow (*Chilopsis linearis*), Arizona yellow bells, and assorted *Eucalyptus* species. Soaptree yucca casts noticeable shade, which many other species of agaves, aloes, and flowering perennials appreciate.

Yucca decipiens is a tree-form species that has long, dark green leaves with pronounced threads. It is delightfully fast growing and gets to be about the same size as a soaptree in half the time. For those with little patience who still desire an arborescent accent, this is the yucca to grow. It is slightly less cold hardy than the soaptree, tolerating temperatures down to 10° F.

For those who do not want the treelike form of a large yucca, there are midsized species from which to choose. *Yucca rostrata* is the favorite of many who find its color, texture, and user-friendly aspect to be charming. Thin, blue, flexible leaves with a fine yellow edging tend to spiral out of a compact head. Backlighting illuminates the gilt edge of the leaves. Young plants make a blue, spherical sculpture that is great to design about with assorted colors of flowers and textures of foliage. Red-spine cactus and mescal ceniza contrast the fine, linear foliage of *Y. rostrata*, and angelita daisy echoes the yellow on the leaves without being overbearing. Older individuals maintain the same globose head perched upon a tall, columnar trunk, looking for all the world like a Dr. Seuss creation.

The wide, flaccid, dark green leaves of *Yucca recurvifolia* spill out from an erect central core, giving the plant a fluid appearance. Foliage persists for years, so it does not gain a naked or shaggy trunk with time, just added height (to five or six feet). This southeast native is an unarmed species with good, clean foliage, and it is able to tolerate some shade as well as excess moisture. *Y. recurvifolia* makes an ideal shrub alternative in

Yucca rostrata **(foreground) makes a beautiful centerpiece in a dry gravel bed of my garden.**

265

A strapping clump of banana yucca forms a strong focal point in the garden or landscape. (Photo by Charles Mann.)

a wide variety of settings and is idiot-proof to design around. It is also easy to work around and in my garden is center stage in a bed that entertains dozens of other shrubs, palms, grasses, perennials, and annuals.

In contrast, there is the blue yucca (*Y. rigida*), which is not very easy to plant around without wearing heavy armor. My first encounter with this plant drew blood—I do have the tendency to touch new plants when I see them. I was captivated by the cool blue, 18-inch-long leaves radiating out from the stem of this stout yucca. A quick inspection of its constitution showed me how it got the name *rigida*, and that it also has very sharp tips. My garden is too small and intimate for an eight- to ten-foot-tall yucca that screams "lawsuit," but I'd love to have one. Certainly in larger gardens there's a need for barriers, restricted access, or protection from intruders (one planted under a window will keep you safe at night). Pastel pink oleander and pink-flowered *Leucophyllum* 'Green Cloud' would look great with the blue yucca.

A smaller-statured, even demure, hardy yucca for any garden is, unfortunately, rarely seen. *Yucca pallida* is a low-growing, clumping treasure with wide, blue leaves bearing golden trim, displayed openly with each leaf slightly twisting. Individual plants only get one to two feet tall and wide, and they blossom faithfully each spring like any other perennial, with big, ivory bells, making them fit into gardens gracefully. The open habit of pastel blue leaves is wonderful to interplant with a host of delicate flowers for summer and winter bloom.

Close cousin to the preceding is the twisted-leaf yucca (*Y. rupicola*). This small, ground-hugging clump-former has a simple, elegant profile with each soft, dark green (sometimes blue) leaf gently twisting (hence the name). This shade-tolerant yucca is yet another resource for planting in the sunless embrace of trees, where its festive foliage can romp with Texas betony, desert plumbago, and tropical sage.

Banana yucca (*Y. baccata*) is a midsized, swarthy plant with thick, fleshy leaves that more resemble an agave. The two- to four-foot-tall, spine-tipped plants form little trunk but will clump indeterminately, forming a massive, formidable barrier in time. Their bold, statuesque air is welcome relief, even in western settings with Zone

5 winters, and is a counterpoint to the loose informal aspect of flowering shrubs and perennials. I like to contrast the formidable foliage with drifts of delicate flowers.

SOTOLS

Dasylirion, known as sotol or desert spoon, is a spectacular addition to any hot-weather garden, and for southern European gardeners—who relish the plants—it was love at first sight. Their firm but flexible leaves explode from the plant's core in whimsical symmetry. *Dasylirion wheeleri* sports flattened, powder-blue foliage and dizzying symmetry that art pure art, although art armed with sharp teeth along the edges. Leaves emerge with dry, frayed tips, leaving some to wonder if the plant is healthy, but this is normal and adds to the ambiance. Remarkable cold and moisture tolerance allows this desert plant to be used even in North Carolina (Zone 7), where an endless array of flowers can parade before the cool blue foil. Pink globe mallow (*Spaeralcea ambigua*) is a pastel consort in spring, and the coral-pink form of tropical sage (*Salvia coccinea*) surrenders to its prickly blue embrace in summer.

Dasylirion texanum is a shiny green version with the same splendid, explosive form. Its verdant resilience in the face of adverse conditions makes it a perfect addition to the lush, dry garden where green foliage seems less arid. Texas sotol is also hardy to Zone 7 and should be planted in more gardens throughout the sunbelt. Mixed with palms, bear grass, and ornamental grasses, the Texas sotol imparts the illusion of an oasis without the water.

Mexican grass tree (*Dasylirion longissimum*) is a departure from the American species in that the long green leaves are round instead of flattened, and without a single spine or thorn. The rigid but flexible evergreen leaves gently arch up and outward from the center of the plant. These persist even at the base as the trunk develops (up to five feet in height) until there is a see-through pillar of fine, quivering foliage resulting in a hypnotic effect. Wild red Drummond's phlox is particularly effective dancing amid the thin, rigid leaves of the Mexican grass tree in spring, and the tall wands of siren-red *Salvia darcyi* welcome its company in summer. It is cold hardy in Zone 8 and makes an exceptional container plant.

When used artfully and planted with colorful counterparts, agaves, cacti, yuccas, and sotols are jewels in the heart of the southwest garden. The fact that they are tolerant of heat and drought only adds to my enjoyment of these exceptional plants. Hopefully more people will see rich, diverse plantings with these desert beauties and enjoy the rewards of including them in their gardens. It is time for us to breathe new life into old motifs and celebrate the dynamic and unique beauty of these choice plants.

Several Mexican grass trees cast a green veil around a central agave plant.

CHAPTER 19

CONTAINER GARDENING IN THE SOUTHWEST

There are many reasons, both aesthetic and practical, for growing plants in containers. The pot itself makes a statement, and if one goes beyond the usual terra-cotta, the varied choices are impressive. The color of the pot itself can be neutral, subtle, or outlandishly brilliant. The containers can blend into the surroundings, echoing already used structural materials, or be

a contrasting element. Indeed, the container is sometimes art in itself and can even be celebrated on its own without plants. But when the right specimen is grown in it, the resulting combination is a spectacular addition to the patio, courtyard, terrace, or the garden itself.

Containers allow us to leave the restrictions of the two-dimensional ground and explore new heights in the garden. Especially when using several pots of various sizes clustered together, depth and additional dimension are born. In hot, dry climates it is possible to use some small containers as long as succulents and cacti are the plants chosen to grow in them. On the whole it is best to use larger pots for growing plants in summer so that they will not dry out too quickly.

I need to grow some of my desert denizens in pots for cultural reasons. Some plants need the extra drainage afforded, and some require mobility to whisk them in to safety when a hard freeze is imminent. I make the most of it by celebrating the individual architectural form and structure of each cactus and agave specimen by growing it in its own pot. Quality white clay pots are the unifying theme that ties this assortment together; they also blend with the limestone used in my patio and terrace.

Some choice plants might be lost in the ensuing jungle that is the summer garden, and growing these in pots allows them to be free from competition, both physical and visual. Frost-tender, heat-loving desert tropicals include colorful flowering plants like the desert rose (*Adenium obesum*), which is a showy relation of the frangipani. Simple leaves crown the bold, succulent stems upon a fat, swollen base of this exotic, which blooms gloriously during the summer months. Also in this category is the crown of thorns (*Euphorbia milii*), which has been hybridized past the ubiquitous red of the species to include pastel yellow, pink, peach, and orange strains that bloom periodically throughout the year on a stage of fat, spiny branches.

Exotic South African specialties include a vast array of *Aloe* species and their kin, *Haworthia* and *Gasteria* (all of which have dozens of species). Incredible foliage color, texture, and plant structure are valuable enough, but these have great flowers, too. The common medicine plant (*Aloe barbadensis*) doesn't excite me, but I keep it around for more pragmatic reasons. However, other species of Aloe large and small dazzle and amaze me in their variety of forms and colorful blooms. Most are worthy of container culture even if it doesn't get chilly

OVERLEAF: A corner of the pot patio with multilevel staging.

ABOVE: Elegant, sophisticated containers expand James David's Austin garden up to the front door.

enough in winter (like it does where I live) to warrant keeping them mobile for a quick retreat from killing cold.

Also from the dark continent, the intriguing and varied *Stapelia* species also make great, easy specimens for containers as they snake their way over the pot's edge (you may want to move them downwind when they start blooming). Another succulent species, elephant food (*Portulacaria afra*), makes a tight shrublet with tiny lime-green leaves and reddish stems. It is splendid on its own in a pot, where it sculpts itself and changes shape as it grows. Although not grown just for its sweet, colorful flowers (it is a close cousin to *Adenium*), the outrageous spiny trunk crowned with leaves from Madagascar that is *Pachypodium* makes a dramatic statement against a barren wall.

Numerous species of succulent-leafed plants from all over the world hold their own in containers and impart spectacular, colorful foliage textures in a variety of plant shapes and forms. These can be grown to perfection alone or mixed together in containers to create an exciting display. The genera *Crassula*, *Kalanchoe*, *Senicio*, *Echeveria*, *Cotyledon*, *Aeonium*, *Pachyphytum*, and *Graptopetalum* all have many species each to contribute to the foliar mélange in containers. These plants can be given the horticultural treatment that they require for unexcelled growth since pots allow for special soil considerations as well as effortless, perfect placement in sun or shade.

For shady locations nothing beats the fail-safe mother-in-law's tongue (*Sansevieria trifasciata*), which loves hot, dry shade. The twisting, spiky, variegated leaves make punctuation points in pots, and the plants are hard to kill. Many more species of this interesting succulent tropical are available. Some are short rosettes looking like bird's nests, others are tall and cylindrical, and still others look like beaver's tails. The color range also goes beyond yellow and green to white and silvery shades.

Whereas tropical bromeliad species make quick and easy pot plants for humid environments, there are also desert bromeliads that excel in containers in the dry

Southwest. The genera *Hectia, Dyckia,* and *Puya* are all quite sculptural, albeit rigidly spiny. They are best grown in pots with good drainage, and they look sophisticated and complete with the appropriate choice of container. Some of the cycads and their kind that grace tropical gardens also revel in dry heat. Virgin's palm *(Dioon edule)* is a slow-growing horticultural gem for those who are capable of long-term relationships. The bluish-green, feathery leaves are quite durable, yet the overall air of a large specimen is regal.

Of course cacti make exemplary container specimens as they enjoy baking dry during summer (they need water during growth, however). The smaller species, especially, are showcased in the right pot. Pincushion cactus *(Mammillaria)*, Bishop's cap and silver dollar cactus *(Astrophytum)*, and *Trichocereus* are three of the best, and each genus has quite a few species from which to choose. All are charming, easy to maintain, and yield the added bonanza of blossoms in spring and summer. A noncactus xeriphyte with grassy foliage sprouting from a swollen, woody base (caudex) is *Calabanus hookeri.* It is perfect for adding linear texture to cactus combos in pots.

It is also possible to grow water-loving plants in containers. Large pots, especially those without drainage holes, are ideal for bog gardens and the culture of plants that would be difficult to keep wet otherwise. Cannas thrive in the dry heat as long as there is ample water, and a containerized water garden is the easiest means to grow them. Likewise, umbrella sedge *(Cyperus alternifolius)* and its cousin Egyptian papyrus *(Cyperus papyrus)* grown in a water-holding container add a certain *"je ne c'est quatic"* to the desert terrace or courtyard. Spider lilies *(Hymenocallis* spp.) also love wet feet and prosper in pots. Their dark green, straplike foliage is beautiful before and after the fragrant white blooms.

Because sun and soil can be impeccably controlled when growing in containers, it is easy to grow an assortment of heat-loving annuals in pots for flashes of color. Of course, these will need to be watered more than succulents and much of the desert fare, but good, water-retentive soil and a large pot guarantee success. Since these pots will be on the terrace or near the home, it is easy to situate them where they receive some shade from the hottest sun. One of the beauties of container gardening is the ability to move the pots about as conditions change and needs dictate.

As much as I love to garden in the soil of beds and borders, I see the growing of flowers and plants in pots as essential to give added depth and interest to the garden. The new dimensions created by moving plants off the ground and into pots are most refreshing. In a hot, dry climate, many easy-to-grow plants thrive in containers and impart different colors, textures, and flowers, too. Especially in the Southwest, a vast array of symmetrical plant species make artistic statements with their sculptural qualities enhanced by the right pot.

EPILOGUE

GARDENING IS AN ONGOING PROCESS, and my garden—small as it is—will never be done. The plants that succeed and flourish will continue to increase in size, consuming more of the available space and changing the proportions and scale of the entire garden. The plants that fail will be replaced and tried again in a different site (I never throw my hands up until I've killed a particular plant three times), or I will try new ones.

There seems to be an ever-lengthening list of annuals, perennials, and bulbs for either the hot or cool season that I wish to try in my garden. There are also different cacti, agaves, aloes, and yuccas that I will certainly take a fancy to and try fitting into my overstuffed beds and pots (small spades also do well as shoehorns).

Of course, more lawn will have to go, as it does each season, little by little, but don't tell my wife that. New trees and shrubs for my garden cannot ever be considered unless I annex the bleak and unused lawns of my neighbors.

The best that I can hope for is to see these and other exciting plants growing somewhere in other people's gardens and landscapes. I don't need to possess every wonderful plant appropriate for my climate and soil, but I nevertheless still seem headed in that direction. I'm thrilled to see other gardeners motivated to try new plants and even rethink old ones. Hopefully this book will inspire many gardeners to bravely go forward with their own patches of paradise, trying new plants and in new combinations. Don't let a plant's mortality discourage you: As long as we learn from our mistakes, death is just part of gardening (although a more challenging part).

Perhaps more sunbelt gardeners will discover the joys of cool-season horticulture. Especially in hot climates, it is refreshing to be able to wander the garden with newfound enthusiasm for a host of enchanting, demure flowers. And it is wonderful to feel the warmth of the winter sun as a blessing rather than as the curse it is in summer. When involved in cool-season gardening, the process is just as fulfilling and valuable as the resulting flowers.

LEFT: Bear grass, cacti, agaves, and more in a passionate planting that exemplifies an understanding and love of gardening. Entrance to Boyce Thompson Arboretum.

PLANT SOURCES

The Antique Rose Emporium
Route 5, Box 143
Brenham, TX 77833
Old garden roses and perennials

B & B Cactus Farm
11550 East Speedway
Tucson, AZ 85748
(520) 721-4687
Cacti, agaves, yuccas, sotols, nolina

**Bluebird Nursery, Inc.
(Wholesale)**
P.O. Box 460
Clarkson, NB 68629
(800) 356-9164
Perennials

Blue Meadow Farm
184 Meadow Road
Montague Center, MA 01351
(413) 367-2394
Perennials and annuals

Brent and Becky's Bulbs
7463 Heath Trail
Gloucester, VA 23061
(877) 661-2852
Cool-season and warm-season bulbs

Carol Gardens
P.O. Box 310
Westminister, MD 21157
Woody ornamentals and perennials

Cistus Design Greenhouses
2827 NE 11th Avenue
Portland, OR 97212
www.cistus.com

Desert to Jungle Nursery
3211 West Beverly Boulevard
Montebello, CA 90640
(323) 722-3976
On-site sales only—the name says everything

Forestfarm
990 Tetherhow Road
Williams, OR 97544
(541) 846-7269
Woody ornamentals and perennials

High Country Gardens
2902 Rufina Street
Santa Fe, NM 87505
(800) 925-9387
Perennials

J. L. Hudson, Seedsman
P.O. Box 1058
Redwood City, CA 94064
Seeds of perennial and annual species

Logee's Greenhoouses, LTD.
141 North Street
Danielson, CT 06239
(888) 330-8038
Tender perennials and subtropicals

Louisiana Nursery
5853 Highway 182
Opelousas, LA 70570
(318) 948-3696
Woody ornamentals, bamboo, perennials, and bulbs

Mesa Garden
P.O. Box 72
Belen, NM 87002
(505) 864-3131
Cacti and succulents

Niche Gardens
1111 Dawson Road
Chapel Hill, NC 27516
(919) 967-0078
Woody ornamentals, perennials, and grasses

Thompson & Morgan Inc.
P.O. Box 1308
Jackson, NJ 08527
(800) 274-7333
Seeds of perennials and annuals

Park Seed Co.
1 Parkton Avenue
Greenwood, SC 29647
(800) 845-3369
Seeds of annuals and perennials

Plant Delights Nursery, Inc.
9241 Sauls Road
Raleigh, NC 27603
(919) 772-4794
Perennials and grasses

Plants of the Southwest
Agua Fria, Route 6
Box 11-A
Santa Fe, NM 87501
(505) 471-2212
Seed for Southwestern perennials, annuals, and grasses

Ty Ty Plantation
Box 159
Ty Ty, GA 31795
(912) 382-0404
Subtropical bulbs and perennials

Van Bourgondien & Sons
245 Route 109
P.O. Box 1000
Babylon, NY 11702
(800) 552-9996
Cool-season and warm-season bulbs

Wayside Gardens
1 Garden Lane
Hodges, SC 29695
(800) 845-1124
Vines, woody ornamentals, perennials, and bulbs

Woodlanders
1128 Colleton Avenue
Aiken, SC 29801
Vines, woody ornamentals, and Southeast native perennials

Yucca Do Nursery, Inc.
Route 3, Box 104
Hempstead, TX 77445
(409) 826-4580
Woody ornamentals, perennials, bulbs, agaves, and yuccas

INDEX

(Note: Page numbers in **boldface** indicate photographs.)

Mexican blue palm (*Brahea armata*), 133, 227, 236–37, **238**

Mexican bush sage (*Salvia leucantha*), 112

Mexican firebush (*Hamelia patens*), 107, **136**; heat tolerance by, 27

Mexican flame vine (*Senecio confusus*), 154

Mexican grass tree (*Dasylirion longissimum*), **56**, 218, **267**

Mexican heather (*Cuphea hyssopifolia*), 37, 39, 184, 219

Mexican honeysuckle (*Justicia spicigera*), 218, 233

Mexican milkweed (*Ascelepias curassavica*), 112, 151, 183; 'Silky Gold,' 37, 102, 105, 116

Mexican oregano (*Poliomentha longfloria*), 132; 'Bustamante,' 132

Mexican palmetto (*Sabal mexicana*), 139, **140**

Mexican petunia (*Ruellia brittoniana*), 99, 102, 115, 116; 'Alba,' 105; 'Katy,' 37, 171, 184, 204

Mexican sunflower (*Tithonia rotundifolia*), 178; 'Aztec Sun,' 178

Mexican weeping bamboo (*Otatea acuminata*), 149–50

Microbial populations, limiting, 15

Microenvironments, 23, 28, 51, 94; arid, 19; choosing from, 24; complexity from, 19; varied, 22

Microniches, creating, 19, 26, 28, 197, 208

Milkweeds (*Asclepias* spp.), 101–2, 117

Mina lobata, 156, **157**

Mineral soil beds, hot soil and, 15

Mini-oasis, **201**, 218, 227, 249; containers in, 201; creating, 197, 199, 208, 219, 251

Miniature margurite (*Chrysanthemum paludosum*), 52

Miscanthus, 113, 178, 'Variegatus,' 182

Miscanthus transmorrisonensis, 146–47

Mojave Desert, 261; Joshua tree and, 264; rainfall in, 27

Montbretia, 169, 176

Moonflower, 101

Moon vine (*Calonyction aculeatum*), 156

Morning glory (*Ipomoea tricolor, Ipomoea purpurea*), 155, 156, 171, **174**, 250

Morning glory vine (*Merremia aurea*), **248**, 250–51

Moss rose (*Portulaca grandiflora*), 173, **174**; 'Sundial,' 173

Mother-in-law's tongue (*Sansevieria trifasciata*), 270

Muhlenbergia, 239, 241, 241

Mustard, 79; 'Osaka Red,' 72, 73

N

Naked ladies, 166

Naples onion (*Allium neapolitanum*), 39

Narcissus, 35, 108; 'Avalanche,' **58**; 'Baby Doll,' 61; 'Peeping Tom,' 61; 'Trevithian,' **62**

Native plants: classification of, 21; garden potential for, 21

Needle palm (*Rhapidiophyllum hystrix*), 140–41, **142**

Nemesia, **50**, 51–52, 87, **89**

Nemophila, 55

Neoregelia, 193

Net toadflax (*Linaria reticulata*), **22**, **57**, 263

New Guinea impatiens (*I. hawkeri*), **15**, 190; 'Tango,' 190

New Zealand flax (*Phormium tenax*): 'Pink Stripe,' 51; 'Purpureum,' 51

Night-blooming jessamine (*Cestrum nocturnum*), 133

Nitrogen levels, in hot soil, 15

Nolina, 235, 261

Nolina longifolia, 247

Nolina nelsoni, 246

O

Oakleaf hydrangea (*H. quercifolia*), 123, 126, 145, 151, 186; 'Snow Queen,' 129

Observation, 23–24

Octopus agave (*Agave vilmoriniana*), **258**–59

Oenothera, 263

O'Keeffe, Georgia, 107, 205

Oleander (*Nerium oleander*), 230–31, 266; 'Little Red,' 231; 'Petite Pink,' 217, 227, 231, 237; 'Sister Agnes,' 231

Onions (*Allium drummondi, Allium stellatum*), 35, 39

Opium poppies (*Papaver somnifernum*), 39, 46–47, 63

Orange River lily (*Crinum bulbispermum* 'Alba'), 163

Orchid pansies (*Achimenes grandiflora*), 186; 'Atropurpurea,' 161; 'Purple King,' 161

Oregano, 80, 82

Oriental poppies, 43, 44

Origins, understanding, 21–24

Ornamental amaranth (*A. paniculatus*), 189

Ornamental cabbages, 80

Ornamental grasses (*Muhlenbergia*), 97, 113, 116, 121, 127, 142–48, 177, 189, 230, 231, 235, 238–39, 241–43, 245; 'Aurea,' 207; 'Burgundy,' 207; drought tolerance of, 143; gigantic, 108; 'Yellow Queen,' 207

Ornamental kales (*Brassica oleracea*), 80; 'Red Bor,' 80; 'Red Russian,' 80

Ornamental sweet potato (*Ipomoea batatas*): 'Blackie,' 156; 'Margarita,' 100, 105, 156, 165; 'pink frost,' 156

Oxalis, 76, 161–62

ABOUT THE AUTHOR

Photo by Peggy Parks.

TOM MONGER PEACE HAS SPENT HIS LIFE growing flowers, shrubs, and trees, which entertained him even when a small boy growing up in the San Francisco Bay area. He later studied forest biology and botany in college. Combining his degree with inherent wanderlust, Tom participated in a forestry program in Nepal as a Peace Corps volunteer, before returning to the United States to garden in earnest. He managed a cutflower greenhouse for six years, growing a multitude of different and innovative plants before making garden design his profession. After marriage to his wife, Diane, Tom moved to Texas where he began to learn about gardening in hot climates. Travel from coast to coast has helped broaden his experience and exposure to the wide world of sunbelt horticulture.

Tom currently operates a small but diverse wholesale nursery in south-central Texas where he grows a variety of plants for use in his garden as well as for sale to local retail outlets. He has designed gardens for others in California, Arizona, New Mexico, Colorado, Texas, Louisiana, and Florida. Tom also has written for several regional and national publications, and currently writes for *Country Living Gardener* magazine. Speaking engagements and lecture tours are additional facets of Tom's profession in horticulture, and he has spoken about gardening to audiences across the country.